THE UNIVERSAL ASPECTS OF FASCISM

&

FASCISM

James Strachey BARNES

Foreword by Roberto FIORE

THE UNIVERSAL ASPECTS OF FASCISM

Preface by Benito MUSSOLINI

followed by

FASCISM

Reconquista Press

ISBN 978-1-912853-22-9

Watch ye, stand fast in the faith,
do manfully, and be strengthened.
St. Paul, I Cor. XVI, 13.

TABLE OF CONTENTS

FOREWORD

THERE are precious few people interested in political and ideological history who have not heard of Fascism. There is an
immense number of books on this subject world-wide, in different languages, offering sometimes totally opposing political
views and analysis. Many are clearly biased in their views of
Benito Mussolini and his Fascist Party, combining myth, distor-
tion and lies, to the extent that subjectivity, rather than historical
accuracy, has become the absolute norm. This stems from the
fact that the majority of historians are on the left wing of the
political spectrum — if you believe in Left, Right and Centre —
and motivated accordingly, consciously or otherwise. Their
principal aim is to distort the reality of Fascism, and to denigrate
the truths inherent to this ideology. They have been so successful in their efforts that only a minority of people ever come
across the true historical facts. However, there are always some
few writers who attempt to adopt a non-partisan view, allowing
interested readers to compare and evaluate the truth in this
debate.

Two books in recent decades have sought to paint Fascism
in a fairer and more balanced light, rather than the 'wild' party
implied in the muck-raking political potboilers of recent years. I
suggest that this is not so much an attempt to rehabilitate Fascism, rather to carve out a niche as an 'expert' in a minority
field. I have chosen a book written by Tim Redman, entitled
Ezra Pound and Italian Fascism published by Cambridge University Press in 1991. It seems to me that this book expresses the

author's disenchantment with the repetitive historical nonsense still in circulation. It is a partial, but sincere, effort to clear Pound of all sorts of accusations made by other writers, for which, for that minimal slap on the cheek of the establishment narrative, one suspects that he has suffered. The second book is Robert Paxton's *The Anatomy of Fascism* published in 2005 by Penguin Books. It is radically different in that it attempts to define what Fascism was and how it contrasted with National Socialism in Germany and other nationalist movements in Europe, where the uniforms, banners and methods are some-what similar, but the ends don't always mesh. Ultimately, each has drawn upon the other in their development, either superfi-cially or in depth.

Although Fascism is technically confined to twenty-three years, it is not a dead creed, but rather a developing saga as new perspectives arise in articles, books and conferences. For exam-ple, in Italy in recent decades, more academics are revising their views of Fascism in the light of new research. The result is that Fascism is being revisited, and it brings out episodes of the past that, in hindsight, now look rather different from previous inter-pretations, leading to a growing historical revisionism. In this new field, it often happens that a reader will stumble upon some-thing unexpected, promoting a change in the way certain per-sons are perceived. Alternatively, personal conversation with another might stimulate us to change our previous beliefs, an example of which I will relate, and which would have been impossible years ago. A few months ago I was waiting to appear on a political programme in Italy and I happened to speak to a very well-known communist leader. Lowering his voice and whispering, he started telling me disturbing political 'secrets', such as Hitler allied with the capitalists and suffocated the real revolutionaries — the Stormtroopers. Moreover, the best speech he ever heard was the one that Mussolini pronounced in the Lirico Theatre in Milan in 1944: republican socialist, anti-capitalist and anti-masonic. My communist friend does not want people to know that such a well-known communist could harbour great sympathy for a certain type of Fascism, but, as history reveals there is nothing new under the sun.

Mussolini was the first to recognize the Soviet Union, having met Russian communists in Switzerland where there were vigorous debates and revolutionary tones, and later both Lenin and Stalin were enraged with their Italian counterparts for having let Mussolini go — the Russians regarding him as the only real socialist and one who founded a new doctrine. Mussolini destroyed Communism in Italy, but kept a muted respect for certain leaders. He welcomed Bombacci, leader of the communists, who in turn wanted to die alongside the Duce, which in fact he did in 1945, both being shot and hanged by Italian partisan communists. His last words were 'Long live Communism, long live Mussolini!' When Mussolini took power he sought at the beginning of his régime to make peace with the socialists, but that ended when Matteotti was killed. It is now a recognized fact that the killing of Matteotti was orchestrated by a circle of agent provocateurs under the orders of the King, but it was a fact that he wanted to strengthen his 'democratic regime' (1922-1924) with a socialist-fascist alliance. Communism understood that Fascism shared some of its seeds and thus was mortally dangerous. Where Fascism won, Communism disappeared, and when after the war Fascism was defeated, Communism resurfaced with enormous strength.

When in the Seventies Italy began to live in a 'civil war of low intensity', as a teenager I had to deal with the communists who at one stage suddenly decided to stop any debate with fascists... It was totally forbidden to allow fascists to speak or to speak to them. Why? They had suddenly realized that the debate was lost, and that the idea of Distributism (*socializzazione*) was superior to the utopian Communism because it was common sense to the ordinary man and woman. Revolution was no longer the domain of Che Guevara, but of Evita whose creed had become a legend of Liberation and anti-Americanism, while the Communist Party in Argentina was allowed to exist under the criminal régime of General Videla.

The conflict and relationship between Fascism and Communism can be explained in a very simplistic way through use of a picture. With the expanding of Capitalism, the reaction was materialistic, anti-Christian and based upon anti-Nationalism, Marxism. The only serious attempt to give an answer to these errors was made by Pope Leo XIII who advocated a Third Way, Guilds against class struggle and in favour of widespread property. Mussolini initially a socialist (with Marxist tendencies) became a nationalist and picked up on the encyclical *Rerum Novarum*, and founded Fascism. The result was that Marxism was finished ideologically and militarily because natural love of homeland is in most people, and the influence of Nationalism is stronger than class hatred. Today, Marx has been replaced by the likes of Soros, and Mussolini by Putin, another convert.

When the new millennium opened with a new Russian Prime Minister, the whole scenario changed. Russia adopted Christian and patriotic flags and anthems; young couples were given money and land to encourage more children; the Russian State welcomes nationalist refugees. Russia is becoming slowly but decisively a Christian country; Russian tanks firmly support Assad in Syria in the first place to defend Christian communities, and certain circles define Putin as 'The Defender of the Faith'. Even the Communist Party became Christian and nationalist in order to survive. Putin had done exactly what Mussolini had done eighty years earlier. He has turned Communism into Nationalism. The same is happening with some rapidity in other countries like Hungary and Poland where millions march in the streets under the Banner of God and Fatherland. Marxism is blotted out of the country, Liberalism is defeated, and the country is in the hands of national Catholics with a team of hard-line radicals that have entered the Parliament. The fight between Communism and Fascism has been the central element of European history, and after exactly 100 years, seem to be at the crucial and final stage.

The book in your hands is unique for the good reason that James Strachey Barnes was an Englishman with Italian ancestry, who after World War I, in which he fought alongside the British Armed Forces, returned to Italy and enrolled in the Fascist Party, becoming a close friend of Mussolini. Unlike other books on this subject, Barnes sheds light on Fascism from within, offering a new perspective which transforms the generally accepted views of academics, whose works are largely a patchwork of the work of other academics, often biased and superficial. This book has nothing to contrast with other works out there, because it presents a new version of Fascism, something unique in our time.

Roberto Fiore

THE UNIVERSAL
ASPECTS OF
FASCISM

To
My Grandfather,
SIR JOHN STRACHEY, G.C.S.I., C.I.E, D.C.L.

*Absolute Liberalism contradicts our common
humanity,*
Absolute Democracy our obvious inequality.

Ramiro DE MAEZTU

TABLE OF CONTENTS

AUTHOR'S PREFACE

FIRST and foremost I have to thank His Excellency, Signor Benito Mussolini, for honouring my book with a Preface. I am particularly grateful to him for this honour because I am anxious that my book shall indeed represent for English readers an authentic account of Fascism, as the authors of the movement and those who gave it its name understand it. So this book goes out with the Duce's *imprimatur,* and thereby I hope to repay him in some small measure for his kindness, in that my readers and critics will now know that what I have to say is not merely the expression of my own personal standpoint towards politics for which I have appropriated the name "Fascism," but also that of the man who holds the moral copyright, so to speak, for the term, who has moulded the movement as it has become. Hence, whatever people may think of the principles of Fascism, they will be bound to take them into consideration as they really are acknowledged in Italy and not as they would fancy them to be, with the result that a great deal of hostile criticism beside the point should henceforth be eliminated once and for all.

I wish also to tender my thanks very particularly to the Rev. A. Vermeersch, Professor of Dogmatic Theology at the Gregorian University in Rome, for his kindness in reading through my first draft and for the many suggestions he has contributed to make the text more philosophically accurate. I am, moreover, very much indebted to my friend, His Excellency, Signor Emilio Bodrero, Under Secretary of State for Public

Instruction, who has helped me to elucidate a number of delicate points touching the exact interpretation of fascist doctrine;
and to my young friend, Mr. Henry John, for numerous useful
suggestions and for having introduced me to the works of
Jacques Maritain and Albert Valensin. These two writers base
their thought on that of their master, St. Thomas Aquinas, and
I have made conspicuous use of them; for I have found no happier combination exists for producing a lucid exposition of difficult philosophical points than that which is the outcome of the
acute French logic of these essentially modern Frenchmen,
exquisitely neat French expression and the incomparable wisdom of the Angelic Doctor.

This itself is an additional reason why I have chosen the
scholastic method by which to expound the political Philosophy
underlying Fascism. It is the method of common sense, the
method, in its elementary stages, most easily assimilated by the
general reader. I consider, too, that Neo-Scholasticism is, taken
as a whole, the most vital school of Philosophy in Europe to-
day, the one which, more than any other, is capable of assimilating what is of value in the other schools and so making for
the greater philosophic progress.

In saying this, however, I do not wish to disparage other
methods. There is no greater admirer than myself of the modern
mathematical school, of which Mr. Whitehead is the most eminent exponent, and although, with respect to Idealism, I consider there is a fatal flaw in Hegelian logic, in which Idealism
has become only too commonly identified; although I consider
the results of Hegelism to be on the whole, and in certain
departments wholly, pernicious, I have the very greatest respect
for Professor Gentile, who is generally classed as a Neo-
Hegelian (though perhaps unduly, since he derives more from
Vico than from Hegel), not only for his imperishable work as an
historian and pedagogue, but as the philosopher, who, in the
generations to come, is likely to be given a special niche of honour by those very schools that now oppose him, on account of
his having paved the way for a genuine reconciliation between
Idealism and Realism. I confess I find great difficulty myself in

always following his thought, and when I do, I by no means always find myself in agreement with him. But I am quite certain that many of his Neo-Scholastic critics very frequently misinterpret him; and I have a shrewd intuition that the above judgment will prove, in the long run, to be the correct one.

For the rest, I have been careful to acknowledge in the text or in footnotes the sources of information on which I have drawn; and at the end of the book I have appended an ample bibliography[1] of the works I have consulted in the course of preparing the present work.

My own knowledge of Italy and of Italians dates from my earliest childhood. Practically the first ten years of my life were spent in Florence in the house of my grandfather, the late Sir John Strachey, to whom this work is dedicated, and with Italy I have never since lost touch. Apart from minor visits, I spent nine months in Italy in 1909, when I was nineteen years of age, ten months in 1911, seven months in 1914 and six months during the War as *liaison* officer between the British and Italian Air Forces. I was in Italy during the seizure of the factories by the workmen in 1920, and since 1923 I have been living continuously in Rome as my headquarters, and have had occasion, during these years, of visiting, without exception, every province of this fair land.

J.S.B.
Rome, September, 1927.

---

[1] Not included in this edition. [Editor's note]

AUTHOR'S PREFACE TO THE SECOND EDITION

IN preparing this book for the second edition, I have limited corrections to the second part only with the object of bringing various matters there treated up-to-date. On the other hand, I take this opportunity of making a short auto-criticism of my own work.

A year's training since I published my book, in the calm and impartial atmosphere of the International Centre of Fascist Studies at Lausanne, has enabled me to take stock of the situation and to acquire a profounder intuition of the bigger truths of Fascism, truths which are apt to escape the notice of many of even the creators of Fascism itself. In fact, it would be difficult to find two Fascists who would be able to give quite the same coherent explanation of the movement; for like all great movements it is something which transcends the wills and personalities of the principal actors, who, though in retrospect they find themselves moved in the same general direction by an irresistible undercurrent, are yet so agitated and so swept hither and thither by innumerable eddies and cross-currents that they often seem at each stage of their journey to be travelling in different directions, each preoccupied with his own problem of adjustment to the main pull of the stream and convinced that his own relative motion corresponds with the direction of the final inevitable plunge.

I am now only too well aware of my book's shortcomings. It was written partly with the object of showing that Fascism is not incompatible with the teaching of the Catholic Church, nay more, that the fundamental principles laid down by the Church with regard to the nature and purpose of the State entirely square with those embraced by that body of fascists who do in fact represent the main current of the movement. I stand by this thesis. Fascism, in my considered opinion, would not deify the State, as would so many other nationalist creeds, but would acknowledge God above the State and the existence of a moral law which is not merely a natural law, such as the law of the survival of the fittest, but a divine law before which the State itself must bow even if by so doing it brings upon itself destruction, a law justified by the faith that no death for an ideal is ultimately unfruitful, that even if all we love appear to perish in one supreme heroic sacrifice, we shall inevitably be sowing thereby the seeds for an eventual and glorious harvest of our heart's desire. This, to me, is the central idea, the moving force of Fascism; the utter repudiation of materialism and every form of naturalistic theory of the State, whether of the type advocated by Maurras or by Marx or by Hegel or by Rousseau or the hundred and one other philosophies which have flowered into fashion since culture ceased to have its roots in Christian thought.

The success of Fascism entirely depends on the extent to which the new generation growing up will be capable of making this transcendental outlook on life part of its very being; for Fascism indefinitely presupposing the existence of a Divine Providence is determined to educate the new generation into one of believers in the supernatural, to make of it a generation of heroes who know not fear because of their faith, who would gladly fly in the face of any danger run in a worthy case, and welcome martyrdom with a smile. This is no exaggeration. This is the root of the Fascist Revolution, which may be described as a furious revolt against the various forms of materialism that have avowedly dominated our civilisation since the era of the Pagan Renaissance.

One of the defects of my own book was to omit to place this fact in evidence as the foundation on which to build up an explanation of all the rest; for this fact explains how Fascism started without any definite theoretical ideas. It explains its fury against everything representative of the old *régime*, it explains its intolerance. It is the key to the understanding of Mussolini's character, it explains all the differences of opinion between those who would attempt to rationalise the movement and at the same time explains their unanimity in action, their desire to be disciplined and led, and to acquiesce even in mistakes of leadership rather than have no leadership.

I pointed out indeed how the revolt against the prevailing materialistic philosophies of the last century was, along with the nationalistic movement of Corradini and the patriotic but revolutionary syndicalist movement, one of the three main causes and antecedents of Fascism. As a matter of fact, it was *the* main cause, the particular antecedent which was the determining motive in the other two. Nationalism and Syndicalism were swept into the irresistible torrent of this great anti-materialistic revolt of the men who had learnt the lesson of sacrifice in the War, when they found themselves becoming masters of the situation and needed a set of theoretical principles to which to refer their actions and a practical programme of reconstruction. Nationalism gave the one, Syndicalism the other; but both were transformed on contact with the consuming fire of the revolution. Their incorporation into the movement was inevitable, partly because neither of these movements was tainted by the hands of the old political cliques, partly because they corresponded to genuinely felt needs, were indeed live issues. But they were transformed: Corradini's Nationalism lost its naturalistic bias, in so far as it possessed this bias—in particular its tendency to advocate the subordination of the individual to the State in an absolute, as distinct from a purely juridical, sense was redressed; for Fascism, in contrast to certain forms of Nationalism, regards man, not in the abstract manner of so many philosophies, but as a concrete being compounded of both the individual and the member of society, who, in order to be in harmony with himself, must make his interests one with those of the society to which he belongs; while Syndicalism, on the other hand, became national and demanded the seal of the State's authority for its functioning.

My book is certainly pregnant with this truth about Fascism; but I failed to make many important distinctions, as, for instance, that the revolt against materialism was manifest in many different ways, by a modernist movement, by the growth of neo-idealism, as well as by a revival of orthodox religion. Fascism is not necessarily bound up with orthodoxy. This is now to me obvious and there are many Italians, fascists, who would energetically repudiate any such assertion. The whole powerful school of neo-idealism, with Gentile at their back, would probably repudiate it, and if I had made this distinction, I would have better explained the universal import of Fascism. Nevertheless, I adhere to my main thesis to this effect: I am convinced that Fascism will become not only the means of reconciling the claims of Church and State in Italy, but provide the impetus necessary to enable the Church to assimilate modern culture. I believe that the consequences of Fascism will prove tremendous for the Church. I believe the orthodox revival within Fascism will prove the winning tendency; that the Church will thereby come soon to realise it is no longer a beleaguered city and that in the process of assimilating modern culture it will lose its diffidence towards modern culture and once more assume the preponderant direction of modern culture; that with growing prestige it will walk hand in hand with a general cultural revolt against materialism, mainly assisted by Fascism, until the ideal of the Holy Roman Empire adapted to modern conditions will cease to be a half-forgotten dream but become a practical aim— while neo-idealism and modernism as complete systems will pass away and be remembered only as symptoms of the revolt and as its discarded instruments during a period of transition. To sum up: I believe Fascism to be the beginning of a new political and cultural synthesis, in which, compared to an ellipse, the Roman tradition of authority, both political and ecclesiastical, will form the foci.

This is prophecy and only time will show whether or not I am right. But it is one thing to affirm the faith that is in one, another to rationalise it, to follow up its implications in the realm of the contingent, to refer it back to the practical business of statesmanship. In attacking these problems, I found myself very insufficiently prepared. I found my conclusions to present a number of paradoxes which I failed altogether to resolve, though I believe they are indeed resolvable along the lines of the method I made use of. My failing to resolve them, however, is the great defect of my book, especially as I leave myself open to criticism by many better equipped neo-idealists, such as Mdlle. Lion, who would fain answer the vital question of the relationship between the State and the moral law along different lines, which, if I am wrong and they are right, would mean the unfulfilment of my prophecy. But at that, for the present, I must leave it. Only it should be noticed that even if my prophecy fails to materialise, my diagnosis of Fascism as mainly an anti-materialist revolt remains unaffected, although I should be disappointed in my highest hopes and have some qualms as to the final result of the struggle in which western civilisation is engaged, with Italy as its cockpit, between the enemies and followers of Christ's visible Church.

J.S.B.

PREFACE BY HIS EXCELLENCY
BENITO MUSSOLINI

THE book which I have the pleasure of prefacing is from the pen of a clear-minded English thinker who knows Italy and the Italians perfectly, and not less perfectly Fascism. It is, therefore, a book destined to dissipate—among men of good faith—that halo of incomprehension which for so many years has surrounded Fascism in the world at large and is due to many causes, of which the principal are the following.

Before all things, a new movement that announces itself as the destroyer, not only in doctrine but also in practice, of principles universally considered and followed, is bound to arouse violent hostility. It is wholly in the logic of things that the international Socialist, Democratic, Liberal, Masonic and Bolshevist world should be furiously anti-Fascist. The extent of the fury is the measure of the upheaval of ideas brought about by the Fascist Revolution. It is also logical that the anti-Fascist forces throughout the world should seek to keep men's minds in ignorance of what Fascism really stands for both in respect of its doctrine and its reality. This explains the crass stupidity which embellishes the articles and speeches of certain men who have the reputation of being eminent in their own countries.

The misunderstanding of Fascism is due, besides, to journalistic literature which has seized hold of the exterior, episodical, picturesque and interesting aspects of the Fascist Revolution, and has not paused to look deeply into the matter; the consequence is that the public at large is left either in darkness or has obtained a notion of Fascism that is superficial.

Lastly, there is the semi-philosophical hostility of those who refuse to admit that Italy is capable of initiating—for the third time in her history—new forms of political civilisation. For these, history came irrevocably to an end in 1789.

These three causes—with the minor ones it is useless to concern ourselves—are sufficient to explain how it is that, after five years of Fascist rule, the world is still full of anti-Fascist prejudices.

Nevertheless, as bit by bit Fascist rule reveals its formidable will and capacity to *endure*, the speculations which people used to make about its *transitoriness* are collapsing; and the interest which thinking persons are beginning to take in it becomes evident. Lately there appeared a book by a German professor, Gutkind, and now his book is followed by this solid, interesting, exhaustive volume by Barnes, an Englishman.

Whoever reads it will convince himself that Barnes is well prepared for his task. His work is, in fact, the product of a direct knowledge of the question: Barnes knows Fascism both in its doctrinal elaboration and in its practical realisation. His book is not the result of a rapid tour or a brief sojourn in Italy, but is the witness of a man who, having lived long in Italy, and knowing the language and mind of Italians, is able to penetrate into the intimacy of things and see what a hurried and distracted traveller cannot see.

This valuable testimony of Barnes is expressed in the title which he has given his book. He has sought to make clear and to illustrate the universal aspects of Fascism; and he has succeeded. These aspects exist. Fascism is a purely Italian phenomenon in its historical expression, but its doctrinal postulates have a universal character. Fascism sets and solves problems which are common to many peoples, and precisely to those peoples who have experienced and are tired of Demo-Liberal rule and of the conventional lies attached thereto. The fact that the application of Demo-Liberal principles (the individual outside and opposed to the State) has varied from nation to nation, in no wise destroys the character of universality which these principles have enjoyed from 1848 to 1914. In the same way the fact that Fascism possesses a specific and original Italian stamp does not prevent its principles having an application in other countries, in other forms, as indeed has already occurred. It is our proud prophecy that Fascism will come to fill the present century with itself even as Liberalism filled the nineteenth century. Through the experiment of two Revolutions, the modern world has sought to escape from Demo-Liberalism and the tragic contradictions of Marx—that is, the Russian and Italian Revolutions. On the first has already fallen the judgment of civilised peoples: the experiment has been shown to be more destructive than creative. For the second, ours, the Fascist or Roman one, the experiment has been running five years with eminently creative results: in the institutions, the laws, the works, the very psychology of a whole people. The Fascist experiment is so sure of itself that it has been able to set out its programme of political reform during the next few years. The Fascist experiment is marching on: from the Labour Charter to the new representation in the legislature. Russia, on the other hand, is going back: there the Revolution is undergoing a process of denying itself both economically and politically. The Communist system of economy has failed and the dream of a world Revolution has set. Bolshevism, after ten years, is standing hat in hand, begging the western middle classes for experts and dollars.

I thank Barnes for his noble effort and wish his volume the very best success among the English public, for the sake also of the truly traditional friendship between Great Britain and Italy. It is necessary, among other things, for statesmen to convince themselves that it is impossible to have a foreign policy if they ignore Fascism, given that Fascism identifies itself and will identify itself for many tens of years with the whole Italian nation.

Mussolini

INTRODUCTION

§ I

Efforts have been made, more or less successfully, to create a Science of Politics—*Sociology*, as it has been aptly called—based solely on the facts of observation and, where possible, of experiment; facts duly classified and analysed, from which emerge certain natural laws governing the life of human society. By natural laws are meant uniformities in the ordinary scientific sense, that is, generalities having the character of successive approximations to the truth.[2]

A Science of this kind is essentially amoral. It follows a method wholly inductive and empirical, asking of history and of observation answers to such questions as the following: Are there any general and constant conditions, and, if so, what are they, that entail the decadence or corruption of the body politic? Are there other conditions, and, if so, what, that are invariably associated with the health and prosperity of human societies?[3]

---

[2] It was Herbert Spencer, I believe, who first popularised the term "Sociology"; but in his ambitious *Principles of Sociology* he failed, perhaps willy-nilly, to keep the Science within the narrow meaning here defined, although there are many indications that lead one to suppose that he had an intuition of this being both possible and desirable. The same may be said of Comte with respect to his *Positivist* Philosophy.

[3] *Cf.* Jacques Maritain, *Une opinion sur Charles Maurras et le devoir des Catholiques*, p. 22 (Librairie Plon, Paris, 1926).

Such a Science may be calculated, also, to throw light, if only indirectly, on a number of practical questions. For example: Given an end proposed by a given Government in given conditions, what choice of means are there by which that end may be furthered? And again: Given certain pathological conditions affecting a particular community, what remedies are available, if any, to restore to that community its health?

Machiavelli may, with justice, be regarded as the founder of Sociology. It is true that he was more of a physician prescribing remedies for the ills from which his country was suffering at the time than a man of Science concerned mainly with the discovery of general laws. But his nostrums were the fruit of the then newly-stirring scientific spirit, fertilised by a passionate desire to free Italy from foreign dominion—that is, they were the result of inductive and empirical reasoning upon a number of carefully classified and analysed facts bearing upon collective human nature and applied to the end he had in view—facts, moreover, culled from a direct and acute observation of the society of his day and from history. He was the first eminent writer on politics who adopted the modern scientific method, and, though many of the means he recommended can only be described as infamous, his various treatises remain a storehouse of worldly wisdom, which, even now, no reflective and practical statesman can afford altogether to neglect.

In modern times, another Italian, Vilfredo Pareto, gifted with something of Machiavelli's wit and economy of style, but possessed of the fully developed scientific spirit of the present generation, has, with very considerable success, endeavoured to lay a secure foundation for this Science.[4] And there are others, only less distinguished, who have essayed the same task, notably Durkheim, Le Play and Maurras, to mention three names with whose works I am personally acquainted. Students, too, of mob-psychology, like Gustave Le Bon and Graham Wallas, may be considered a branch of the same root.

---

[4] *Cf.* Vilfredo Pareto, *Trattato di Sociologia.*

This "Sociology" may be described, indeed, as the Physiology of society; and, as the handmaiden of Physiology is the practising physician, so the handmaiden of Sociology is the practical statesman.

No one will deny that a Science of this kind (assuming, as I think we have the right to assume, that it has already shown itself capable of elucidating a number of important laws and promises to achieve a considerable development) deserves to be encouraged as an extremely useful branch of study, being the synthesis, as Pareto defines it (while admitting the definition to be imperfect) of the special social Sciences of History, Jurisprudence, Economics, etc.[5] To be versed in it should sharpen the intuition and widen the experience of a statesman and provide him with landmarks to guide him in the piloting of the Ship of State, tempering his idealism with the stern facts of reality.

Sociology, however, is itself only a branch of Political Science in the wide sense of the term. It is of importance to make this distinction, whether or not we regard Political Science as an autonomous Science or as the general term applicable to the whole group of Sciences that bear directly upon politics. However this may be, I insist that there can be no real Political Science without at least a working theory of the true ends of human existence, whereby a Moral Philosophy is implied, ends which Sociology, properly speaking, wholly ignores. Rational progress is only possible when it is known to what end it is desired to

---

[5] It is generally considered that the father of modem Economics is the Englishman, Adam Smith. It was the Romans, on the other hand, who laid the foundations of modem Jurisprudence; while the pioneer of the Science or "Philosophy" of History was the Italian Gian. Battista Vico (1688-1744), whose most prominent modern representatives are two of his own countrymen, Benedetto Croce and Giovanni Gentile. Later on I shall have occasion to discuss certain aspects of these three special social sciences; for Fascism stands for a repudiation of certain doctrines developed in the course of the nineteenth century in a direction at variance with the classical principles informing these sciences, developments associated with Philosophical Idealism, the positive theory of Rights and the Manchester School of Economics.

progress. So that Political Science, as I take it, may be said, on the one hand, to comprise Sociology, and, on the other, to be comprised by Philosophy, that is, by an Ethic, if not by a Metaphysic also. If I were to attempt a definition, I would put it thus: Political Science has as its object, on the one hand, the investigation of the essential characteristics of human society, regarded as a natural phenomenon, together with the demonstration of such uniformities as emerge from the study of human society under various conditions and phases of development (Sociology); and, on the other hand, the ascertaining of the ends that society fulfils, is capable of fulfilling or ought to fulfil, together with the principles governing right conduct with respect to the actions of public authorities (Philosophy).

Let me illustrate this distinction, in the first place, by an analogy. Physiology tells us of the construction and functioning of the human body, from which we may deduce certain rules of physical health, granted that we set ourselves the practical question, in the light of the facts elucidated by Physiology, how to maintain ourselves in physical health. If we include within this Science an examination of the effects of moral states of mind on physical health, pathology and so forth, our rules of health should be fairly comprehensive. Similarly, rules of health and rules of material prosperity may be deduced from Sociology for the body politic. Did we assume, however, that physical health were the sole end of human existence and, conversely, that material prosperity were the sole end of human society, we should already be stepping outside the respective domains of Physiology and Sociology. We should be subscribing to a materialistic Philosophy. It follows, therefore, that Sociology, as defined, cannot really stand by itself as the Science of Politics.

The truth is that Sociology, like every other empirical science, is incapable itself of leading us anywhere in the practical affairs of life. These Sciences merely increase our hold over nature and so enable us to do more easily and with less risk of failure what we *choose*. They do not choose for us. They contain no categorical imperative. They merely say, "If you do this or that, such and such a consequence or consequences may be regarded as more or less certain to ensue."[6]

Sociology, for example, may affirm in a particular case—to give now an example illustrative of this important distinction— that if a given Nation's population continues to increase in conditions which preclude adequate facilities for emigration or absorption through a parallel increase in industrial development, either a war or a plague or a famine or a general lowering of the standard of life must, other things being equal, result. Itself does not, cannot prescribe the precise remedy. As we have seen, however, I do not deny that Sociology may open our eyes to the means by which a given end may be effected; but almost invariably it points to a wide choice of means, and, if we subscribe to a Moral Philosophy, not all these means may be legitimate. Thus, in the example just given, it might be supposed by some that the solution pointed to was the artificial restriction of births, the end in view being the avoidance of the evils enumerated. But is this means legitimate? Whether we answer "yes" or "no," we imply some Moral Philosophy. And, again, is it the only remedy available? Not at all, it seems. For Sociology has a good deal more to say on the subject. It may lay down, in the first place, with equal truth, that if the artificial restriction of births be resorted to, certain other consequences are likely to follow, such as the encouragement of vice and of selfishness, the decline of population beyond the limits of prudence, the rapid depopulation of the country-side (for a well-populated country-side depends on a system of peasant proprietorship or of yeoman farmers, who are only capable of maintaining themselves by means of large families), a disproportionate increase of wage-earners at the expense of that section of the population which controls its own means of livelihood, the concentration of the population in cities with the attendant evil results of lowered

---

[6] G. K. Chesterton has put this point somewhere, very neatly, to the effect that a law of nature can be recognised as much by resisting it as by submitting to it, by out-manoeuvring it or even using it against itself, as in the case of the arch.

vitality, the influx of foreign elements on a scale calculated to injure the ethnical homogeneity of the race, the weakening of the military strength of the nation *vis-à-vis* rival powers, etc., all of which consequences, for instance, France, where the artificial restriction of births is widely practised, is in process of undergoing. In the second place it points to other remedies, on all of which it can offer some instruction, as, for instance, the raising by other processes of the general standard of living, coupled with an increase of opportunity for economic advancement, resulting in later marriages and therefore smaller average families and in greater opportunities to sublimate the sexual passions, which constitute the predominant vent for psychic energy only where the standard of life is low, that is, with regard not only to material conditions but in the absence of opportunities for pursuing intellectual pursuits and healthy physical recreation. There is also the remedy of education in the highest sense of the word, the inculcation of habits of self-control, of a frugal life, of respect for one's women-kind, etc., to which end there is no influence more powerful than that of Religion.

I do not intend, however, to follow this point into greater detail. I afford it as an illustration of the limits to the teachings of Sociology and in order to emphasise the fact that we must indeed know the ends for which society is instituted, and subscribe to some kind of Moral Philosophy before Sociology can be of the least use to us.

"Naturalism" is the term used to denote that school of sociologists who fall into the error of supposing that Sociology is the master-key of Political Science. Students should be well warned of this danger. Sociologists like Durkheim, Maurras and others, have too often thus confused the issue. Why is it that Machiavelli has earned for himself so evil a name? Because, although he had clear and, taken by themselves, admirable aims in view, he had no true Philosophy nor Religion, by which he could synthesise his aims and estimate the true value of the means which he recommended. *Au point de vue de la Science Politique, il y a ainsi danger de s'enclore dans l'empirisme comme dans une doctrine suffisante, et de refuser les synthèses plus hautes qui seules peuvent conduire à la science proprement dite. L'erreur où l'on risque alors de tomber est celle du "naturalisme" politique.*[7] Sociology, *in fine, "n'est que la préparation, la phase de déblaiement expérimental qui précède la science."*[8] It may be, like Machiavelli's Principe, a treasure-house of worldly wisdom; or it may reveal to us, in masterly fashion, as in Pareto's *Trattato di Sociologia*, the effects on the general health and prosperity of the body politic of different institutions, constitutions, laws, customs, religions, philosophies, habits of thought and emotion, systems of economy, climate, topography, etc., etc., in varying or analogous conditions. It may be deemed, indeed, the *vade-mecum* of the practical statesman. But unless the statesman possess also a Religion or a Philosophy, even if it be only a practical philosophy or one intuitioned as through a glass darkly, or, to say the least, a definite *Weltanschauung*, Sociology can be of no practical use to him whatever.

§ II

It follows, therefore, that every political school or movement must have an underlying, if not altogether a conscious, political Philosophy; and if a political movement is to have any permanent or universal worth, it is of the utmost importance that the political Philosophy underlying it should be true.

The purpose of this book, as the title denotes, is to expound the universal aspects of Fascism. Now, the only absolutely universal aspects of Fascism are the Philosophy underlying the movement, and its *Weltanschauung*. In a sense it is stretching it a little far to call either of these things Fascism, particularly the

---

[7] Jacques Maritain, *Une opinion sur Charles Maurras et le devoir des Catholiques*, p. 47 (Librairie Plon, Paris, 1926).

[8] *Ibid.*, p. 24. *Cf.* Aristotle, *Metaphysics*, I, 980, b. 26.

first; for the Philosophy underlying Fascism existed before Fascism;[9] and its *Weltanschauung* is only an emphasis on certain qualities of the human spirit, the value of which, taken by themselves, has never been called in question.

Nevertheless, I have decided to call these things Fascism, if only because they are, indeed, the stuff of which Fascism is made and the rock upon which Fascism is building a new political order and a new type of State. Moreover, it is this movement, called Fascism, which is bringing once more into honour, in men's minds, the truths enshrined in the old Philosophy.

Then there is another quasi-universal aspect of Fascism. This is the new political order, the new type of State—in other words, the new institutions, which the movement is bringing into existence—an aspect which is not absolutely universal, because what suits one Nation will not necessarily suit another, living in different conditions, at different times, with different characteristics and different needs. But all the greater civilised States of the present day have much in common, perhaps more in common than is usually supposed. The industrialisation of production, distribution and exchange, and the rapid means of transport and communication, have levelled the world up and down. We are all ill with much the same kind of maladies, less virulent here than there, but most of them prevalent everywhere. Most of the great Powers have the same order of problems requiring solution, the problems of Capital and Labour, of the glaring inequalities in the distribution of property, of the greater or lesser inefficacy of the parliamentary system, of the instability of Governments, of general discontent and restlessness, etc., etc., etc. Most people are perplexed and know not where to turn for a solution. State Socialism, which is the *reductio ad absurdum* of

---

[9] Its existence before Fascism does not imply that, in the meantime, it has not developed, nor that Fascism itself may not have given a special impetus to its development. Truth is a vital principle. If it is not lost it grows, it develops; but it grows consistently. Within the acorn is the image of the oak.

Capitalism[10] in that it would level everybody down to a salaried, propertyless, proletarian class, is more and more coming to be recognised as a bankrupt policy, Red Syndicalism and Bolshevism as spelling red ruin. Liberalism is everywhere an anæmic plant, and most of the so-called Conservative Parties all the world over differ little in principle from the Liberal, except as being less inclined to flirt with Socialism. Fascism, on the other hand, claims to be an alternative remedy for the present discontents to that offered by the extremists of the Left, and it is the only important alternative remedy in the field, if we discount the false optimism of "wait and see." For it may well be possible that the institutions which Fascism is cautiously bringing into existence in Italy and slowly perfecting may prove to be adaptable elsewhere. In so far as they are, Fascism has here too a kind of universal message. Part of the present work will accordingly deal with the Fascist programme and its concrete achievements; but the core of the book will deal with the Philosophy underlying the movement, the truth of which, I hope, if not altogether to prove—space alone excludes such a task—at least to illustrate in a convincing manner.

---

[10] I use the term "Capitalism" here in its restricted sense, as contrasted with "Distributism," *e.g.*, as that economic system which tends to concentrate the means of production into the hands of the few and to reduce the vast majority of people to the status of wage-earners, with little opportunity for saving—each according to his class—beyond what is barely necessary to keep body and soul together when old age, sickness or temporary unemployment becomes their lot. There are of course other characteristics of "Capitalism" (against which Fascism sets its face), as for instance: the habit of mind of regarding production in terms of profits only, of regarding labour solely as a commodity and prices as being properly determinable by the interplay of supply and demand rather than with reference to the cost of production.

§ III

What I shall refrain from discussing outside this introduction are the vicissitudes of the fascist Revolution; the ephemeral episodes of its development; the pros and cons of the transitory measures adopted to secure its triumph; its various excesses; its picturesque aspects, and so forth. Something, on the other hand, will be said here of the personality of Mussolini; while a chapter will be dedicated to the history of the movement, more, however, with the object of demonstrating its traditional character than to set out a chronicle of events.

Fascism has come as a Revolution. Italy is still in a state of Revolution. We have here, in fact, a Revolution in many ways as fundamental as the French or Russian Revolutions. We have a Revolution, not because there has been brought into power a new economic class of people (though, indeed, an altogether different type of people has been brought into power); not because the philosophical order of ideas underlying Fascism, nor yet its *Weltanschauung*, possess any startling novelty; but because Fascism represents a complete reversal of the fundamental principles governing the theory of politics that have increasingly held sway in most civilised countries during the past few generations, and because it is bringing into being a new kind of political organisation, utterly different from the prevailing order and copied in no sense (in spite of certain resemblances) from anything that has been attempted hitherto. Lastly, we have here a Revolution because changes are being effected more or less abruptly and extra-constitutionally (however well it may be camouflaged), and this through the action of a minority, possessed of a creed and the zeal of missionaries, who seized power in the first instance by violence, albeit with the passive consent of the vast majority of Italian citizens, sick to death of the old order. Since it is the fashion among certain sections of the Opposition in Italy to deny that any Revolution has taken place, in order to allow no excuses for certain fascist excesses, I can only ask, having stated the case with exactness, what then, indeed, constitutes a Revolution?[11]

Unfortunately excesses are the inevitable accompaniments of every great Revolution. Excesses—by which I mean acts of violence or persecution committed by private persons or groups of persons, with or without the tolerance of an extra-legal revolutionary authority—are never morally justifiable. But every fair-minded man, with a knowledge of human nature as it is, will, in the circumstances of a Revolution, make allowances for them.

A Revolution lets loose human passions. Fundamental principles are at stake, which both sides regard as vitally affecting the well-being of society, of all that they hold in reverence. Every Revolution presents opportunities to unscrupulous and undesirable persons for attempting to exploit the situation to their personal advantage and for indulging in crime. Numbers of *agents provocateurs* insinuate themselves into the ranks of the revolutionary Party and attempt to discredit the movement from within by one disreputable means or another. New men, adventurous spirits, who, at the time of insurrection, gained distinction by qualities of leadership in the field, come to occupy positions of authority in Government, for which they are morally or temperamentally unfitted. Abuses of power consequently result; and only gradually is it possible for the higher authority, however well-intentioned and however strong, to eliminate them, except at the risk of jeopardising the whole movement—for each of these revolutionary chiefs, by the very fact of their gift for leadership (not commensurate, however, with their sense of discipline or responsibility) will have a considerable local personal following, which it might be fatal to alienate.

To be fair, the excesses of a Revolution must be judged in comparison with the excesses of other equally important Revolutions, by the progressive diminution of the excesses as the

---

[11] As Georges Sorel amply shows in his *La Révolution dreyfusienne*, the essence of a Revolution is a change of ideas.

Revolution runs its course, and by the efforts made by the Government to put a stop to them. The following paragraphs will deal with these points.

There are many persons, opposed to Fascism, who consider the French Revolution as a great emancipating movement which has conveyed immense benefits on mankind. Yet consider the awful horrors that occurred when the principles of that Revolution were at stake! Would these persons wish them away if, by so doing, they simultaneously wished away what they consider the beneficial results? And what of the horrors of the recent Irish Rebellion? The atrocities committed by Fascists are mild in comparison with those committed by the Irish; and if the latter may be comparable to those committed in Italy by the Communists,[12] the reprisals sanctioned by the British Government and committed by a specially recruited force of *bravoes*, when other more regular, though possibly more costly, means might have been employed to deal with the situation, are far more reprehensible than those ordered by the Fascists, who, before becoming themselves the Government, and in the face of an impotent Liberal Ministry, had no other alternative means at their disposal, if Italy were to be saved from economic ruin. Thirdly, what of the unparalleled horrors of the Russian Revolution?

The truth is there is hardly an example in history of a Revolution so little abounding in excesses as the fascist Revolution. Moreover, the worst excesses have been committed by the other side. Again, the fascist excesses have been sporadic. They have never been part of the fascist programme except at the time when the Fascists were breaking the power of the Communists by reprisal, before the reins of Government fell into their hands. Since then every effort has been made by the Government to put them down (including every kind of reprisal committed by local fascist organisations). It was not easy at first to wean certain

---

[12] *Cf.* Luigi Villari, *The Awakening of Italy* (Methuen, London, 1924), in which an accurate and documented account is included of the Communist outrages committed in Italy before the Fascist march on Rome.

elements from the mentality engendered during the period preceding the march on Rome; and for reasons stated above, it was not always possible to impose discipline. But the fact remains that each year, since the advent of Fascism to power, the excesses have diminished. This fact is incontestable. Gradually the irresponsible and undisciplined elements have been and are still being eliminated. Between the years 1923-1927, literally thousands of Fascists have been imprisoned for committing excesses; thousands, for no other reason, have been expelled from the ranks of the Party. Literally scores of Prefects have been retired for failing to maintain order when Fascist bands, acting, albeit, under gross provocation, vented their wrath from time to time on members and organisations of the Opposition.

The last excesses committed of any considerable gravity are already, at the time of going to print, nearly one year old, namely, those following the two consecutive attempts on Mussolini's life in the autumn of 1926. What was the answer of the Fascist Government? The prosecution and imprisonment of hundreds of Fascists, the expulsion from the ranks of the Party of hundreds more, the dismissal of a large number of Prefects, the strengthening of the numbers and authority of the regular police, and the assumption of the Ministry of the Interior by Mussolini himself, in order that his great prestige and authority might be exercised directly on the preservation of order and the enforcement of discipline.[13]

Finally, it may be said, in this connection, to the credit of the fascist Revolution, that the death-roll has been exceedingly small in comparison with that entailed by other great Revolutions. The total death-roll of the Revolution is little more than 4,000; and of these 4,000 deaths, half have been incurred by the revolutionaries themselves. The victims of the Revolution number scarcely 2,000! Compare the figures of the French and

---

[13] The circular issued to the Prefects by Mussolini on his assuming office as Minister of the Interior is a document pregnant with evidence of the will of the Government to put an end to every kind of excesses.

Russian Revolutions, and the result must be regarded as quite exceptional.[14]

There is another similar point, which may be cited in favour of the Fascist Revolution. The economic life of Italy has in no way suffered in the process. On the contrary, the country, which perhaps more than any other country suffered economically from the effects of the War, has in the interval been set magnificently on its feet again. Italy has actually recovered more rapidly and from a worse position than any other of the big European Powers involved in the Great War. The Government deficit has been converted into a surplus. The same is true of the railway budget. Inflation has ceased; the commercial budget has greatly improved; the value of the lira has been maintained relatively steady. Unemployment has diminished, despite a continued, remarkable decrease in emigration, and a formidable increase in the population each year by close on half a million souls—facts which point to the ability of Italian industry to absorb a rapidly increasing demand for employment, without any appreciable lowering of wages as measured by their purchasing power. Government services, too, have conspicuously bettered their efficiency; hygiene and housing conditions have improved; while the conditions of the working classes with respect to opportunities for recreation, to insurance against old age, invalidity, accident and unemployment, and to hours of labour, have all made distinct progress.

This is, indeed, a remarkable achievement for a Revolution. And if there are causes for Italy's rapid recovery and present relative prosperity independent of the action and legislation of the fascist Government, no impartial observer can deny the greater part of the credit to Mussolini and his collaborators. The doing away of strikes and lock-outs, the new spirit of goodwill engendered between masters and men, the economies effected in the bureaucratic machine, the corn "campaign," the drastic collection of taxes, the comprehensive measures adopted to improve

---

[14] According to the official figures issued by the Moscow Government, there were executed over 1,800,000 persons between 1918 and 1923.

the lot of Southern Italy, are six points for which Fascism can legitimately take all the credit; and together they account for most of the economic ground gained.

Then there is another point with which I wish to deal here and here alone. Fascism is held up by its opponents as the enemy of Liberty. The principles governing the fascist conception of Liberty will be dealt with later on in the proper place. Here I only wish to emphasise the fact that exceptional restrictions of Liberty are necessitated in revolutionary times, just as they are in war-time. A Revolution is a fight, a fight between two opposing principles for the soul of the Nation. No compromise is possible between Parties who hold diametrically opposite principles, considered as fundamentally affecting the welfare and happiness of society. Hence a revolutionary Government cannot tolerate, while the issues are still at stake, the unrestricted propaganda of its enemies. Toleration of fundamentally adverse principles is, if we examine our consciences aright, usually due either to lack of conviction, to impotence making a virtue of necessity, or to contempt. None of these conditions apply to a revolutionary state of affairs. There would be no Revolution in the absence of conviction, there would be open civil war in the absence of authority, while contempt for the power of the enemy, when he is still in the field, would spell suicide.

Many restrictions of liberties by the fascist Government are indeed necessitated by the very nature of the case. It is the condition of every Revolution. But as soon as the yeast of the Revolution has leavened the whole country, as soon as the changes effected have become perfectly constitutionalised, many of the liberties of which citizens have been deprived will undoubtedly be restored, in exactly the same way as the Defence of the Realm Act was rescinded in England after the War. Not that this will entail a return to the liberal regime. As I have implied, the fascist conception of Liberty differs fundamentally from the liberal. Here I am merely drawing attention to the fact that it would be wrong to regard, as anti-Fascists are continually asserting, that *all* the restrictions of Liberty at present imposed in Italy are inherent in Fascism. The very idea is absurd. Anyone with the smallest historical sense will readily concede this point.[15]

It would be well for the reader to remember, too, that Fascism has contemporaneously restored many liberties to the Italian subject—for one thing, the liberty to worship God in public in accordance with the ancient customs of the people, a liberty which the former freemasonic Governments had rendered precarious. Fascism has also restored the greatest guarantee of personal freedom that we possess, the security of property. Lastly, the ordinary citizen is, I veritably believe, more concerned with his liberty to go about his ordinary business, to travel with the expectation of certainly arriving punctually at his destination and to communicate with his friends through the public services without fear of interruption, than he is about the dissemination of his political opinions in the columns of the Press or on the hustings. Those liberties at least the ordinary citizen is now assured in Italy as he has never been assured before.

§ IV

Before passing on to my first chapter, which will deal with the historical aspects of Fascism, it may be as well to conclude this introduction with a short sketch of the principal actor in the drama, Benito Mussolini. At the same time—for this is the main purpose of the Introduction—I can continue to clear the ground for the consideration of the universal aspects of Fascism, by removing one or two further popular misconceptions of the movement.

Mussolini occupies the position of a Dictator. But the idea of dictatorship has nothing whatever to do with Fascism, either

---

[15] Certain restrictions, for instance, on the liberty of the Press are, admittedly, of a temporary nature, while other measures affecting the liberty of the subject automatically lapse after a stated period of time, unless expressly renewed.

as a doctrine or as a programme. Mussolini's dictatorship is the instrument of the Revolution. When the revolutionary period comes to an end, there will be no place, properly speaking, for a Dictator in Italy. Thus, if Mussolini continues to direct the affairs of State under a perfectly constitutionalised fascist *régime*, he may still dominate, by his ability, his personality, his prestige, but he will cease to dominate by virtue of his office, as leader of the fascist revolutionary organisation, whose word at present is law. As Prime Minister he would still occupy a position of commanding authority, for the motto which Fascism has substituted for the "Liberty, Equality, Fraternity" of revolutionary France is *Responsibility, Hierarchy and Discipline*.[16] Under the new laws the Prime Minister will be a vastly more important person than he was under the liberal *régime*. The restoration of the principle of State authority will be shown to be one of the main, if not the main, feature of the fascist Revolution, and the Prime Minister will stand at the apex of the hierarchy of the State executive. Nevertheless above him there will stand the King, with reinforced and clearly defined prerogatives, placing certain constitutional bounds to the power of the Prime Minister. Nor will the King's prerogatives be the only constitutional checks. There will be others, forming a balance of powers, such as would commend itself to the most exacting of constitutional lawyers. So there will be no dictatorship when the revolutionary period is over. Fascism does not stand for a dictatorship, neither of a person nor of a class. It is a movement which in no sense may be called reactionary, however much it may insist on the importance of State authority. It is of the greatest importance, if Fascism is to be rightly understood, to distinguish between the two notions. If there is a dictatorship in Italy now, it is because the revolutionary organisation has taken this form by an accident of history.

The accident in question is the presence of a genius, a man of the people, with that medium-like gift of intuitioning and

---

[16] *Cf.* Emilio Bodrero, *Vittorie dottrinali del Fascismo* (Biblioteca dell'Istituto Fascista di Cultura in Milano, 1926).

interpreting the vast subconscious ideals of historical Italy dormant in the heart of every true Italian. This, I believe, is the secret of his success, this and his passionate sincerity and disinterestedness. The Italian adores a saint who shows himself to be no fool either to boot.

Nobody will deny that Mussolini has a remarkably practical head on his shoulders; he is a born organiser with big sweeps of ideas coupled with a ready power of grasping and ordering detail. He has immense powers of work and concentration. His versatility is astonishing. He has the gift of a fine, economical, Michael-Angelesque eloquence, which, together with his exuberant personal magnetism is of the stuff that leads men and multitudes. All these talents even his enemies concede him. Nor will anyone deny him a prodigious tenacity of will, great courage, a rare capacity for learning from experience, and the power of swift decision at the psychological moment, coupled with an acute instinct for judging the psychological moment.

Nevertheless, a very erroneous opinion of him appears to have been conceived abroad. I am not referring to those caricatures which represent him as a pinchbeck Napoleon, a glorified mountebank or a reduced edition of the Renaissance tyrant of the kidney of Eccelino da Romano.[17] There are also serious people who appreciate his unquestionable genius, but represent him as a materialist, or as a monster of egoism and of personal ambition, or place him in the same category of selfish, albeit glorious adventurers, as they place Napoleon. Mr. Maynard Keynes, in that admirable essay of his, *A Short View of Russia*, published last year by the Hogarth Press, appears to take something of these views. He places Trotsky, Mr. Bernard Shaw and Mr. Baldwin, each in his way, amongst the most religious of men. He appears unwilling to add Mussolini to this list and thereby falls into a vulgar error. The passage referred to (in the

---

[17] *Cf.* A recent effusion of Mr. H. G. Wells, which, were it not for the wide reputation gained by Mr. Wells as a popular and distinguished novelist, no self-respecting publisher would consider worthy of reproduction.

Preface to Mr. Keynes' Essay) comes immediately after the following sentences: "There are two distinct sublimations of materialistic egotism—one in which the ego is merged in the nameless mystic union, another in which it is merged in the pursuit of an ideal life for the whole community of men." But that such is the pursuit of Mussolini is not only my own conviction, who know him, but the conviction of everyone, unexceptionally, who has had to do with him, the conviction which is at the root of the people's love for him. In this his psyche differs profoundly from Napoleon's.

All great men of action hold in common certain qualities, such as have been enumerated above. What is more interesting are their differences, their individual character and their moral outlook. In these respects Mussolini and Napoleon are at opposite poles. If both share certain national characteristics, such as the complexity of the Italian mind, the Italian sense of realism, the one is a typical Romagnol, the other a typical Corsican— and one of the pleasant facts about Italy is the divergence of character that exists between Province and Province. The Corsican is outwardly cold, too often calculating, little susceptible to the influences of Art, of Religion, of others' personalities; and he has little sense of humour. The Romagnol has a great, palpitating human heart, a very keen sense of humour, is generous to a fault, is dangerously susceptible to outside influences. The Corsican makes an implacable enemy, the Romagnol makes loyal, life-long friendships.

If Mussolini has a weakness, it is his susceptibility to personal influences. He may judge fallen human nature pretty shrewdly in the mass; but he has the impulse to go out to meet the best in each individual with whom he comes in contact, and the realisation of the good in each is apt to obscure for him the bad. He is too apt to judge others by his own generous self. He will readily forgive an injury, readily excuse an apparent disloyalty; too often for the sake of an old friendship he will give a man another chance, who has let him badly down. Napoleon, never. Mussolini is well aware of this weakness. Bitter experience has taught him to be on his guard against it. But there it is, the defect of a quality, which we would not wish away. For if Napoleon was loved because he could intoxicate men's minds, as he led them up to share with him and through him the exhilaration and glory of his achievements, Mussolini is loved because he loves.

Napoleon was the centre of his universe; God is the centre of Mussolini's. He exults in the feeling that the whole of him is being used, the whole of his mortal self used up, for the cause in which he believes. His constant prayer is, "O, my God, let me perish if thereby Italy may be made great in the eyes of the world and in Thine eyes," and, "forgive me my trespasses, as I forgive them that trespass against me." For he knows that the path to Heaven of the statesman is only too often paved but with good intentions. The end does not justify the means; but when all is contingent, the lesser evil has often to be chosen. But if evil has always to be hated, what then? Courage to go on notwithstanding and faith in God's mercy. That is the attitude of Mussolini in the face of the practical problems of life: a deep consciousness of good and evil, a great sense of responsibility and realisation of the fallibility of human judgment in the choice of worthy means; hence a continual self-criticism and self-martyrdom, which, if it were not for his faith, his sense of duty to his vocation, and his moral courage, would drive him to a contemplative life. Not Napoleon but, rather, St. Ignatius is Mussolini's spiritual companion.

Every day he grows in wisdom and moral stature. The quality of consistency in the character of anyone is to be judged rather by a consistent evolution of his ideas than by a fixity of opinions. This is especially true of a man of action, whose practical Philosophy comes to maturity and clarity in the course of acquired experience, intensified by the burden of responsibility when it comes to him.

Mussolini, who began his life as a Socialist, has passed through many stages of opinion in the course of his evolution. But his evolution may be likened to an ascending straight line. This is his true consistency; and it would be absurd to quote any stage of his past, even of his comparatively recent past, against his present.

The same may be said of the political doctrines underlying Fascism. Fascism never possessed a ready-made Philosophy. It arose as a Party of action. Its aims at first appeared obscure to the ordinary man in the street, apart from the immediate aim of re-establishing the authority of the State. Consequently, recruits joined the movement in the beginning from every kind of source; or many others, for fear of committing themselves to the unknown, held themselves aloof. But very gradually at first, more swiftly after the march on Rome, the true significance of the movement became clearer, with the result that many of the first recruits, when they were honest, had no alternative but to abandon it; while others, with their original doubts removed, took their place. Its significance has now emerged into the full light of day. Mussolini, in the course of his own latter-day evolution, as he clarified his own ideas, clarified them also for the whole Party and made them finally a consistent whole. This entailed a continuous scrapping of impure doctrinal ingredients, and at the same time, independently of those who, of their own will, left the movement, a continuous scrapping of impure human elements—a most difficult, ungrateful task, requiring infinite judgment, firmness and tact, and carried out only at the cost of much heart-burning, disappointment and worry. This has been Mussolini's passion; but it has also been his schooling. He has suffered in a way which it is difficult to exaggerate from the moral failings of others, many of whom he had reckoned as his friends, men who betrayed him and his best hopes by their self-seeking, their envy, their shallowness. But hereby he himself has come to understand, in a way which five years ago perhaps he only dimly grasped, that the only way to serve one's country best is to serve God first.

PART I

CHAPTER I

FASCISM IN THE LIGHT OF HISTORY

F ASCISM may be defined generally as a political and social movement having as its object the re-establishment of a political and social order, based upon the main current of traditions that have formed our European civilisation, traditions created by Rome, first by the Empire and subsequently by the Catholic Church. Conversely, Fascism may be described as the repudiation of that individualist mentality that found expression first in the Pagan Renaissance, then in the Reformation and later in the French Revolution, not to speak of the Industrial Revolution, which issued in "Capitalism,"[18] itself the product of the Reformation.[19]

Thus, according to our definition, which has Mussolini's sanction, the accusation made by certain persons that Fascism, in its defence of the Church and its restoration of Religion to a place of honour in the State, is acting from purely opportunistic motives, falls to the ground.

In order to be quite clear, what is meant by "opportunistic motives?" They are three: First, that by defending the Church with its wide-flung influence, Italy may be enabled to spread her influence, too.[20] Secondly, that, by upholding Religion, the

---

[18] *Cf.* footnote defining "Capitalism," on p. 47 of the Introduction.

[19] *Cf.* Curzio Suckert, *L'Europa Vivente* (Valecchi, Florence, 1923).

[20] Compare official atheist France's patronage of French Catholic Schools and Missions abroad, the while discouraging Catholic action

cause of Fascism may gain the popular support of Italian Catholics, who form the vast majority of the population.[21] Thirdly, the mere appreciation of the fact that Religion is a powerful aid in the maintenance of social order, in the disciplining of men's selfish appetites and in instilling in them the virtue of self-sacrifice.

Although the above definition is an accurate one, nevertheless there is a universal aspect of Fascism independent, in a certain sense, of the Roman tradition. What I mean to say is simply this: that, although Japan, for instance, is in no sense an heir to Rome, nevertheless Japan, while maintaining her own traditions, might yet be, in a certain sense, a fascist State. This point will be dealt with later. It is sufficient for the reader to bear it in mind, lest he should, at this stage, draw too absolute conclusions from my definition.

Every acute and sensitive observer in Italy as far back as 1911,[22] or even earlier, was aware of the extraordinary vitality of the Italian people of this generation, and was consequently on the alert to see what was to be the outcome of it. He must also have been aware of three and increasingly growing movements; a revival of Catholic life, Syndicalism and Nationalism—three movements which prepared the ground for the advent of Fascism.

The revival of Catholic life had no leanings towards Clericalism, which may be defined as a political order wherein the influence of the Priest predominates, nor yet towards Ultramontanism (the aim of which was the restoration of Rome in full

---

at home.

[21] Compare the Catholic policy of Napoleon III, who sought thereby to gain the Catholic vote.

[22] I fix on the date 1911, because it was in that year that I first intuitioned something of what was to follow; and this intuition I found was shared by numbers of Italians, standing outside politics, with whom I came in contact in the course of my wanderings throughout the peninsula. It was the year of the fiftieth anniversary of the unification of Italy.

sovereignty to the Pope—a term which explains itself, in that all its principal advocates lived beyond the Alps).

Catholic opinion, after the taking of Rome in 1870, took a long time to become absorbed into the new State; for Catholics were torn at first in their allegiance, or, more accurately, Catholic opinion was rendered impotent for some time (especially before the relaxation, by Pius X, of the ban contained in the Papal Decree *Non Expedit*, which formally prohibited Catholics from taking part in parliamentary elections),[23] owing to the distraction caused by the fears entertained for the Papacy as a result of the fall of the temporal power. Only gradually, as it was realised that the Church was in no sense weakened by the change, in spite of the highly unsatisfactory and anomalous position in which the Pope has been placed by the wholly inadequate and purely unilateral Italian Law of Guarantees, and, finally, by the destruction of the Austrian Empire, the stronghold of the Ultra-montanes, did it become possible for Catholic opinion fully to re-assert itself. Meanwhile, the anti-Catholic Freemasons, the Positivists, the Hedonists, the Materialists, had had a long run for their money. They had dominated the State for close on two generations; but despite the religious vacuum they had sought to create in the heyday of their opportunity, the people had maintained their faith. No sooner, therefore, did the Catholics begin to find themselves again, than their influences grew and grew. Already in 1911 there were vivid signs of their coming triumph, which signified also the triumph of tradition.[24]

---

[23] The ban was finally removed altogether by Benedict XV.

[24] I am not concerned here with a chronicle of events, or it would be necessary to give some account of the birth of the Catholic Party, as distinct from the general revival of Catholic life; the development of the Catholic Party into the Popular Party, which became, after the War, the strongest organised Party after the Socialists; its moral degeneration in competition with the Socialists, together with its inoculation with the virus of Internationalism and Democratism (a definition of which will be given in due course); its split into two sections after the advent of Fascism, resulting in the absorption of the national and conservative

Secondly, Syndicalism, before the War, was of the red variety, preparing the ground for the day when the factories would come to be handed over to the workers without compensation to the owners, and the Red Syndicalist Republic proclaimed. Associated with the socialist party, it shared, at first, with the latter its materialistic view of life and paid homage to the name of Marx. Socialism, however, by 1911 was showing signs of losing ground to Syndicalism; and Syndicalism itself was changing. Sorel had become its prophet; Corridoni had become its most inspiring leader, Corridoni who was afterwards killed in France, while serving with an Italian voluntary contingent before Italy herself entered the War. Syndicalism indeed was becoming less internationalist, less materialist. The Mazzinian idealism of the Republican party, whose stronghold was big-hearted Romagna, was affecting it.

It had already become apparent that there was a sane side to Syndicalism; it had become apparent that a Syndicalism could exist which need deny neither Religion, nor Patriotism, nor Justice to the owners of property. Syndicalism, away from any special application of the term, may indeed be described as an effort to give the wage-earner a property interest in his industry and so a sense of responsibility for the well-being of that industry. As such, it is a movement instinct with the Roman, the Catholic tradition.

Modern industry necessitates the employment of large bodies of men as wage-earners; but the Traditionalist, ever since the great mediæval civilisation which was the outcome of the Christianisation of the Roman Empire, with difficulty acquiesces in the position of a mere wage-earner. This is particularly so in the case of the Italian; for Italy has remained the heart of the Roman, the Catholic tradition, as being the home of the Papacy and the country nearest to the fountain head of the traditions that moulded Europe.

---

elements by Fascism and the wandering in the wilderness of the remainder.

Some solution by which, for the masses, the sense of property may be reconciled with the requirements of modern industry, has accordingly long been a markedly instinctive desire in the hearts of modern Italians. Property means Liberty in the best, concrete sense. The protection which Fascism gives to property and the encouragement which it gives to the worker who owns his own means of livelihood, has contributed much to the popularity of Fascism; for there exists, in Italy, a very large proportion of the people who remain their own masters.[25] The average Italian would far prefer to be relatively poor, but his own master, than relatively rich and at the beck and call of another. Fascism would defend and encourage this healthy inclination. Fascist economic policy is, in fact, a moderate, realistic "Distributism." But it recognises that in the struggle for existence between States in the modern world a place must be found for the great industries within the national economy. These also must be encouraged and at the same time a solution found for the present invidious position of the wage-earner.

Fascism, however, has the good sense to realise, too, that there is no simple solution of the problem, no short cut to Utopia. Much depends on creating, first, the proper moral state of mind in both masters and men. Much, therefore, depends on gradual education and judicious propaganda. Moreover, each industry in its particular circumstances must solve the problem, largely for itself, and in different ways; there can be no cut-and-dried scheme applicable to all and sundry. There are lessons to be learnt from innumerable and diverse sources, such as experiments in co-operation, guild organisation, co-partnership, profit-sharing, workers' investment schemes, etc., etc. Progress

---

[25] According to the census of 1921, nearly fifty per cent, of the population belong to the following classes: small and great agricultural proprietors; *mezzadri* (who have a co-operative interest in the land and great security of tenure); owners of small and large shops, stores, workshops or factories; artisans owning their own tools; persons deriving their sole income from investments or pensions; and professional men, who have chosen their vocation largely from the love of the work itself.

must be effected slowly as experience dictates. Finally, much depends on organisation; and the creation of the great fascist Corporations of Employers and Employees, a description of which will be given in the second part of this book, the institution of Labour Courts and the promulgation of the fascist "Labour Charter," have already laid the foundations of a new economic order, both national and traditional in spirit, which it would not be amiss to call "Fascist Syndicalism"; and it is confidently expected that, through these organisations, the desired solutions will eventually be found.

I now come to the consideration of Nationalism, a movement requiring careful analysis, if we wish to avoid misunderstandings and gauge its import.

Before analysing, however, the various meanings of the term "Nationalism," let us consider for a moment the meaning of such terms as "State," "Nation," "Race," "Empire," and trace in broad outline the origins of the great national States of Europe to-day, which arose out to the wreck of the Roman Empire. Such a survey will exemplify the traditionalist character of fascist Nationalism.

A State may be deemed that system of Government, administration and laws, the supreme authority of which is recognised by a body of men, a Nation or group of Nations. This is the special meaning of the term "State" that we find frequently adopted by eminent writers. In this sense, it was scarcely an exaggeration when an absolute monarch like Louis XIV of France declared: *"L'État, c'est moi."*

On the other hand, in common usage, the term "State" signifies something broader; it is identified with the community which recognises the supreme authority of a particular system of Government, administration and laws. Both definitions, in my opinion, should be allowed to stand. The two ideas reciprocally imply each other, and we can safely leave it to the context to prevent any confusion of thought.

We may say accordingly that a national State is one with authority over a single Nation; an Imperial State one with authority over a group of Nations or a heterogeneous assortment of peoples.

A "Nation" must not be confused with "Race." Nor is it merely the sum of individuals, a body politic at a given moment and recognising the authority of the State. If this were so, the easily-understood term "body politic" could be substituted for the more subtle term "Nation." A "Nation" is much more than this. "It is that living, moral entity, which, though composed of individuals, transcends the scope and life of its components, identifying itself with the history and finalities of an uninterrupted series of generations. It is a moral entity, since it is composed of human beings; for man is not solely matter, and the ends of the human species, far from being the materialistic ones we have in common with other animals, are, rather, and predominantly, the spiritual finalities which are peculiar to man and which every form of society strives to attain as well as its stage of development allows. It is an entity with a unity brought about by common traditions among the people that compose it, traditions formed in the course of time owing to the pervasion of a variety of influences (*not all of which, however, need be present*), such as community of topographical and climatic conditions, of language, race, culture, religion, laws, customs, history, feelings and volitions, economic interests and territory having clearly marked geographical boundaries."[26]

By "Race" I mean the various ethnographical groups of which society is formed.

An "Empire" is a group of Nations or peoples recognising the authority of an Imperial State.

To give examples: modern Greece is a Nation, united by common traditions based on a community of language, race,

---

[26] *Cf.* the speech delivered by His Excellency, Alfredo Rocco, Italian Minister of Justice, delivered at Perugia on 30th August, 1925, published in an English version by the Carnegie Endowment for International Peace, October, 1926; and included in the work by the same author, *La Trasformazione dello Stato* (Libreria della "Voce," Florence, 1927).

religion and other factors. Switzerland is also a Nation, though composed of different races, speaking different languages and practising different religions. It is united, however, by common traditions of history, topographical conditions, etc., etc. Thus, too, the Greek Nation recognises the authority of the Greek State; the Swiss Nation that of the Swiss State or Confederation of States (Swiss and Cantonal Government, administration and laws). Again, France is both a Nation and an Empire, a national State and an imperial State, with its far-flung subject Nations and peoples. Britain is likewise a Nation and an Empire, a national State and an imperial State, associated, into the bargain, with a number of national sister States, who share, with the Mother-country, some portion of the burden and privileges of the imperial State.

A city State or a tribal State might be held, in certain circumstances, to fall under the above definition of a national State. But this would contrast with ordinary usage, because of its primitive character. Hence I shall reserve the term "national" State as applying to relatively large national units only, and use the terms "city" or "tribal" State to denote a distinct class, differentiated by common sense.

The growth and integration of a national State characterises political progress, as distinct from social progress; for these two kinds of progress need by no means march hand in hand. Thus, where we have an Empire, political progress is a process of assimilation of the various Nations or peoples composing that Empire. Similarly, an Empire exhibits political decadence when the various Nations or peoples composing that Empire tend to break away and become independent societies recognising separate States of their own. Germany is an example of a politically progressive imperial system: for the German Empire, the German Imperial State, has by now practically become a single German Nation, a purely national State. The Austro-Hungarian Empire, on the other hand, was throughout the nineteenth century in a decadent condition. The British Empire appears, too, at first sight, to be decadent in this sense; but the appearance may very likely prove illusory; for the conditions of the British

Empire are peculiar, owing to the founding of colonies of British men and women in empty spaces overseas, and to its great geographical diversity. Britain, indeed, is conducting a momentous experiment in developing independent national sister States out of her Empire, sister States for whom there is every good hope of remaining sisters and of working up, in the generations to come, their joint association with the Mother-country into a higher national and imperial unity. It is not merely a question of State decentralisation, a policy which many Empires, including Rome, have profitably practised before Britain. It is something quite new in the history of the world. Whether she will succeed in converting India, however, into an independent national State, desirous of remaining within the Empire and of working up eventually into a higher unity with her sisters, is, it must be confessed, extremely problematical. Great Britain has not exhibited a great talent for assimilation, a talent wherein the Latin Nations appear, rather, to excel; and the success of Britain's task in India would seem to depend much on the power of assimilation.[27]

The Latin talent for assimilation was exhibited in a remarkable degree by ancient Rome. The Roman Empire, embracing, at first, countless Nations and peoples, had, in its prime, practically transformed itself into a single Roman Nation. Not altogether, however. The process was never quite completed. Two big divisions remained, the Latin and the Greek, besides a number of minor ones; and in this connection it is interesting to note that in the Church, which is the heir to ancient Rome, a survival of the various unassimilated Nations that composed the Roman Empire at the time of its decay is preserved to this day in her various rites.[28] So, when the Empire declined, it inevitably split

---

[27] *Cf.* Britain's notable failure hitherto, after centuries of domination, to assimilate Ireland, in spite of the conquest of Ireland by the English language, and the large community of interests, not to speak of the geographical unity, of the two islands.

[28] The Latin rite and the Greek rite correspond, of course, to the main divisions into which the Empire fell, the Armenian and Coptic rites,

along the lines traced where the process of assimilation had ended, and there became two Romes, the Rome of Romulus and the Rome of Constantine.

The Roman Empire may thus be considered the prototype of the great imperial State, and, for us Westerners, the prototype also of the great national State. It was a vital organism distinguished by its unity in variety, the firm foundation on which our European civilisation has been built, the mother of us all. Its vast extent, its pre-eminent civilisation, its dominating strength, its long duration, gave it a prestige which outlasted its concrete existence. Before its virtual demise it had already become Christian, so that Catholic and Roman in ordinary parlance had become interchangeable terms;[29] and out of it there grew, in the West, the Holy Roman Empire, at first a concrete fact under Charlemagne, but gradually to become little more than an outward form and an aspiration. In theory it continued to exist right down to the Napoleonic era, long, long after its very shadow had become obscured; and it continued to exist thus because the hearts of men turned back with longing, as in a dream, to the time when all civilisation was united under a single paternal Government; a past to which men clung as if reluctant to give up the hope of one day reconstituting the unity they had lost. This was especially so among those peoples who had remained Catholic; for the spiritual side of the great Empire had not only never decayed, but on the contrary had grown from strength to strength and spread its wings to the uttermost corners of the earth.

Now, as the Roman State decayed (and this is particularly true of the Western half of the Empire, where, with the removal of the seat of the Empire to Constantinople, political decay was both earlier and more thorough), the central heart ceased to beat out the life-blood required to nourish the body politic; and since

---

etc., to those Nations of the Eastern Empire which had not been perfectly assimilated by the Greek civilisation.

[29] *Cf.* James Bryce's masterpiece, *The Holy Roman Empire* (MacMillan & Co., London, revised edition, 1922).

the Western Roman world had been practically assimilated into a single Nation during the preceding period of political progress, the decay here could not take the form of a mere split-up into national States, for more than one, the Roman one, there could hardly be said to exist. So decay took the form, rather, of a slow sinking into civil chaos, relieved from time to time and locally by the strong rule of some forceful viceroy or condottiere. These were the "Dark Ages." But gradually, out of the dark, came the light, the great mediæval civilisation, the product of feudalism and the city State (the latter itself a tradition from the ancient world), into which society had crystallised anew by a process of adaptation to the conditions inherent in a Nation wherein the State had abdicated its authority. The Roman Empire as a State had virtually ceased, although the outward form of it survived and its prestige still held, especially in Germany and in Italy, where the Pope and the Emperor held their Courts. The sway of the Church was predominant, however, and gave to the whole a spiritual unity, which, in turn, helped to keep alive the fiction as well as the ideal of civil unity.

Politically, Europe, taken as a whole, had markedly regressed, as compared with the great days of the Empire, however much she may have picked up again in comparison with the darkest years of the Dark Ages. But Christianity, the while, had worked a social miracle, a social transformation. Mediæval social conditions, considered independently of political conditions, represented undoubtedly a marked advance on Roman social conditions.[30] So, whereas Europe had decayed politically, she had advanced socially; and this social advance, carrying with it a rich harvest of intellectual and artistic achievements, economic development and comparative security, brought about in turn a new impulse towards political progress.

In the outlying portions of the Empire, or of what had formerly constituted the Empire, in Spain, in France, in England,

---

[30] *Cf.* Alfredo Oriani's great work in three volumes, *La Lotta Politica in Italia* (Libreria della "Voce," Florence, 1917).

for example, this impulse was particularly favoured. The aspiration towards reconstituting the Empire as a reality was here less strongly felt and realised more and more clearly as an impracticable dream. Consequently the impulse towards political progress caused gradually to come into existence among these outlying peoples, where a certain homogeneity of language, race and economic interests had in the course of time become established and where the tradition of the city State was weaker, local political unities that transcended the fief and the city, and finally engendered a number of national States, which, some sooner, some later, broke loose altogether from the idea of the Empire, made themselves the centre of their peculiar aspirations and developed into the corresponding great national States of to-day.

At the centre of things, on the other hand, the impulse towards political progress was less favoured, chiefly because it was there that the form of the Empire still persisted in a visible manner, where the prestige of the Empire and the surviving sense of Roman nationality was still so strongly felt that men continued vainly to aspire to the Empire's reconstruction. The idea of the universal Catholic State, the Roman State, with its local municipal organisation, that had once comprised, and, as it was fondly hoped, was destined again to comprise, the whole of civilisation, overshadowed the narrower national State idea. Political progress was accordingly less marked (though by no means stagnant), for having aspired too high.

Nevertheless, small regional States did indeed form themselves, in Italy often quasi-national or else in the shape of miniature Empires, with a city State at their head, like Venice, or like Florence, which gradually absorbed Tuscany, or like the Papal States; while, in the Germanies, either the same phenomenon occurred, or, more often, regional States grew out of the feudal system without transcending it, and in central Europe a local imperial system, a concrete Empire in the very lap of the ideal Holy Roman Empire, formed out of a group of such regional States, under the aegis of the Austrian Monarchy, came also gradually into being. This Austrian Empire, in fact, may be regarded as the extent to which the aspiration to reconstitute the Roman Empire had succeeded. But it was a barbarous production, incapable of assimilating the more cultured peoples of Italy or of satisfying the Italian imperial ideal. Throughout its history, it was characterised by arrested growth, and ever contained within itself the germs of decay. Further East, the Turkish conquest had meantime laid a dead hand on what had once been Byzantium.

Then, bit by bit, as the Western national States consolidated their power, they too began to develop imperial tendencies, imperial tendencies, however, which in no way sought to recreate the old imperial unity; and Italy, who had failed to form either a new imperial system for herself or to crystallise into a united modern national State, became the contested prize of all her neighbours. Europe became the battlefield of large rival States, each struggling for ascendancy. The Pagan Renaissance left behind it a sorry legacy of cynicism. Right became identified with Might, and lust for power and glory the driving ambition of rulers. The consequence was the oppression of the people by their rulers on the one hand, the failure to achieve any further political progress on the other. Domination, not assimilation, became the knowledged end of Empire and whole Nations were callously handed over from one domination to another, bartered away, sold or partitioned, without any regard for the proper ends of society. Religion was a decaying force and with its decay social conditions decayed everywhere too. Nor have we succeeded in regaining the social ground lost during those fateful centuries which culminated in the French Revolution.

This great upheaval was the revolt of the French people against what had indeed become an intolerable condition of affairs. In so far as it was this, it was healthy enough. It was a heaven-sent punishment on the heads of those in authority, who had forgotten their very *raison d'être*, the promotion of the welfare of the whole people over whom they ruled. It was a morally legitimate breaking of the privileged class-system into which the State had degenerated, and it undoubtedly resulted in a number of permanent conquests for the cause of civilisation. The world badly needed a breath of Liberty and it was in the name of Liberty that the Revolution was made.

The political Philosophy, however, which fed the revolutionary movement was still the child of the cynical, individualistic, purely rationalistic atmosphere of the eighteenth century, tempered only by the thin broth of Humanitarianism. Though it had power to destroy, though it provoked the stimulus required to enable peoples to throw off the yoke of self-seeking rulers, it had no power to construct a healthy State system in the place of the old one. It merely cleared the ground for some other order to take its place, for better or for worse. It hastened rather than arrested the catastrophic course taken by Europe in the sixteenth, seventeenth and eighteenth centuries, of which the epilogue was the Great War.

The revolutionary and Napoleonic wars—to pick up again the thread of our argument—spread the ideas of the Revolution all over Europe. Napoleon himself blew the last vestige of the Holy Roman imperial shadow into smoke and thereby relieved central Europe of an incubus. Thus were created, at last, the conditions which led to the establishment of modern national States in Italy and Germany, and, with the decay of the Austrian and Turkish Empires, to the establishment of various other national States out of their respective components. The late Great War is really, in effect, the end of a chapter, the beginning of which was the decay of Rome. Europe has been finally split up into national unities. Within the confines of Europe there practically exist no more Empires. The great power of assimilation which Rome exhibited has delayed, even till this day, the complete reconstruction of Europe in accordance with differentiated national groups. It still remains a question whether the legacy of traditions which Rome left behind her and still survive are sufficient to form a cement strong enough to bind these national groups together again into one genuine political unity. Fascism would answer: *Yes, but on the one condition that these various national groups, before it is too late, recant the political and religious heresies, which have deformed the true traditions. Europe, it affirms, can only be re-united on the basis of the Roman tradition. Reinforce this great common tradition—the only common tradition—by a general conformation to the Roman political and religious traditions, and we may yet have good reason to hope.*

* * * *

This historical sketch is necessarily a very summary one; but I think it brings out pretty clearly the main facts for my purpose. An important point to remember, in connection with it, is that nineteenth-century European Nationalism, and with it the Italian Risorgimento, was largely nourished on and found its stimulus from the doctrines of Liberalism. This alliance, however, nay, confusion between Nationalism and Liberalism was of an entirely accidental nature, owing to the fact that the latter, being the dominating political tendency of the times, constituted a trump card for the Nationalists to play in their efforts to weaken the resistance of those Powers, whose continual existence depended on the preservation of the territorial *status quo*. The Nationalism, on the other hand, which could be seen to be stirring in Italy in the years preceding the War, was of a different kind. It was a Nationalism completely severed from Liberalism, of which Corradini may be regarded as the founder, one that looked back for its inspiration on ancient Rome. Like the Nationalism which characterised the political progress following the mediæval era, it had laid hold of the truth that large, thoroughly assimilated national States are a measure of political progress; and it sought, accordingly, to make Italy a genuinely united land. In this sense it repudiated the Middle Ages. Italy had been made, but the Italians as a genuinely united people had still to be made. It therefore laid great stress on the juristic and religious traditions of the Nation; proclaimed once more the principle of State authority, which Liberalism had undermined; and repudiated the agnostic State, which dashed with the cherished traditions of Italians and made for disunity. More particularly did it enter the lists against the international gospel of the Socialists. It was this Nationalism which Fascism caught up into itself, purified, developed and made its own.

Descending to analysis, there are three chief meanings to the word "Nationalism," two of which are, when translated into practice, morally justifiable, one of which is not. Italian Nationalism, before the War, was not altogether free from the implications of the third meaning, which was made in Germany. German *Kultur* tended then to dominate the universities of Europe. The influence of Hegel, to choose the most eminent of the German philosophers, whose philosophy led to the exaltation of the third type of Nationalism, was very rampant in Italy; and although his Italian disciples had already transformed his theories into something less pernicious, although Corradini himself had nothing in him of the Teuton, the taint remained. The taint remains, though fast disappearing, among even a certain set of self-styled Fascists of this day; and it is still important for students of Fascism to be on their guard against taking the utterances of this group, who propound doctrines similar to those advocated by Charles Maurras and the *Action Française*, as representing the fascist movement. I am not referring so much to the Italian neo-Hegelians themselves, least of all to Professor Gentile, who would be the first to repudiate Charles Maurras, as to the less instructed nationalist enthusiasts, who, not as philosophical students, but as men of the world, have been inoculated unconsciously by the political fruits of Hegelism, long after (as is the wont of men of the world!) such doctrines have become worn out, old-fashioned *vieux jeux* among thinking men.

I will now analyse the three meanings of Nationalism, so that there should be no mistake about it; and to this end I cannot do better than paraphrase at length passages from that wonderful little book, already referred to, *Une opinion sur Charles Maurras et le devoir des Catholiques*, by Jacques Maritain.

1. Nationalism may simply mean—in opposition to the humanitarian myths—that the Nation, taken as synonymous with the terms *civitas* or *fatherland*, is the highest natural social unity.

2. Or it may mean—in opposition to the fallacious individualistic conception of society—that the common good is "more
divine," as Aristotle and St. Thomas[31] lay down, than the individual good; and that it is something by nature different from
the simple sum or collection of individual goods; that natural
law enjoins on us (as indeed also the 4th Commandment) to love
the good of the fatherland more than our own private interests.

This meaning of Nationalism in no sense implies any consent to the doctrine of *Racism*, which holds that unity of racial
origin is the main principle of unity for civil society and that the
members of each ethnical branch should properly aim at group-
ing themselves together into so many national States. Although
it is desirable that strongly-felt national aspirations, which often
depend on community of race, should be satisfied, as far as this
may be compatible with justice, *Racism* or the Principle of
Racial Self-determination, as it has been called in recent years,
is a materialistic illusion, contrary to natural law and destructive
of civilisation. It is the *reductio ad absurdum* of Nationalism; any
truly logical application of it is farcical and impracticable.[32]

---

[31] *Summa Theol.* 2, 2ae, q. 31, art. 3 ad 2um.

[32] The principle of Self-determination, in any sense—whether racial or
national—can only be admitted as a very secondary principle in the
determination of State frontiers, even if it can be admitted at all. The
reason why it can only be admitted as a secondary principle, if at all, is
that we must necessarily first define our area within which the principle
is to be applied, before we can even begin to apply it; and on the definition of this area, which must depend on other principles, will depend
the practical results of self-determination.

Take, for instance, the old Irish question. Had Ireland or any portion
of Ireland any right to secede? Imagine this question put to the test of
a plebiscite, as, in effect, it was. What area is to be chosen for the plebiscite? If we take the larger geographical unity, which is the British Isles,
the result of the plebiscite would be the sacrifice of the vast majority of
Irish opinion. If we restrict the plebiscite to the lesser geographical
unity, which is Ireland, on the other hand, we sacrifice, in the first
place, the claim of the English, the Welsh and the Scots, whose interests may be very deeply affected by the question, to have any say in the

3. The third sense in which the term "Nationalism" may be used is the corrupt form of its legitimate meaning. It then signifies the blind worship of the Nation, taken as something superior to all moral or religious Law—that kind of Nationalism which is in opposition to God and to the Kingdom of God—the cult of the Nation-God or State-God.

Fascism has definitely repudiated this interpretation and is in course of rejecting from its ranks those who would identify

---

matter; in the second place, we sacrifice the scattered unionist minorities in Southern Ireland and the compact unionist element in the North. If the vote were taken likewise in the separate historical divisions of Ulster, Munster, Leinster and Connaught, we should get the same unsatisfactory result. But if the vote were taken by counties, only four counties would contract to remain within the United Kingdom; and that being so, would they not, for economic reasons, soon repent of their action? Again, if the vote were taken by parishes, we should get a still different result. Or we should get different results again if the vote were taken on the question limited by certain guarantees. As it is, with, in effect, two simple plebiscites, choosing as our areas what are now Southern and Northern Ireland, we have, in the result, first sacrificed the general opinion of the other British Island, we have then sacrificed the opinion of Southern Ireland and finally we have done violence to the principle itself along the whole border. Where, indeed, is the process to stop? What, indeed, is the blessed principle at all, when it comes to be analysed? Surely one that becomes immediately resolved into a number of others, involving questions of geography, economics, convenience, justice and common sense. In these circumstances, need it ever be invoked? Maybe the present Irish solution is a good one. But it is not a good one merely because the majority in Northern Ireland are for the Union and the majority in Southern Ireland are for the Free State. For, on the same principle, it could be considered a bad one, because the majority of the British Isles are for the Union, because the majority of Ireland are for the Free State, because the majority of Ulster are for the Free State, because the majority of two of the counties forming part of Northern Ireland are against the Union—and so on. No. If the present solution is a good one, it is because it has brought useless blood-shed, at least for the time being, to an end, without doing violence to the unity of the British Empire, which is the most important of all the unities involved.

Fascism with this reprehensible idea. Fascism regards God as the only true sovereign, and as Alfredo Rocco, Minister of Justice, has authoritatively declared, [33] "the fascist State must defend and diffuse morality among the People, must occupy itself with religious problems and so confess and safeguard the true Religion, which is the Catholic Religion," the Religion, whose whole history is characterised by an unceasing struggle against all attempts of the civil power to pass God by.

To sum up, Fascism is no improvisation. It has immediate historical antecedents in the three movements: the revival of Catholic life, Syndicalism and Corradini's Nationalism, already growing from strength to strength before the War.[34] It has gathered these three movements together, purified them and harmonised them. Its roots lie in the historical traditions of the Italian people (traditions which all Europe in a greater or lesser degree shares), so much so that nothing could be truer than the following remark by Harold E. Goad, Secretary of the British Institute in Florence, taken from his recent review of Commendatore Luigi Villari's book, *The Fascist Experiment* (Faber & Gwyre, London, 1926) in the Journal of the Royal Institute of International Affairs: "Had there been no European War, no bolshevist Revolution, a movement such as Fascism would sooner or later have taken place in Italy, although it would probably have been less popular and theatrical and certainly less 'repressive,' because it would not have had to combat alien ideas." The postwar crisis, in fact, brought matters to a head; liberal statecraft was found bankrupt; and to save Italy from economic ruin there

---

[33] Alfredo Rocco, *La Trasformazione dello Stato* (Libreria della "Voce," Florence, 1927).

[34] It should be noted here that Marinetti's "Futurist" movement also but in a minor degree, unquestionably contributed to the formation of Fascism. D'Annunzio, too, has exercised a great influence on the practical development of Fascism, the programme of which has in many respects, been inspired by D'Annunzio's ideas embodied in his constitution for the State of Fiume—ideas very akin to those of Guild Socialism. *Cf.* Odon Por, *Fascism* (Labour Publishing Co., London, 1923).

was nothing for it but for a minority of intrepid souls, acting in advance of, but not against, public opinion, to seize the State and to achieve Fascism by Revolution. By great fortune, the movement also produced the man, gifted with all the true marks of a leader, a man of the people, who could read deep into the soul of the people and thereby be able to drive the movement closer and closer to the Italian Nation's true traditions, ridding it, as it developed, of its impurities and moderating its excesses.

For this reason alone Fascism has come to stay in Italy. For Europe it stands at the cross-roads looking back towards the two Romes, Imperial and Catholic, that made her civilisation, and pointing to its straight continuation as the only safe road by which to advance. Thus its historical function and mission is simply this: to prepare the ground for a new European political and social synthesis, founded on the sure traditions of the past, when Europe was yet one.

CHAPTER II

THE STATE

"MAN'S natural instinct moves him to live in civil society, for he cannot, if dwelling apart, provide himself with the necessary requirements of life, nor procure the means of developing his mental and moral faculties. Hence it is divinely ordained that he should lead his life—be it family, social or civil—with his fellow-men, amongst whom alone his several wants can be adequately supplied. But as no society can hold together unless someone be over all, directing all to strive earnestly for the common good, every civilised community must have a ruling authority, and this authority, no less than society itself has its source in nature, and has, consequently, God for its author. Hence it follows that all public power must proceed from God—for God alone is the true supreme Lord of the World. Everything, without exception, must be subject to Him, and must serve Him, so that whatsoever holds the right to govern holds it from one sole and single source, namely, God, the Sovereign Ruler of all. *There is no power but from God* (Rom. XIII, 1). The right to rule, however, is not necessarily bound up with any special mode of Government. It may take this or that form, provided only that it be of a nature to insure the general welfare."[35]

---

[35] From Leo XIII's Encyclical *Immorlale Dei* on the Constitution of States, 20th June, 1888.

Cf. also Aristotle, *Politics*, III, 2, "Man is by nature a political animal,"

This trenchant and succinct paragraph from the pen of Leo XIII summarises the burden of the following chapter; and so well is the classic, Catholic, traditionalist idea of the State therein expressed and proved, that it would almost seem superfluous to add anything to it. But for the sake of the profane general reader, it would be well, nevertheless, to beat round the questions involved in order to make quite certain that no point be misunderstood; and to use the opportunity thereby given to criticise certain opposing theories and to make some few little excursions into regions closely connected, if only indirectly, with the main theory. I shall accordingly divide the remainder of the chapter under a series of headings.

1. Whenever a ruling authority, not humanly subject to any higher ruling authority, exists over a given society of human families, that society constitutes a State, however barbarous, however primitive it may be. Here we have an accurate definition of the State in accordance with the broader meaning of the term. It is a society juridically organised, "a political unity, whose *raison d'être* is the promotion of the general good."[36]

The State, accordingly, is not simply a national unity, nor a racial unity, nor a religious or moral unity, nor yet an intellectual or emotional unity. A given State may coincide with these unities; it may, in the course of historical development, arise from one or more of these unities, either alone or combined; it may, and almost certainly will, tend to establish these unities. But these unities do not in fact constitute the State, because they can exist independently of the State. The essence of the State is political unity—juridical unity; and it is a "perfect" society in that it admits no superior authority to itself save alone the Moral Law, which is the Law of God. Nevertheless, as I stated in the previous chapter, an indication of political progress is the

---

and St. Thomas Aquinas, *Summa Theol.* 2^a, 2^{ae}, q. 109, art. 3 and 6 ad 1um, 3 q. 65, art. 1.

[36] *Cf.* A. Valensin, *Traité de Droit naturel*, Vol. II, Chap. IV, par. 2 (Éditions Spes, Paris, 1925).

growth and integration of national States, that is, the assimilation by a given State of the various national groups or peoples of which it may be composed, into one single Nation under the authority of its juridical institutions, which are an aspect of itself; and the extension of the State, wherever extension leads to assimilation of the parts to which its authority is extended.[37] National unity, therefore, is indeed a measure of political progress. But the State may well be independent of national unity; and its independence of national unity may be justified, "provided it be of a nature to insure the general welfare," and demonstrates its vitality by its cohesion and by its power of assimilation. The power of assimilation is, in fact, the general justification of Empire, of which more will be said in due course.

"The political unity which is the State, arises from the co-operation of two causes, of which one is the very nature of things, the other the conscious human will—so that one may rightly say of the State that it is, taken as a whole, both a natural and voluntary society."[38]

The establishment of States is not due to men's caprice. Historically speaking, the establishment of States has not followed upon an era of anarchy. Their establishment is a product of nature, the consequence of man being by nature a social animal, in that no society of families can hold together without a supreme ruling authority, the presence of which makes of that society a State and man a political animal. In other words, States have not arisen and do not arise by the mere conscious willing of human beings; but having arisen or arising, men's will consciously acquiesce in their establishment, in that their establishment fulfils purposes inherent in human nature, and seeks more or less successfully to perfect them. For the whole human race, by the Grace of God, is born members one of another; and

---

[37] It is important for the reader here to recall to mind the definition of "Nation" given in the last chapter, lest any misconceptions should arise owing to his associating any other meaning with that term.

[38] *Cf.* A. Valensin, *Traité de Droit Naturel*, Vol. II, Chap. IV, par. 2 (Éditions Spes, Paris, 1925).

the natural tendency of mankind to form States, to acquiesce consciously in their formation and to perfect them, is a reflection of this fact. It is only due to fallen human nature, in other words to *original sin*, that the whole of humanity has failed to grow up or crystallise into a single State. The universal State, however, is the goal of political progress, an aspiration which, owing to man's very nature, it is impossible to cancel from his heart. But such progress, in so far as it may be promoted by man's conscious will, even if we discount actual selfish ambitions, is hindered by the very diversity of existing States, in size, degree of civilisation and culture; by distrust of one another; by the fear of oppression; above all, by disagreement over what constitutes moral worth; for no State will willingly allow itself to become merged in another higher authority, if it experiences even the smallest suspicion that thereby a code of Moral Law, other than that which itself holds to be true, would become ascendant, and so corrupt in its eyes the ends for which the State is constituted.[39] It is too often forgotten that many wars are waged in perfect good faith, whether in fact justified or not, owing to the fear of succumbing to a power thought to be morally inferior.

So the State is a political unity, the juridical institutions of which are an aspect of itself. Thus, too, the notion of a State and of authority go together; for the exercise of a supreme ruling authority is the function of the State. The State, moreover, is an organism (as indeed are all human societies, but more specifically the State as being the most perfect and formal of human societies), albeit an organism *sui generis*, a fact which Sociology

---

[39] For this reason the establishment of religious unity would, more than anything else, in an age of political progress, promote the establishment of an universal State. But no religious unity is possible without the acceptance of the principle of religious authority—not that religious authority can coerce individual judgment, but because the presence of a religious authority preserves the given deposit of doctrine from becoming lost or corrupted, insures its consistent development and is the only effective check on the process of indefinite disintegration.

demonstrates, in that the State may be observed to be a living unity, subject to growth and decay, like any other living organism. Hence it is not the mere sum of its parts, but the resultant thereof, with an autonomy of its own, having as the object of its existence the general good.

As Herbert Spencer has pointed out: "The State undergoes, like every living organism, a continuous growth. As it grows, its parts become unlike; it exhibits increase of structure. The unlike parts simultaneously assume activities of unlike kinds. These activities are not simply different, but their differences are so related as to make one another possible. The reciprocal aid thus given causes mutual dependence of the parts, and the mutually dependent parts, living by and for one another, form an aggregate constituted on the same general principle as is an individual organism. . . . The analogy of a society (State) to an organism becomes clearer on learning that every organism of appreciable size is a society; and on further learning that, in both, the lives of the units continue for some time if the life of the aggregate becomes suddenly arrested, while, if the aggregate is not destroyed by violence, its life greatly exceeds the life of its units."[40]

The natural tendency of all organisms is to fight for their continued existence; and Sociology demonstrates that States exhibit this natural tendency as powerfully and instinctively as any other living organism. This is a natural law, which the Moral Law transcends, but does not lay aside. The Moral Law can never be in essential conflict with Natural Law. So here we have a law of life; and the manner in which the Moral Law transcends it is by sanctioning the sacrifice of individual life whenever thereby a richer, more vigorous life and a generally higher (more moral) life is rightly judged to be the consequence. Thus the justification of the State's right to promote a spirit of self-sacrifice among its members for the common good, or to call upon its members to risk, or even lay down, their lives in

---

[40] Herbert Spencer, *Principles of Sociology. Cf.* St. Thomas Aquinas, *De Regimine Princ.*, 4. 33.

order to insure its survival, depends on the fact of the fulfilment by the State of the purposes for which it is divinely constituted, the promotion of the general well-being, that is, a higher, richer and more vigorous life for the aggregate that succeeds the generation of which the sacrifices are demanded.[41] The same principle may be held likewise to justify many coercive laws, provided such laws do not in any way infringe on an individual's "natural" rights, arising out of the conditions in which and the purposes for which the individual, endowed with a soul and a rational mind, has been created.

But Government is an art exercised by human beings, who are apt to fail, even with the best intentions, in their judgment of right and wrong means. Laws may, in fact, be unjust or defeat their own purpose, however well intended. When we leave general principles and enter the realm of the contingent, we are often beset by insurmountable difficulties. Practically we seem often to be placed in the dilemma of a choice between two evils, so that, as I have said, the path to Heaven of the practical statesman is only too often paved by good intentions. There is, of course, the Science of Casuistry, a specialised branch of Moral Philosophy, to guide practical men along the right path. And if, for no adequate reason, this Science has earned a somewhat evil reputation, this is but the homage which it pays to the difficulties which are to be met with in the realm of the contingent. Much of it necessarily constitutes debatable ground; but the world owes a debt of infinite gratitude to the great Jesuit thinkers, to whom, more than anyone else, is due the elaboration of this Science. Those who pretend to scoff at it are generally those who have never taken the trouble to enquire into the subject or are so proud as to imagine that their own uninstructed reason, instinct or experience are an invariably infallible guide. I assure these folk that private judgment on moral questions is the death of all morality. If this were not so, there would be good cause to allow criminals to act as judges in their own cases.

---

[41] *Cf.* St. Thomas Aquinas, *Summa Theol.* 2ª, 2ᵃᵉ, q. 31, art. 3 ad 2ᵘᵐ.

2. Authority is essential to any form of society, whether it be domestic or civil, barbarous or civilised, legitimate or illegitimate, free or necessary. Authority will invariably be present in some form or society will cease to be.[42]

The definition of authority and proof of the above statement are given very forcibly by Albert Valensin, as follows:

> "*Les hommes ne sauraient vivre normalement isolés les uns des autres. Il est dans leur nature de vivre en société, c'est-à-dire en unissant leurs activités en vue d'une fin commune. Mais pour tendre efficacement à cette fin commune, ils ont essentiellement besoin de recevoir l'impulsion d'un principe d'unité qui ne soit pas seulement extérieur, mais intérieur, touchant à leur volonté même et la liant par le seul lien qui convienne à des êtres intelligents, et par conséquent libres : je veux dire, par le lien moral de l'obligation.*
>
> "*Or, ce principe, cette faculté, ce pouvoir* d'obliger *est précisément ce qu'on entend par autorité.*"[43]

So authority consists in the right of Government. It is a moral power, a reasonable, a unifying and beneficent principle, to which respect is due on the one hand, which requires a consciousness of responsibility in those who exercise it on the other.[44] Most of all is this true respecting the State, the supreme ruling authority in a civil society. So the State does not originally arise, as some would pretend, as a consequence of the

---

[42] *Cf.* Leibnitz, quoted by A. Valensin, *Traité de Droit Naturel.*

[43] A. Valensin, *Traité de Droit Naturel*, Vol. II, Chap. IV, par. 3. Reason is man's title to freedom; and if reason binds him to observe the Moral Law, he loses thereby nothing of his freedom. *Whosoever committeth sin*—who denies what is reasonable—*is the slave of sin* or of Unreason (John, VIII, 34). So that submission to authority, which Reason demonstrates to be necessary whereby man may live peacefully in society, is no loss of freedom. The question of a given authority losing its right to govern owing to its own neglect of reason's dictates, is dealt with in due course.

[44] *Cf. Ibid.*

presence of a national instinct. I do not mean by this that, in the course of historical development, a State may not be formed out of elements having a clearly-defined national consciousness, following the dissolution or partial dissolution of another State or States. This, of course, happens frequently, though by no means invariably. More often than not within the State, established originally with complete disregard of national consciousness, a sense of nationality among those composing the State is brought gradually into being, especially if the State shows itself to be a strong and vital organism and fulfils adequately the purposes for which it is constituted.[45] The inability on the part of a State to assimilate the national groups or peoples of which it may originally be composed into a single Nation is due, in most cases, to a combination of weakness and bad, unreasonable, unsympathetic Government, leading to disintegration from within by the rebellion of the disaffected or to disintegration from without as a consequence of defeat in war.

The theory that the presence of a national instinct gave rise originally to States is flatly contrary to the facts, which anyone with historical knowledge will readily admit. It is putting the cart before the horse. On the other hand, there may be good enough reasons, without having to fall back upon this theory, why, in particular cases, a particular imperial system should be combated, or why the aspirations of a people, strongly united by a common national sentiment, should be encouraged to break away, by every legitimate means, from the dominion of an imperial State and form a State of their own, either alone or in conjunction with another outside group sharing with them the same or similar national consciousness. If the imperial State

---

[45] Compare Switzerland. Modem Italy itself affords another example. Originally only a few imaginative minds had any feeling of common nationality for the whole of Italy. Even at the time of the Risorgimento it was only a minority who felt anything of the kind. It has been the Great War and Fascism which have really created, for the first time, in Italy a powerful sense of common nationality among the people at large.

in question be flagrantly misgoverning its members, or some of them; if it be exhibiting an obvious incapacity for assimilation; if its weakness be such that there is constituted a continual menace to its safety or cohesion, the creation of new States by a regrouping of the members of the imperial State along the lines dictated by national sentiment, or in accordance with some other principle of unity, may be legitimately advocated as a measure to insure better Government, more stable political conditions, greater or swifter political progress, or peace. There is nothing, however, inherently wrong, unstable or aggressive in an imperial system. On the contrary, a sound imperial system, like the Roman, for one, requires no apology. An imperial system is in countless cases the prelude to greater unity, to the creation of a wider national consciousness, to the establishment of peaceful conditions over a wider area, to greater well-being through the lessening of restrictions on trading, and to the maintenance of peace in the world at large. Who can deny that the British Empire is not eminently fulfilling these functions? Again, the splitting up of Central and South-Eastern Europe, as a consequence of the Great War, into a large number of national States, though, maybe, a necessary and even salutary process of historical development (given the facts of Turkish misrule and the decadent conditions of the Austro-Hungarian Empire), is by no means an unmixed blessing to the peoples concerned. So we may rightly conclude that, to argue from the particular case, which may be justified, to the general case as a principle to be universally applied, is a complete and dangerous *non sequitur.*

Another false theory in juxtaposition to ours is that States arose in the first instance through some actual or tacit social contract entered into between the individual members of a society. This theory is no less false historically. It was popularised, if not invented, by Rousseau for the purpose of providing some historical and reasonable foundation in support of the contention that Democracy and the "Sovereignty of the People" were matters of universal validity. In a later chapter I shall have occasion to discuss in some detail these two principles. Here I am only concerned with exposing the falsity of the theory which purports to make these principles necessarily acceptable, because inherent in the origin of States and of authority— though to punish a corpse, in all conscience, is a sad waste of breath; for no serious student of politics entertains the theory of the *Social Contract* any longer for an instant. But in that there are many people (and among these some serious students of politics), who believe passionately in the ideal of Democracy; and since Rousseau's theory had so much to do with the promotion of this ideal during the last century, that it survives still among the uninstructed,[46] we may as well recapitulate a few of the main reasons that expose its futility.

A.—The existence of a contract, either actual or tacit, originating the State, especially among primitive peoples, is not confirmed by history. On the contrary, all the historical evidence points the other way.

B.—The notion that man is "born free," by which Rousseau evidently means "independent," is contrary to experience. Man is born a member of a family, and is subjected in infancy to the authority of his parents. Moreover, if it has become the custom for grown men and women nowadays to emancipate themselves from all parental authority, this was not so in earlier times, especially among primitive peoples, where the authority of the head of the family usually remained in force until death terminated it. It is true that, in a sense, as we have seen, man is "born free" by virtue of his reason, with which he is endowed.[47] If this were all that Rousseau meant by his hypothesis of a pact, namely, that in all forms of society man's reason leads him to acquiesce in some form of authority, I should have no objection to make; but Rousseau must mean more than this, or why elaborate an historically untrue hypothesis in order to justify something which could be stated much more simply without it? The

---

[46] Popular journalism is continually guilty of repeating similar errors, witness Mr. H. G. Wells in his *Outline of History* with respect to the theory of natural selection as solely accounting for evolution.

[47] See footnote p. 89.

truth is that he is searching at all costs for some argument that would necessarily bind man to be the slave of the "general will," that is, to an instinctive force rather than to a rational one. Consequently Rousseau's freedom has no rational significance; he would say in effect: "I am free to do whatever I will, even to the extent of renouncing my freedom, or of selling my own soul." Such freedom, however, is the very negation of freedom. It is licence.

C.—The notion of a "state of nature," where man was happy in his complete independence, existing anterior to the formation of the State, is an entirely arbitrary presupposition. It is not merely contrary to the teachings of the Church, but contrary to the conclusions of ethnography. (N.B.—A "state of innocence" is not the same thing as a "state of nature.") Even Voltaire, who shared some of Rousseau's conclusions, considered this notion of his as a piece of prodigious nonsense, as indeed it is. "Non-social man would be a miserable, naked, helpless biped, exposed to the rapacity of beasts and to the elements."[48]

D.—Rousseau declares the necessity of a pact in order to account for the State and in order to legitimise authority. In other words, he commits himself to the following untenable position: Assuming that a given State came into existence following a pact, unless the pact be renewed every twenty years, as Sieyès logically suggested, that State cannot continue *de jure*, but only *de facto*. For why should a pact, even supposing it were once made and brought a State originally into existence, bind indefinitely future generations of men "born free," that is, born essentially independent? And what of children and women and of all those men who happen to be disenfranchised? Is any pact valid without their concurrence? On what criterion, moreover, were the original voters enfranchised? Did these include women? What in fact are the limits within which the equality of all men, whereby they become entitled to have a say in making

---

[48] *Cf.* Richard Aldington, *Voltaire*, Part II, Chap. XIII (George Kentledge, London, 1925).

the pact, is to be practically admitted? The possession of Reason? But what, in the absence of some original authority, is to decide at what age and in what circumstances men and women are to be considered sufficiently reasonable to be accorded the suffrage? All along the question is being hopelessly begged or eluded. For even supposing an agreed universal system of suffrage, is any pact valid between enfranchised members unless accepted unanimously? Of course, if all men were endowed with perfect reasonableness, unanimity would result. But then there would be no need for a pact. And in the absence of unanimity, has a minority not thereby an indefeasible right to secede? Rousseau refused to admit this right. Yet the supposed indefeasible right of the majority to rule, which has proved to be the practical consequence of Rousseauism, is in reality a denial of Rousseau's basic thesis! Never, indeed, was a theory so utterly paradoxical, inconsistent, self-contradictory and contrary to established facts and common sense.[49] It wallows from one fallacy to another, perhaps because Rousseau failed, in the first instance, to make this most important distinction, namely, that the two propositions: (1) that man is a rational animal, and (2) that man must needs act reasonably, do not mean the same thing. The first proposition is true. The second is false. The first supports the theory that good Government should be reasonable, that Reason is the criterion of good Government, that any Government, however formed, is legitimate if reasonable—all three true propositions. The second supports the theory that the popular will must be right, that a Government not based on the popular will must be wrong—both false propositions.

3. So far we have treated the question of authority in the abstract. In the concrete the question poses itself as follows: What man, or body of men, has the right to exercise authority? In other words, who has the right to perform the functions of the State?

We have seen that authority arises spontaneously as a condition of society. Historically speaking, the actual sovereign

---

[49] *Cf.* A. Valensin, *Traité de Droit Naturel*, Part II, Chap. XIV, par. 11.

power is found to be wielded in innumerably different ways. In primitive societies it is often wielded under a patriarchal system or by a council of Elders. Or the constitution of a State, whether established in accordance with Law or Custom having the force of Law, may be based on the rule of one or of the few or of the many, according to circumstances. Have any of these forms of Government more than another the right to exercise authority? The answer given, in accordance with the doctrines so much advertised during the past century, whether Rousseau's theory be subscribed to or not, is that only the many have the right to exercise authority, in the sense that the "general will" is the only legitimate authority.

The most plausible reason given for this answer is that, the general good being the object of Government, the "general will" can alone insure the general good. But nobody has ever been able to give a satisfactory answer to the question why this should necessarily be so. Why should the "general will," assuming that it is possible to determine it, be considered infallible? Is there any reason to suppose that the instinct of the mass is usually superior to the reason of the individual? Or have we to suppose that the mass acts reasonably? Of course, if we assume that mass action is always, or even generally, dictated by reasonable fore-thought, we might justly conclude that, having no other interest than to promote the general well-being, the authority of the mass has a better title to authority than any other. Unfortu-nately, however, it is precisely mass-action that is, in fact, the most unreasonable of human actions. In other words, if we trust the "general will," we trust to a blind instinct, which, given that society is an organism, may indeed be one of *Nature's* means of preserving the organism's life: animals are endowed by a very acute instinct of the kind. But men are not merely animals, though man in the mass acts very like an animal. Is the State then to be guided in the last resort by instinct, when Reason is available—Reason, which, to say the least, is unquestionably a fitter instrument for preserving life?

Again, how is the "general will" to be determined? The State is not an organism endowed with a natural means of articulation. Some kind of artificial machinery has got to be established by which the "general will" may be made manifest. But if we appeal to each individual singly and make a sum of the results, we do not obtain a general verdict; we obtain a sum of individual verdicts, which is not the same thing. Any mathematician will confirm this, though it may not be self-evident to the layman at a glance.[50] Of course, if we obtained, as the result of such an appeal, a unanimous verdict, and assumed, at the same time, that all members of the State, unwilling to exercise or incapable of exercising the suffrage (including minors, criminals, lunatics and domestic animals) tacitly supported the unanimous verdict of those who exercised the right to vote, the result might perhaps be regarded as an approximate equivalent to the "general will." But even so, it would only be approximate, unless we further presupposed that each member, in registering his vote, solemnly and truly voted for what he considered the interests of the community at large, in the full realisation that the life of the community goes beyond that of a single generation, rather than in favour of his own personal interests or of those of his immediate generation. But such a presupposition is a fantasy; and how can we ever obtain unanimity in practice? Even in exceptional cases of crisis, engendering great excitement, with a single issue at stake, and when the decision to be taken is one practically decided in advance by the circumstances, would there be any hope of obtaining unanimity even in a small community? As for majority rule, it is still further removed from one determined by the "general will"; for, unless the majority be so large as to approach unanimity, a condition of affairs only less difficult to obtain than unanimity itself, the divergence between what is implied by the sum of individual wills and what is implied by

---

[50] *Cf.* William Sanderson, *Statecraft* (Methuen, London, 1927): "To grant the franchise to ordinary citizens as individuals is to invite political decisions based on myriads of eccentric opinions, no two of which can be exactly alike and none correct."

the "general will" becomes all the more marked. In fact, therefore, there is no sure means of determining the "general will,"
save, possibly, in tiny States where the whole of its members are
able to assemble together in one place and there act *en masse*,
after being duly excited in order to allow a full measure of elec-
tricity to circulate. Perhaps the surest way of gauging the "general will" would be by employing a medium.[51] But I have not
heard yet of any serious suggestion to employ a medium as a
method of Government; although the greatest statesmen are
usually endowed with a medium-like sense, by which, within
limits, they are enabled, so to speak, to sound the "general will."
For by all means let the "general will" be sounded in so far as
this be possible. But there is no reason whatever for necessarily
allowing the actions of Government to be dictated by it.

The truth is that any such notion respecting the inherent
right of the people as a whole to govern is manifestly absurd.[52]
This does not mean, however, that I deny all merit to the "general will," especially when it is understood as that *esprit de corps*,
issuing in patriotic sentiment.[53] On the contrary, this may be a
great force for good, and its latent presence is a sign of political

---

[51] The ancient device of consulting oracles may, perhaps, be cited an
attempt to consult the "general will" by means of a medium.

[52] As Mussolini himself has put it, the "Sovereignty of the People" is a
myth, nothing more nor less than an ideological abstraction.

[53] It may be argued with a good deal of reason that the force of *public
opinion*, on the other hand, is something very different to the instinctive
mass reaction to certain circumstances which I have identified with the
"general will"; that, on the contrary, public opinion is a rational force,
against which no Government should act. It should be noted, however,
that apart from the practical difficulty of gauging public opinion and
especially the degree of its unanimity; apart from the fact that a strong
expression of public opinion, whether right or wrong, necessarily sets
limits to the powers of any Government; its value is very relative,
because its value depends entirely on the kind and degree of public
education. So it is not so much a question of the right of public opinion
to control Government, as it is a question of the duty of Government
to create a really healthy public opinion.

maturity. Neither does what I have said mean that a popular form of Government may not be highly desirable. This is quite another question, which will be dealt with in its proper place. Here I am solely concerned with the concrete question as to what it is that sanctions the *right* to govern.

The right answer is a very simple one: The Moral Law, which is based on Reason. Different forms of Government arise according to circumstances. Government may take one form or another, as we have seen, whether popular or otherwise. But, whatever its form may be, there is only one thing that will give the right to govern: the Moral Law, Reason. If those who hold the reins of power have acquired their power in accordance with a just principle and govern in accordance with Reason, implying a due regard to the general welfare, which, above all, presupposes the moral welfare of the people, no one has the right to call in question the right of that Government to govern. This is the Divine Right of any Government, whether of Kings or of Parliaments—Divine because to act reasonably and in accordance with the Moral Law is to fulfil the will of God. It is an appalling thought if examined closely, this idea of enthroning the "general will" as sovereign, a ferocious beast in the place that Reason should occupy. We know what a terrible thing a mob, unrestrained by authority, can be—blind, excessive, cruel. We know how dangerous and how contagious is war-fever, when peace is hanging in the balance. However such a theory, in fact, as that which ascribes the only true title to authority to the "general will," ever came to be accepted by reasonable men, it is difficult to imagine. The truth is, as Whitehead—in the author's humble opinion perhaps the greatest living philosopher and to-day by far the most eminent among non-Catholic philosophers—has pointed out in his *Science and the Modern World*,[54] ours is not an Age of Reason, still less the eighteenth century, despite its "rationalism," but an Age of Science; and that Sci-

---

[54] Alfred North Whitehead, *Science and the Modern World* (Cambridge University Press, 1925).

ence, vulgarly held to be the inseparable handmaiden of Reason, has made its greatest advances in an age characterised by its lack of interest in dialectics. "The Ages of Faith," as he says, "were the Ages of Reason." A truly reasonable age would surely have found sharper weapons from the armoury of the old Philosophy than the above shoddy implements wherewith to depose the Kings and oligarchies, who, in recent centuries were abusing the authority they held by governing flagrantly in the interests of a class rather than that of the whole people. It has been left to Fascism to revive the use of the old weapons and, in driving by their means from high place Ineptitude and Folly, to prove their eternal efficacy.

4. Of course, sweet reasonableness, as we have had occasion to point out, is not always in practice to the fore. This fact alone is sufficient to condemn the principle that a majority possesses necessarily the right to rule, or, to take the opposite extreme, that an absolute Kingship is the only proper form of Government. No particular form of Government is, so to speak, presanctified. To govern in the interests of the general welfare is not, in fact, an easy matter. Government is an art, the exercise of which depends first and foremost on right principles and right intention, whatever the form of Government may be. Practical questions therefore arise as to how we are to secure rulers who will act constantly in accordance with right principles, with right intention; or as to how we are to secure, given right intention, the maximum of reasonableness in practice. And at what point has anyone the right to refuse allegiance to a constituted authority which appears to be erring in one or both of the above senses?

The answers which I propose to give to these questions are as follows: First, being practical questions, certain practical tests, certain practical ways and means, can propose the solutions to the difficulties they adumbrate. No Government, for instance, can in practice remain indefinitely in power if it continually and flagrantly misgoverns society. The instinctive "general will" comes in such cases, if the sense of self-preservation of the Government fails to bring about reform, or if common sense fails to accommodate matters, to be provoked into action at the instigation of, or in support of, a minority ready to suffer martyrdom in the name of what they hold to be reasonable. Reason and instinct in such cases, in fact, tend to combine and the *Vox Populi* to become the *Vox Dei*—and we have Revolution in or Dissolution of the State. Again, practical rules can be formed and should be formed, based upon experience and upon Reason, as to the proper constitution of Governments, in order to allow of their improvement, to allow of their progressive adaptation to changing conditions, and so as to admit of reasonable criticism and provide means by which incompetence and abuse of power may be minimised, that is, incompetent or tyrannous members of Government substituted in accordance with some constitutional device to meet the case in point. On the other hand, we have the test of Moral Law, which alone sets limits to the authority of the State and should be the main safeguard against the abuse of power, in that any flagrant and continuous violation of the Moral Law by the State sets individuals free to disobey the constituted authority.

Now I am aware that it may be objected to this last point that, where no independent moral authority is admitted, man has either to rely on his individual moral judgment, with nothing more than the choice of some Moral Philosophy and the Science of Casuistry to help him, or he must submit blindly to the authority of the State. I admit the dilemma; and when it arises, we are indeed theoretically reduced to allowing the criminal, so to speak, either way to act as judge in his own case. The absence of an independent moral authority affords excuses for both tyranny and irresponsible rebellion. But there is no theoretical alternative to these evils that I can see, when no independent moral authority is admitted. The practical tests are then the only tests. But where an independent moral authority is admitted, the full solution is available. Then we have the State on the one hand, supreme in temporal matters, the Church on the other, supreme in spiritual matters, the court of appeal of the oppressed, the moderator of tyrants. Thus, I maintain, the ideal of the Middle Ages, then never more than most imperfectly realised, of a Universal State conterminous with a Universal Church remains *à l'ordre du jour*, the ideal to which any true theory of the State must inevitably pay homage and command us to aspire.

This reflection leads us to deal with another important, though none the less fallacious theory, of the State, in juxtaposition to ours and conveniently dealt with under the heading of the present section. I refer to that "Gothic" theory of the State,[55] repellent to the Latin mind, but which has not been without its influence in Latin countries, elaborated by Hegel, Schelling and Fichte, who would make "reasons of State" the sole moral sanction. Needless to say, such a theory would subordinate the individual entirely to the State and justify any form of tyranny resulting in the successful survival of a State and in its aggrandisement.

The theory entails that perverted form of "Nationalism" to which we alluded in the last chapter, and is a particular form of that political "Naturalism" to which we alluded in the introduction. It is based on a Metaphysic, which substitutes for a transcendent God, an immanent God, a God who manifests himself

---

[55] "A Gothic theory of the State repellent to the Latin mind." This is how my friend, His Excellency Dr. Emilio Bodrero, Under-Secretary of State for Public Instruction, in a letter addressed to me in February 1927, commented on "Naturalism" and that false form of Nationalism which is the form of Naturalism advocated by the *Action Française*. Daudet and Maurras, with all their French Patriotism, appear indeed to have become in this respect the adepts of the German professors who contributed so largely to creating German Militarism. This is, of course, the logical consequence of their alliance with and tolerance of Atheism, combined with their just horror of the individualist doctrines that are carrying their country to ruin. In other words, if you posit the need of authority, but are prepared to rule out God, you have no theoretical alternative but to enthrone the State in God's place. It is in the acknowledgment of God as the Supreme Sovereign, and all Governments, however constituted, as merely the temporal vicars of Christ, where Fascism parts company with the doctrines advocated by the *Action Française*.

as an eternal "becoming"; a Metaphysic that endorses a kind of Pantheism and concludes that because God and Nature are in some way confounded, whatever is must be right. It further raises the idea of power to the place occupied by the idea of love in Christian Metaphysics. The "will to power" becomes the proper law of action. It would make a state of war the natural and inevitable condition of man, that is, it would sanctify that condition. Hegel actually does attempt to do so. It may, in fact, be said to be the very theory that led Lucifer to let loose war in Heaven.[56]

Hegel's represents, indeed, the quintessence of all the doctrines which, in the course of the last centuries, propagated in one form or another the idea of the State being an end in itself, and identified, as did the Pagans, the moral with the civil law. His Philosophy is the ripe fruit of the Pagan Renaissance. It is the eldest child of eighteenth-century cynicism and the father of German Militarism, while it affords a bait for all that is criminal in us, in that it consists of a hash of Materialism (positivist, utilitarian, and evolutionist), dished up under the disguise of a false Idealism that appeals to man's only too easily aroused predatory instincts, pride and the lust for power.

There are various forms of this pernicious Philosophy and it is impossible to follow these various forms into detail. The Italian so-called neo-Hegelians, Spaventa, Benedetto Croce and Giovanni Gentile, have each in turn contributed much to attenuate the German theses, to purge them of their gross materialism. They have also valiantly served the urgent historical purpose of working the German theses out into a bare thread; although, as a result, I must confess from my own point of view, which may indeed be due to my own limitations, they leave behind such a tangled skein that it is somewhat difficult to make head or tail of their conclusions.

German Idealism unfortunately arrived to endorse "Historical Fatalism," which is Italy's most conspicuous contribution to the philosophical heresies that have dominated European

---

[56] *Cf.* Hegel, *Rechtsphilosophie*, par. 321.

thought since the Renaissance, a contribution of which Vico, with all his grand gifts to the world, cannot be wholly acquitted.

Vico is generally considered the founder of the "Philosophy of History." But although there may be a true History of Philosophy, there can be, strictly speaking, no true Philosophy of History. History is, when all is said and done, merely an accurate description of past events. A good historian is one who, besides accurately describing the events, possesses sound judgment in the choice for the purposes he has in view of the relative importance of events he describes and of their inter-relationship. From History, it is true, certain social laws may be deduced, that is, certain uniformities in the scientific sense. But such laws belong to the conclusions of Sociology, a Science not a Philosophy, a Science moreover based only partly on historical data.

The endowment of an historical sense is the marked characteristic of the Italian mind; and in the riot which attempted to overthrow Orthodoxy from the sixteenth century onwards, it was natural that Italy should make a personal contribution to the specious half-truths which only too commonly passed muster for Philosophy during the following generations in the form of philosophico-historical theses. And now, in getting back to Orthodoxy "Historical Fatalism" (as one would have a right to expect, given the Italian hallmark), which teaches in effect that history is but an unfolding, inevitable pageant, containing no might-have-beens, so that all social and political systems (and Philosophies) have their full justification, whatever their intrinsic merit, in accordance with their mere power of survival, looms as a particularly nasty obstacle in her path. The school of Gentile is, however, gradually sifting the truth from the falsehood embodied in this obstacle; and when this is done, the obstacle will doubtless crumble.

For my part, I believe that dynamite—a general assault on Hegelian logic—would, as a matter of fact, do the work quicker and, in the long run, probably better too. I have a notion that Hegel and his bedfellows have sucked out of the Italian heresy most of the falsehood, so that a frontal attack on Hegel would do more good in Italy than anything else. This, however, is beyond the scope of this book to undertake; and as Hegel's theory of the State and all kindred heresies can only be fully exposed by criticising his general Philosophy, I am afraid I must refer the reader elsewhere for a refutation.[57] Let him be quite certain, nevertheless, that the notion of the State as an end in itself forms no part whatever of orthodox Fascism.[58]

---

[57] *Cf.* Benedetto Croce's *Saggio sullo Hegel* (Laterza, Bari), which, if it does not go as far as I would wish, remains a most admirable criticism.
[58] All the so-called "Idealist" philosophies seem to me to exhibit one fatal flaw, by which the commonest pitfall into which logicians are apt to fall is erected into a logical principle, as G. E. Moore, of Cambridge, has shown in the most brilliant of his essays, "The Refutation of Idealism" (*Philosophical Studies*, Kegan Paul, Trench, Trubner & Co., London, 1922). The following is, perhaps, the most arresting paragraph of this essay, well worth quoting if it will lead the reader to study the question which I have here raised but cannot conclude:
"A distinction is asserted, but it is *also* asserted that the things distinguished form an 'organic unity.' But, forming such a unity, it is held, each would not be what it is *apart from its relation to the other*. Hence to consider either by itself is to make an *illegitimate abstraction*. The recognition that these are 'organic unities' and 'illegitimate abstractions' in this sense is regarded as one of the chief conquests of modern philosophy. But what is the sense attached to these terms? An abstraction is illegitimate when, and only when, we attempt to assert of *a part*—of something abstracted—that which is true of the whole to which it belongs; and it may, perhaps, be useful to point out that this should not be done. But the application actually made of this principle and what perhaps would be expressly acknowledged as its meaning, is something much the reverse of useful. The principle is used to assert that certain abstractions are *in all cases* illegitimate; that, whenever you try to assert *anything whatever* of that which is part of an organic whole, what you assert can only be true of the whole. And this principle, so far from being a useful truth, is necessarily false. For if the whole can, nay *must*, be substituted for the part in all propositions and for all purposes, this can only be because the whole is absolutely identical with the part. When, therefore, we are told that green and the sensation of green are certainly distinct but yet are not separable, or that it is an illegitimate

abstraction to consider the one apart from the other, what these provisos are used to assert is that, though the two things are distinct, yet you not only can, but must treat them as if they were not. Many philosophers, therefore, when they admit a distinction, yet (following the lead of Hegel) boldly assert their right, in a slightly more obscure form of words, also to deny it. The principle of organic unities, like that of combined analysis and synthesis, is mainly used to defend the practice of holding *both* of two contradictory propositions, wherever this may seem convenient. In this, as in other matters, Hegel's main service to philosophy has consisted in giving a name to and erecting into a principle, a type of fallacy to which experience had shown philosophers, along with the rest of mankind, to be addicted. No wonder that he has followers and admirers."

CHAPTER III

THE MAIN PRINCIPLES OF FASCISM

THE general theory of the State enunciated in the last chapter may be truthfully said to be the one endorsed by Fascism, by Mussolini. The present chapter accordingly will, at the risk of some repetition, present a summary of the salient principles that form part and parcel of this theory, together with a number of others, dependent thereon, on which Fascism lays particular stress.

I. Man is by nature a social animal. Living in society is the natural condition of mankind. Society cannot hold together, however, without there being some authority ruling it. Authority is implicit in every society. Authority therefore belongs to the natural order of things as much as society itself, and, having thus its source in nature, it has God for its author. So the principle of authority is a divine principle. Wherever a supreme authority exists, acknowledging no higher authority save the sovereignty of God alone, we call that authority the State, which is society juridically organised for the purpose of promoting the general good. The State is thus a political unity, and every political unity is an organism, with a life which transcends that of the individuals who compose it, and outlasts that of any particular generation of men. For this reason, the family is the true unit of the State, not single individuals. The State, owing to its acknowledging no higher authority, save God alone, is the highest form of human authority; and since, as we have shown, it belongs, like all authority, to the natural order of things, man may be justly said to be, by nature, not only a social animal but also a political animal.

II. The highest form of State is the national State, because the most perfect harmony is brought about when national unity, based on a community of traditions, coincides with political unity. National unity, moreover, reinforces authority and is an element of vitality in the State. But in the order of evolution (though not necessarily in the order of involution) political unity precedes national unity; that is, political unity creates national unity, at least whenever the State's authority is exercised over a relatively long period of time, firmly and justly for the general good. Thus, also, vital imperial States tend towards losing their imperial character in a process of assimilation and so towards becoming large national States. The political ideal or goal of mankind is, indeed, one universal national State, owning one supreme authority and integrated by one common national consciousness, however varied and intense might be the local differences and loyalties.

Fascism insists that progress towards this goal can only be made by upholding the principle of authority in existing States, and not, as would humanitarian Internationalists, by weakening authority and national sentiment, which sustains authority. It seems to stand to reason that man cannot hope to construct a higher authority by a process of destruction that brings the very principle of authority into contempt. It is surely only through the physically binding force of Law and the morally binding force of Religion, that mankind can be brought together into wider unities—and since both of these forces derive their power only from the sanctions provided by authority, progress can only come through sustaining authority, wherever it may be found. Fascism also lays stress on the consciousness of nationality being one of the main bases, in the concrete case of a national State, of any imperative claim on the part of the individual to take a share in Government. The national State, in short, is St. Thomas's *Communitas Perfecta*, that is, that truly unified political society grown conscious of itself and of its ends, the object of the common good, which is the supreme end of any community juridically organised.

III. Authority, arising spontaneously as a necessary condition of society, arises in various forms, according to circumstances. Original State authority appears to have been patriarchal in character.[59] However this may be, respect is invariably due to the State authority, whatever form it may take, provided it is, with due allowances for human fallibility, acting with right intention and in accordance with right principles. The form that the State authority may take evolves, or should evolve, in accordance with the requirements of evolving society, adapting itself *motu proprio* to changing conditions. If it fails to do this, it will fatally come, sooner or later, to fail in its object, the promotion of the general good, and it will therefore lose the right to govern, lose the right to be owed respect and become the cause of social dissolution through rebellion or war. Such evolution of the State authority from within adapting itself to outward conditions is a manifestation of organic growth. Where it is not manifest, the State organism must be reckoned decadent or ill.

Taparelli somewhere sums up very neatly the questions arising out of this conception of authority. He says that authority resides in the community, because where there is no community there is no authority; that authority is exercised *for the sake of* the community, because this is the very principle of its unity; but that authority *is not derived from* the community, because the community is incapable of either creating it or abolishing it, since it is inseparable from the very notion of community. The precise form which authority takes, however, is a question, as I have said, of organic growth, authority being a vital principle of all society. To the question, *who is to decide the form of Government*, the answer is, *whoever is, in fact, the efficient authority at any given phase of social development*. Wherever a nominal

---

[59] Some experts, notably in Germany, are now denying this! Whether this view be true or false, however, the argument here is not affected.

authority has practically abdicated, a real authority must necessarily arise spontaneously to take its place, or society falls into dissolution. This, in effect, was the process which gave rise to the fascist Government.

Once this idea is grasped, it will be seen how futile was Austin's attempt to solve the question juridically of where sovereignty ultimately resides. As Ramiro de Maeztu, in his stimulating book on Guild Socialism (*Authority, Liberty and Function*, Allen and Unwin, London, 1916), clearly shows, the question of sovereignty is a question of power. The body wielding it is continually shifting and it is for the historian and not the jurist to designate the body that happens to be wielding the sovereign power at any particular moment. In this connection de Maeztu quotes Duguit, Professor of Constitutional Law in the University of Bordeaux: "Law is a discipline of fact which social interdependence imposes on every member of the group." The social rule, in other words, can be shown objectively to be based on solidarity, and solidarity on the fact of man's interdependence.[60]

IV. Private moral judgment, if it is not founded on true doctrine, on a true Moral Philosophy, means moral chaos. In the absence, therefore, of an admitted independent moral authority, such as is the Church, the practical tests are the only tests, by which to judge the extent to which the State authority is performing its duty. In any case, the State has no right to arrogate to itself the right to judge itself; nor has the individual the right to lay down capricious standards. Both the all-sufficing and the agnostic State, therefore, reflect a false principle. So the State, to say the least, must conform to a Moral Philosophy and be judged according to that Moral Philosophy. Hence it is important that the Moral Philosophy, acknowledged, protected and vulgarised by the State, should be a true Moral Philosophy;

---

[60] It is as well to point out here, on the other hand, that many of Duguit's views on the subject of State authority—views which de Maeztu also very largely endorses—are very different, not to say utterly opposed, to Fascism.

but any Moral Philosophy is probably better than no Moral Philosophy, provided it be an independent Moral Philosophy, that is, one of universal application and not identified with the notion of State infallibility.

Thus the Scylla and Charybdis of State Agnosticism and State Infallibility must in any case be equally avoided. In practice, this means the recognition by the State Constitution of a Religion of the State. The recognition of the principles of some Moral Philosophy only may work to a certain extent in practice, especially if it reflects the general moral consciousness of the age. But such a makeshift is vague and consequently highly unsatisfactory. By the recognition of a definite Religion the case is otherwise, provided the Religion in question be under the direction of a body independent of the State.

Fascism has formally recognised the Catholic Religion as the Religion of the State in Italy, and has thereby chosen well, not only because it is the Religion of the vast majority of Italians; not only because the Catholic tradition is part of the very soul of Italy and, given the historical antecedents of Fascism, leaves Fascism really no alternative choice; but because the Catholic Religion is perhaps the only Religion that preserves *in every sense* its complete independence of State authority. I recommend this point particularly to the consideration of thoughtful persons.[61]

The relations between Church and State have not yet, however, been settled in Italy. The "Roman Question" still subsists. I believe, however, the day of its solution is approaching. It is a very difficult, mainly juridical, question, which cannot be discussed here. It would be quite beyond the scope and purpose of this book to do so. But until it is settled, situations may arise which would prevent the Italian Government and the Holy See from agreeing on all points touching matters of policy. Until it

---

[61] It is precisely this independence which those States who desire to be judges in their own case are so afraid of. The cry which, from time to time, is raised against the political interference of Rome is almost invariably the cry of a guilty man who is anxious either to save himself from condemnation or to perpetrate some crime.

is settled, Fascism will not come entirely into its own. Meantime, however, the Catholic Religion will remain in honour in Italy as the State Religion, no longer a dead letter of the Constitution, as it was under previous Governments. The Crucifix is back in the Schools and in the Law Courts. Religious education is again ensured for all Italian children, unless their parents specifically raise objections. Chaplains are back in the Army and Navy and form part of the fascist Boy Scout Organisation, known as the "*Balilla.*"[62] The independence of the Church and its Bishops is recognised. Lastly, public propaganda by other religious sects is forbidden, though, of course, full toleration is granted to the practice of other Religions that are not definitely repugnant to Christian feelings and morals.

V. There is a natural instinctive force possessed by every living organism and directed to maintain that organism's existence. With respect to that organism which is the State, this instinctive force finds expression in the "general will," which is consequently a useful touchstone for every Government to sound, however this may be possible; for the first duty of Government within the Moral Law is to preserve society from dissolution, since society is a necessary condition wherein man may attain his highest development and satisfy his needs. But there is no sure means of ascertaining the "general will," and in any case, unless Reason supports the direction apparently pointed out by the "general will," no cause is shown why that

---

[62] The disbanding of the Catholic Boy Scout organisations in the smaller towns would have been, according to our theory, intolerable, if emphatic and ample provision had not been made in the law governing the "*Balilla*" organisation, for the religious instruction for the boys. In this connection it should be noted, too, that one of the main reasons for the disbanding of the Catholic Boy Scout organisations in the smaller towns was precisely in order to insure that the local "*Balilla*" organisations should not be deprived of the Catholic element and so risk falling into the hands of local anti-clericals or those elements in Fascism who would idolise the State and so bring the "*Balilla*" under the ban of the Church.

direction should be followed. Reason and not instinct must be the final criterion of Government action, as well as of individual action. In this connection, it may be useful also to point out that good Government insures Government with the consent of the governed; for any protracted or widespread discontent is a symptom of bad Government, unless such discontent arises out of an agitation organised by vested interests pursuing selfish ends, that is, particular ends not coincident with the general good.

VI. There are a number of secondary absolute principles to which every form of Government must conform, if it is to be able to carry out efficiently the purpose for which it is constituted. For example, we may say that every good form of Government should be devised so that the central authority may be kept by some means in close contact with all parts of the body politic, like a good nervous system, in order that suffering in any part may be swiftly known at headquarters and measures taken by which the malady may be accurately diagnosed and remedied. Justice should be even. The executive should be vigorous, the bureaucracy expeditious and efficient. The system by which are recruited those who actually exercise the powers of State should be such as to throw up in effect an Aristocracy of intelligence and morality. No system should be too rigid, no system too fluid. Means by which constructive and effective criticism may be brought to bear on the acts and proposed acts of Government, and the Government influenced by such criticism should be provided. Likewise means should be provided to act as checks against the possibility of power being utilised to defeat the real purpose of Government, which is the general good as opposed to any particular good, and to enable incompetent members of Government to be easily substituted by others. Means, too, should be provided to enable a form of Government to adapt itself easily to changing conditions. On the other hand, no Government can carry on the business of the State properly, if it has to take truck of purely captious criticism, or if it is at the mercy of gusts of popular sentiment, or depends for its continuance in power on its popularity only.

The list of such secondary absolute principles to which every form of Government should properly subscribe could be prolonged indefinitely; but no useful purpose would be served here by formulating a greater number. The above will illustrate for the reader the kind of principle intended. Those enumerated are perhaps the more important ones. They are of a kind which almost any school of political thought, whether fascist, liberal or socialist, would regard as practically non-controversial.

VII. The business of the State is to govern. A weak State is a decadent State. The business of the State is, further, to see to it, that the activities of individuals or individual social groups, within the State, are co-ordinated to promote, in so far as this may be possible, the general good. The end of the State being the general good, the particular province of State action, with its eye on the fact that the life of the State outlasts the life of the individuals that compose it, lies in measures having as their object the harmonising of individual ends with the general needs of society. The duty of the individual is to realise that he is not an isolated unit, that he is a member by nature and necessity of a community, that all men are members of one another, that he is consequently responsible in all his actions to his fellow men, and not only to those of his own generation but to future generations. *In fine*, it is his duty to contrive to make coincide his individual interests with the general interest. And it is the business of the State to help him to accomplish this by so arranging the structure of society as to make the pursuit of individual interests as often as possible coincident with the general interest, and to prevent by Law, carrying the necessary sanctions, all such activities of individuals which contrast in their effects with the general good, and so, contemporaneously, protect those individuals who are socially inclined from those who are not.

Individuals possess certain natural rights, of which I will speak in due course. But these natural rights of the individual do not conflict with his duties to the community. On the contrary, these natural rights lie at the very roots of society, so, if the State were to infringe on these natural rights, it would be defeating its own purpose. But apart from these natural rights, the State can be no respecter of persons; so that the State, by the very nature of the case, and with its eye on the general welfare, is concerned only indirectly with the individual's welfare—that is, it requires the individual's welfare to be made one with the general welfare and promotes the individual's welfare through the general welfare, for which alone it is directly responsible. Hence the individual is subordinate to the State, in the sense that he is subject to the authority of the State and restricted in his liberties within the institutions and laws of the State, aiming at the general good. He is not subordinate to the State, on the other hand, in the sense that the State has no limits to its authority over him and makes of itself an end of itself. The promotion of individual happiness may perhaps be regarded indirectly as an end of the State; but true individual happiness is dependent on the general well-being which it is the direct business of the State to promote, and no individual has the right to seek his happiness in a direction contrasting with the general good.

This distinction is fundamental, and at the risk of labouring the point unduly, we may put it again in the following way: Whereas it would be strictly incorrect to say that the laws and institutions of the State, *in fine*, the State uses the individual for its own purposes and subordinates him to the social organism, this would be true if interpreted only as meaning that all laws and institutions are directed to promote individual action along lines coincident with the general interests of society and so require that the individual submit to the authority of the State, except the State betray its trust. Hence, from a purely juridical point of view, which is eminently the State's point of view, we may justly say that the individual is a subordinate factor, not because he is a less considerable factor than the community, but because he lives by the community, and the protection of the community from dissolution is the first practical duty of the State; for without authority, without laws or customs having the force of laws, society ceases to be.[63]

---

[63] As St. Thomas Aquinas points out: "The part indeed desires (and

It is not this conception of solidarity and moral responsibility that is likely to issue in Tyranny. On the contrary, it is precisely Individualism and Agnosticism that has always been (as History amply proves) and always will be the enemy of true freedom.

This becomes immediately apparent if we examine for a moment the practical ideal—unmasked—of what generally goes by the name of Liberalism, which accepts the individualistic and agnostic hypothesis, yet seeks to found thereon a city of happy families. The liberal solution may, in effect, be stated thus: The individual is the centre of the universe (*cogito, ergo sum*). The supreme object of the individual's life is his "self-realisation" according to his peculiar nature (a condition on which his happiness—so it is assumed—necessarily depends); and he alone (it is said to be his natural right) can and should be judge of what his self-realisation consists in. But since, in a state of anarchy, this would result in the efficient self-realisation of only a few (the stronger, the more intelligent and the more unscrupulous) at the expense of the many relatively less well-equipped individuals, the State is posited as the necessary means by which the latter may be assured a relatively better chance of achieving their individual happiness at the expense of a part of the opportunities for achieving a maximum happiness of the few better equipped individuals. This being so, the object of Government (whatever its form may be) should be properly limited to securing by compromise, as far as this may be practicable, the maximum opportunity for individual self-realisation *all round*, or, in other words, the highest realisable mean of opportunity

---

should desire) the good of the whole in so far as it is fitting to itself (*i.e.*, to the part); but not so that the part refers the good of the whole to itself, but rather so that it refers itself to the good of the whole." (*Summa Theol.* 2ᵃ, 2ᵃᵉ, q. 26, art. 3 ad 2ᵘᵐ). Or to paraphrase, on the other hand, Gentile: The conceptions of the individual and of the society to which he belongs are complementary ideas, which form a real, concrete unity, inseparable except in abstraction. The rights and duties of the one are the function of the other's, and *vice versa*.

for the self-realisation of each individual (the formula "the greatest happiness of the greatest number" was an effort to express this ideal).

Thus the ideal of the perfect liberal State becomes merely a kind of opportunistic combine of the feeble and mediocre, of the many who live in fear of exploitation by the few of energy and ambition!

No wonder under this dispensation, rather than acquiesce in such drab mediocrity, so many of the gifted few have hailed Nietzsche as their prophet. No wonder, as different classes in the community gain self-consciousness, class warfare becomes a fact, since each one knows, whether individual or group, that whoever gains control of the State is in a position to increase his opportunities of self-realisation at the expense of his less fortunate neighbour! Nay, he would also be justified in doing so where no universal moral law is admitted and all is a matter of individual judgment!

Liberalism indeed may be accounted for, in a world permeated by Individualism and Agnosticism, as a desperate and vain attempt to escape from Tyranny, which is the logical consequence of such a world. For the Tyranny of the *Ancien Régime* was the direct result of the Individualism and Agnosticism of the Renaissance, operating in a society politically undeveloped and so easily exploited by the bold and unscrupulous. Liberalism, under more evolved political conditions, managed to overthrow this Tyranny, only to prepare the way, however, so it seems, for the alternative dictatorship of a class (Bolshevism), unless it can succeed in stereotyping its colourless ideal in the shape of the socialist slave State, whereby all men may be turned into machines. *In fine*, as its best, Liberalism can propose but an unstable equilibrium. It is a gloomy edifice built upon the shifting sands.

VIII. The acceptance of fascist principles means the end of *laissez-faire* as an absolute principle—that is, the principle of *laissez-faire* ceases to be a dogma into which it had come to be erected in the course of the nineteenth century. Its application becomes merely a matter of expediency, dependent on judgment as to whether or not, in given circumstances, its application in particular cases would more or less contribute to the promotion of the general good. Its general application is by now authoritatively condemned, as indeed experience has condemned it. In this Fascism entirely agrees with Mr. Maynard Keynes, despite the latter's prominent position as a Liberal. In fact, Mr. Keynes' excellent little book, *The End of Laissez-faire* (Hogarth Press, London, 1926), might, so far as it goes, serve as a useful introduction to fascist economics. There is scarcely anything to object to in it and there is much to applaud. He traces the history of *laissez-faire* in a manner that makes every sentence a delight to read and finally takes leave of the principle in a bed of ashes. He acquits the classical economists, Ricardo and Adam Smith, in spite of their language lending itself to the *laissez-faire* interpretation, of actually entertaining the fallacy themselves, and shows that it was "the political campaign for Free Trade, the influence of the so-called Manchester School and of the Benthamite Utilitarians, the utterances of secondary economic authorities, and the educational stories of Miss Martineau and Mrs. Marcet that fixed *laissez-faire* in the popular mind (*of England—and through England the whole world was influenced*) as the practical conclusion of orthodox political economy," and thereby deformed the thought of the great men who had laid the foundations of the Science. He further traces "the peculiar unity of the everyday political philosophy of the nineteenth century to the success with which it harmonised diversified and warring schools and united all good things to a single end. Hume and Paley, Burke and Rousseau, Godwin and Malthus, Cobbett and Huskinson, Bentham and Coleridge, Darwin and the Bishop of Oxford, were all, it was discovered, preaching practically the same thing—Individualism and *laissez-faire*. This was the Church of England and those her apostles, whilst the company of the Economists were there to prove that the least deviation into impiety involved financial ruin." He then shows conclusively (and therein he is supported by every modern economist of weight) that "the world is *not* so governed from above that private and social interest always coincide. . . . It is not a correct deduction from the Principles of Economics that enlightened self-interest always operates in the public interest. . . . We cannot, therefore, settle on abstract grounds, but must handle on its merits in detail what Burke termed *one of the finest problems in legislation, namely, to determine what the State ought to take upon itself to direct by the public wisdom, and what it ought to leave, with as little interference as possible, to individual exertion.*" Finally, he concludes very convincingly that Socialism and Individualism are reactions to the same intellectual atmosphere.

All this is pure fascist premises and I cordially recommend Mr. Keynes to proceed to Italy and there to study Fascism with an open mind and with the same scrupulous care as he has studied Bolshevism. An essay from his pen on Fascism would doubtless prove a most valuable piece of constructive criticism. Dare we say that he would come to acknowledge the fascist principle, which, in the place of the principle of *laissez-faire*: "Each for himself for the good of all," re-proclaims the Christian and Mediæval ideal of "Each for all, and all for God"?

If Mr. Keynes had traced the history of *laissez-faire* still further back than that which he actually does, he would have found that it issues as a logical consequence of the mentality engendered by the Reformation. Then it was that the great revolt of Individualism against authority was made manifest. This and the special influence of Puritanism, the emphasis placed on the lessons to be drawn from Old Testament history, the theory that good works, a moral life and energetic pursuit of one's vocation were a proof of predestination, of election to salvation, gradually transformed society from the form which the influence of the Church had given it during the Middle Ages, to the one we see around us now. The maxim "each for himself, for the good of all" (which contains a fatal *non sequitur*) came thus to take the place of "each for all and all for God." Capital came to be

valued, not for what it could procure in the interests of the community, but as an accumulation of wealth for wealth's sake, the
holders of which, characterised by the virtues of energy, enterprise, independence, zeal and dogged pertinacity, became the
saints of the new order; and so Capitalism came into being, Capitalism which thrives on *laissez-faire*.[64] Fascism would alter this;
but it discards the socialist formula that prescribes, as a remedy,
the nationalisation of the means of production, considering this
as a mere *reductio ad absurdum* of Capitalism.

Mr. Keynes shows in more than one place that he has no
love for Capitalism, the essential characteristic of which he
admits is "an intense appeal to the money-making and money-
loving instincts of individuals as the main motive force of the
economic machine." But he appears to accept it as inevitable.
At any rate, for the moment he appears to limit his vision of the
possible remedies to an improvement in the technique of Capitalism and to judicious control by the State. On the other hand,
he readily admits "that the fiercest contests and the most deeply
felt divisions of opinion are likely to be waged in the coming
years not round technical questions, where the arguments on
either side are mainly economic, but round those which, for
want of better words, may be called psychological or, perhaps,
moral." In this he is undoubtedly right, and it is precisely on a
moral question that Fascism is mainly fighting its battle. Fascism fully realises that the desire for wealth must always remain
a motive force of the economic machine, but denies that it need
be always the main motive force. An intense appeal to Patriotism and Religion are the lines on which it is operating, coupled
with an attempt to give to society a structure wherein, on the
one hand, the artisan, the peasant and the professional man
(into whose work other motives than that of money-getting predominate) may be particularly encouraged, and on the other,
industry and commerce come to be organised on a corporative
basis with definite social and political functions attached to each

---

[64] *Cf.* Eustace Dudley, *National Resurrection* (Longmans, Green & Co.,
London, 1926).

Corporation. Gradually it is hoped that, as these organisations develop, as legislation feels its way more and more effectively in the direction of extirpating the usurer and the manipulator of values, and as, contemporaneously, the religious spirit comes to penetrate again the very bones of society, as it did in the Middle Ages, a transformation of economic conditions away from Capitalism will come to be complete without either reducing the majority of members of society to the position of mere wage-slaves of the State or impairing in any way the productive power of the community.

IX. In much of the above there is already implied the fascist conception of Liberty, which I propose to consider next. The fascist conception of Liberty is very clear and very concrete. As we have already seen, the authority of the State must in any case be limited by the Moral Law. There must be no overstepping of this limit. The individual possesses by nature certain personal rights, rights which belong to him, because, though he cannot live except as a member of society and under the authority of the State, they are not subject to State interference as having authority to do with his position *qua* member of society, but as having solely to do with him as an individual and as a member of a family. This is a corollary of the Moral Law. Hence the *State has no right to coerce an individual in any way beyond what is necessary to safeguard and promote the collective interest; and any form of coercion in excess of what is strictly required to achieve the divinely ordained end of the State, that is, the general good, is to be condemned.*

The line may not always be easy to demarcate in practice; but the principle is clear. The rights of a father over his family, for instance, the family itself, which is the real cell on which the State is built up, the vigour and solidarity of which cannot be, besides, weakened without grave consequences for society itself, must be respected by the State. Children must not be forcibly removed from their parents, without urgent and grave reasons touching the general well-being. The father and mother, moreover, have certain paramount claims with regard to the education of their children, especially with regard to their moral and religious education. No State has the right to persecute an individual with respect to his private opinions and private relations, as long as they remain private. It is impossible to coerce a man's Conscience and Reason; and to attempt to do so is wicked. Nor can the State allow a member to die for want of the means of subsistence; and, as a corollary to this, the right of the individual to acquire property for himself and his heirs becomes intangible. The individual likewise has a right to be protected by the State against slavery or virtual slavery, against interference in his home and in his personal affairs by other individuals; against the invasion of his home by State officials without legal warrant; or against condemnation without fair trial and in accordance with the laws of the land. Rousseau's plea that "all defence, all guarantees against the power of the State are illogical, in that it is impossible for the body to wish to do violence to its members," is a lie. We know it to be possible; and the business of the State, with this general principle before it, is to frame laws to protect the individual against any possibility of such violence. The line of demarcation should be drawn more and more finely, as experience teaches, by a carefully-thought-out code of Law, designed to this end—laws protecting the family, property, the individual Conscience, hired labour and the course of justice, etc.

The liberties which such laws would safeguard are concrete liberties, inherent in the moral notion of an individual's natural rights. But no man possesses the natural right to propagate any personal views he likes, to destroy wealth, to attempt to disrupt society. Any liberties beyond those which appertain to his natural rights and which may be granted to the individual in excess of such rights are such as the State, in legislating, calculates will prove beneficent to the community as a whole, invigorate it, vitalise it, and so give individuals the opportunity for a better and higher life. Such liberties are definite and concrete, as all liberties should be. There is no such thing as freeing man in the abstract.

Liberty is and can only be a concrete thing, a right admitted by principle or conferred and limited by Law in the interest of collectivity. This, indeed, is the old English idea of Liberty. There was a happy time when Englishmen spoke proudly of their liberties. Too often now they vapour about Liberty in the abstract.

Liberty, moreover, is a relative question. As Mussolini has pointed out in one of his most characteristic speeches: "Liberty is not a right, it is a duty. It is not a concession granted to us, it is a conquest. It is not a matter of equality, it is a privilege. The notion of Liberty changes in time. There is a Liberty for times of peace and another Liberty in times of war. There is a Liberty for prosperous times, another for lean times." Serving God, which means identifying our individual good with the good of the whole body of our fellow-men, is the only true freedom.

We have already pointed out that the world is not so governed from above that private and social interests always coincide; and that it is the duty of the individual so to contrive that his private interests do so coincide. When he fails to do this, the State has a right to interfere. Thus, an individual has a right to own and acquire property, but if he systematically destroys the value of his property by impoverishing the soil, for instance, by over-cultivation, or by cutting down the timber unduly in order to realise immediate profits, or even if he merely neglects to develop it, that State has a right to interfere. There is no natural right that confers on man the right to do exactly what he likes with his own, beat his wife, starve his children, work out his property, sell himself into slavery, commit suicide, any more than the State has a right to do anything whatever that it pleases. The Moral Law steps in and must step in everywhere to regulate the limits of what constitutes rights one way or the other. And so it is the State's duty to base its laws on the Moral Law and if in all legislation this principle is systematically kept in view, not many mistakes are likely to be made in practice.

"Liberty," as Leo XIII. said,[65] "is a power perfecting man and hence should have truth and goodness as its object." Liberty to tell lies or propagate evil is licence, not Liberty—and for the State to protect society against lies and against evil is in reality liberating society from the bondage of sin. As Mdlle. Aline Lion, one of Gentile's most able pupils, keeps drumming into her readers in an essay published in the *Hibbert Journal* (January, 1927), "Liberty implies Law." If people would only get this little fact into their heads, they would not only begin to understand Fascism, but begin to see all life in truer colours. People who would disrupt society, break down the State, turn class against class, are the worst enemies of true Liberty. True Liberty is indeed preserved by the very denying of the right of individuals to raise their hands against the State and against God. So, upon this criterion, Fascism has, in effect, brought up to date the old laws of treason, to include every kind of activity engaged in for the purpose of betraying, breaking up, endangering the safety of the State and of public morality—such as the preaching of class warfare, the advocacy of the suppression of private property and of measures which would weaken the family tie, the entering into or recognition of seditious associations or international associations claiming a superior allegiance to that of the authority of the State, artificial birth restriction, pornography, blasphemy, open defiance or contempt of authority, and so forth. Even liberal Governments suppress and censure such things as pornography and physical cruelty to children and attempts to undermine the discipline of the forces of the Realm—in other words, they do draw the line, in practice at least, against gross immorality and treasonable propaganda. Fascism, which does not fear for its popularity, which has not to pander to the velleity of individuals, has merely the courage to dot the i's and cross the t's, to draw the line quite fairly where it logically and reasonably lies. In doing this it promotes no loss of Liberty.

---

[65] Leo XIII, Encyclical *Immortale Dei*, 1885.

The fascist policy of political centralisation coupled with administrative decentralisation is another case in point. There must be no room to allow of the country being divided against itself. But this identification of Liberty with Law is no newly discovered truth. It is an eternal truth, enunciated as long ago as Aristotle, emphasised again and again by the Scholastic philosophers of the Middle Ages. Perhaps, however, only now have political conditions so evolved that its application can become fully realisable, and from the application of this principle by Fascism to modern conditions, a new conception of citizenship may be said to have been inaugurated. I will quote again from Mdlle. Lion: "Liberty implies Law. The citizen implies the State. The employer or the employed implies the productivity of which one employs and the other is employed . . ." so that Fascism has come to proclaim, as the basis of citizenship, the consciousness of citizenship, the sense of responsibility towards others, and the maxim *everything for everyone who shall deserve it through moral sacrifice and productive activity.* Or again, as de Maeztu would put it, man has political rights by virtue of his functional value in society.[66]

X. The next point to emphasise, and a very important point it is, is the sharp distinction which Fascists make, with respect to political principles, between what is absolute and what is contingent. The general theory of the State, such as has been described above, enshrines certain main absolute principles, on which an indefinite number of secondary absolute principles depend. But the greatest care must be taken not to regard as absolute principles those dictating a particular policy, contingent on circumstances. The principle of *laissez-faire* is a case in point. This is entirely a question of policy, of means to a given end. It enshrines no absolute principle, except the negative one that there is no such absolute principle. The same may be said of all forms of Government *per se*, whether popular or otherwise,

---

[66] *Cf.* Ramiro de Maeztu, *Authority, Liberty and Function* (Allen & Unwin, London, 1916).

provided they can claim to fulfil properly the purposes for which Government is divinely instituted.

Mussolini has flattered the compatriots of William James and Charles Pierce by declaring (or so it seems, if we take certain reports as accurate accounts of interviews conceded by him to American journalists) that he is in certain respects a Pragmatist. On various occasions, too, he has praised Fascism for its "freedom from dogma." What does he mean by this? He simply means that Fascism does not dogmatise with respect to any particular form of Government or to any particular policy, provided that, whatever form of Government or policy be chosen, it fulfils the general purposes of the State. One form of Government *per se* has no better claims than another. The pragmatic test, *e.g.*, whether the desired useful consequences, given the purposes in view, result or may be calculated to result, is the only test by which to determine the best form of Government, within the limits imposed by the Moral Law in given circumstances. In other words, Mussolini rightly considers that the best form of Government is the one, which, in the given circumstances of a particular country, works best.[67] So Fascism does

---

[67] There is no doubt, too, that Mussolini himself, in the growth of his interior life, has been greatly assisted by the pragmatic method and, for all I know, even by the works of William James. But William James is, unfortunately, not very felicitous in his mode of expression. He appears to enunciate a number of propositions which, according to the letter of what he says, are easily proved to be false, such as, for instance, that "all true ideas are useful," "all useful ideas are true," "no ideas of ours are true, except those which we can verify," "all truths are mutable, except principles and definitions," etc., etc. (William James, *Pragmatism*, Longmans, Green & Co., London, 1907). The real message of value, it seems to me, that William James appears to desire to "get across" comes to this: certain of our fundamental beliefs—many dogmas of Religion, for instance—are not absolutely verifiable. But they can be tested, as scientific hypotheses are tested. Do they explain the facts better than any other hypothesis? What is the result on conduct in subscribing to them, in that "every theoretical difference somewhere issues in a practical difference?" For it is obviously true that we are

what our honest beliefs make us. Different religions or ways of belief make the whole difference to our mode of life. Turn a Mahommedan country into a Christian one, for instance, or *vice versa*, and in a few generations the place is transformed. If you have, therefore, a clear vision of the type or ideal of life and civilisation you desire to see grow up in or round you, the way of belief which in practice produces that type or ideal will be for you, if not the truth or whole truth, at least that body of doctrine to which, in practice, you allow yourself to submit, even if you allow yourself at the same time to entertain an intellectual doubt as to its actual veracity. From this position it is a very small jump to complete intellectual acquiescence. Many people who have had the misfortune to be deprived of sound doctrinal instruction, have indeed found their way to Christianity, groping, so to speak, along this path; and many more would do so, if they only realised how essentially interdependent are dogmas and conduct. You often hear people, whose reasoning faculties have been inadequately trained, exclaiming that the Christian ideal of life seems perfect to them, but "we are not going to have anything to do with its dogmas." What do they mean by this? They mean that either they have not the courage or intellectual honesty to give up paying homage to a way of life, which, in reality, means nothing to them, or that they are prepared to live on the moral legacy left them by their forbears, but are too illogical or dull to realise that there would have been no legacy at all, were it not for the dogmas believed in by their forbears, and too lazy to trace the inevitable connection. You cannot honestly have it both ways. An honest Unitarian cannot behave quite in the same way or approve quite the same way of life as a man who believes in the Trinity. So if you really believe, as Mussolini came to realise by experience, that the Catholic Christian way of life is the best, you are driven inexorably, if you are of courage and sound logic, to becoming, by the grace of God, a Catholic. And the same might be said, *mutatis mutandis*, of any other form of religion. *Cf.* also G. E. Moore, "William James' Pragmatism" (*Philosophical Studies*, Kegan Paul, Trench, Trubner & Co., London, 1922).

To conclude: Mussolini's admiration for James or, to take other examples, Sorel or Nietzsche, is due to the incidental influence which the opinions of these men happen to have exercised on Mussolini's mind in certain decisive phases of his development. Sorel, for instance, undoubtedly helped to open Mussolini's mind to the pettiness, the not and cannot absolutely condemn popular Government, for instance, or parliamentary Government. Nor does Fascism, conversely, stand absolutely by the idea of the "Corporative State," the form of Government which, in Italy, it is bringing into vogue. These matters are contingent matters, and they remain contingent even if, as in the case in point, certain forms of Government come to be rejected by experience as hopelessly unsuited in general to promote the common good and certain others be calculated as likely to prove efficient instruments. It is all a matter of judgment. Therefore, rules of practical expedience, based on experience and common sense, however they may approximate to absolute principles, must not be confounded with absolute principles.

XI. There remain two important points to elucidate: Fascism and Democracy; and Fascism and Empire. The importance of these points deserves that a whole chapter be given to the consideration of each. Sufficient has, however, already been said to explain what was meant by my allusion in Chapter I to the possibility of some country, like Japan, for

---

materialism, the mean ideology of his socialist contemporaries educated on the doctrines of Marx; while Nietzsche brought home to him the truth that the multitude must be led by the few and hence the necessity of an Aristocracy which represents the refinement, the exaltation, the embodiment of that kind of individualism which is worthy of encouragement, namely, the capacity of individuals to realise themselves in harmony with the good of the community to which they belong, the capacity of transcending themselves, of making themselves worthy of that Communion of Saints, which is the blessed goal of every individual. His admiration for or gratitude to these men, however, does not make him their disciple. A false prophet may very well, despite his heresy—for all heresies having any wide diffusion succeed only by virtue of the truths that they contain—prove to be the turning influence of the life of a true prophet. It would be dangerous, therefore, even if it were not known to the writer to be untrue, to conclude that Mussolini, in praising James, Sorel, or Nietzsche, looks upon the writings of any one of these philosophers as representing in any sense a full or balanced view of the truth.

instance—in no sense an heir to the Roman tradition, conforming its institutions to the fascist conception of the State. If the complete theory of the State which I have propounded is the product of European thought and civilisation, the greater part of it is applicable to all States indiscriminately, even though its full application and development may be impossible outside Christendom, or, in the last resort, outside Catholicism. Here lies the only reservation. Much of it is already universal in practice, wherever Society is found to be in a healthy condition; for it is a theory firmly established on reality and one wholly in conformity with Natural Law. The Peculiar Roman or European element in it begins where Christianity has in its unrivalled manner transcended the Natural Law by the highest Moral Law. Hence a vigorous Eastern State like Japan may in fact be nearer the fascist ideal in practice than many a decadent European or American contemporary, despite the latters' Christian heritage.[68]

---

[68] Unfortunately it is often the corrupted form of the great European heritage (its individualistic egoism, its materialism, its mechanical aspects) that are better known and more frequently imitated in the East. In certain respects, the world being what it is, this may be necessitated in self-defence. But it is a strange paradox that so many Chinese Nationalists, for instance, have europeanised themselves in so many ways just when a true and cultivated European begins to be ashamed of his own example. To take a small matter: European dress. If I were a Japanese or a Chinese Nationalist, I would wear my beautiful national dress, which in most cases is also extremely practical, instead, in the false desire to be modem, of adopting the hideous clothes worn by European men. A Japanese Fascist should look upon the wearing of his national dress throughout the world as a symbol of his sincere faith. The East has much to teach the West and a higher world civilisation depends very largely on the East and the West assimilating the best of each other. Unfortunately often the contrary is the more apparent; and it would be as well for the progressive Nations of the East to acquaint themselves better with the valuable side of the great European heritage, that which is the outcome of Roman and Catholic civilisations, rather than of its corruptions.

Or further light may be thrown on this point if we put it in this way: It is as clearly obvious that a Catholic need not necessarily be a Fascist in any practical sense, as it is obvious that a non-Catholic may, on the other hand, be one. But a non-Catholic Fascist will find himself, within the debatable territory which even the strictest theologian admits, in agreement with the fundamental Catholic conception of the State, and will recognise in the last resort the need for an independent moral authority, such as the Church claims to be, in order to provide the coping stone for any truly perfect polity.

CHAPTER IV

FASCISM AND DEMOCRACY

THE word "Democracy" has various meanings, to many of which Fascism is not only not opposed, but positively favourable; to others it is unfavourable; to one particular meaning it is absolutely opposed. It follows, therefore, that we must carefully distinguish what we mean when we use this familiar word.

Originally the word was always used in a bad sense. Aristotle calls a Democracy that perverted type of State, the normal form of which is a Polity. His well-known classification of the various types of State holds good even now:

(i) States in which authority is concentrated into the hands of one person, *e.g.*, a Monarchy in its normal form; a Tyranny in its perverted form.

(ii) States in which authority is exercised by relatively few persons, or by one or more few classes of persons only, *e.g.*, an Aristocracy in its normal form; an Oligarchy in its perverted form.

(iii) States in which authority is exercised by a relatively large number of persons or by all free subjects irrespective of class distinction, *e.g.*, a Polity, in its normal form, a Democracy, in its perverted form.

It is curious that the word universally adopted in modern times to express a popular form of Government should be precisely the word which in old times designated a corrupted form of popular Government only. It is more than curious. It is significant. It is, to those who have studied History and Philosophy, delightfully ironic.

The perverted form in any case is the one whereby authority is exercised with a wrong intention and according to wrong principles. Consequently, as a matter of fact, a Monarchy, in the absolute sense, may prove every bit as good a form of Government as an Aristocracy or a Polity. Nevertheless, as Aristotle himself is at pains to point out, it is very easy for any of the three types, taken absolutely, to become perverted; and experience shows that some kind of mixed form of Government is likely to prove the less easily perverted. But any form of Government whereby authority is exercised by many would already appear to be a kind of Polity. Therefore we may conclude that a Polity, whereby authority is exercised by many, but in accordance with a system of checks and balances, wherein the more responsible offices are held by an Aristocracy of intelligence and morality, wherein there exists one office of outstanding or unifying authority, is likely to prove, in practice, the best form of Government. With this conclusion Fascism completely agrees. It is a practical conclusion, not an abstract conclusion. It involves no absolute principle, but a sound contingent principle based on common sense and experience.

Using the word "Democracy," therefore, in one of its modern senses, *e.g.*, as equivalent to a "mixed Polity," Fascism may claim to be as democratic as any other political creed. Fascism, in other words, definitely stands, as a practical policy, for a Constitution "broadly based upon the people." Such a practical idea of Democracy as this is essentially traditional. It is advocated, not only by Aristotle in the fourth century before Christ, but by St. Thomas Aquinas in the thirteenth century and by Suárez, the Jesuit, in the seventeenth century. We have no quarrel with Democracy in this sense.

Then there is a second meaning of Democracy with which we have no quarrel, the sense in which homage is paid to the ideal of "equal opportunity," the sense in which we speak of every man "carrying in his knapsack a Marshal's baton."

Now, we know that this ideal is never wholly realisable. Men are not only not born equal, but are also necessarily born into conditions where the opportunities for advancement widely differ. If it were possible or desirable to eliminate the unfit at an early age, remove all children from the control of their parents at the age, say, of six; see to it that up to that age all received equally an adequate amount of nourishment, protection and hygiene; and if, subsequently, all were educated by the State in more or less equally efficient establishments, and none allowed to benefit by the accumulated wealth of relations or friends, we might indeed approach towards the realisation of the ideal. But such an ideal is not only impossible, but undesirable—in that it would mean sacrificing the family, which is the most sacred institution in the State, as well as many other things, which make for responsibility and variety, desirable in themselves.

The ideal of "equal opportunity," therefore, is in any case somewhat of a chimera and, in any absolute sense, both undesirable and contrary to nature. But in the ordinary practical sense of the term there is nothing objectionable in the ideal. On the contrary, there is everything in justice to be said for it. We require that the more responsible offices of the State be filled by the best people, by the people best fitted to occupy such offices, by people conspicuous in intelligence and morality; and such virtues are not the prerogative of any one class. Hence it is right that the State Constitution should allow of its being possible to draw on every class indiscriminately for its officials.

The Catholic Church is an example of an organisation which, in practice, approaches closely to this ideal in its ordinary unexaggerated meaning. The humblest priest, whatever his origin, carries in the folds of his "*ferrajolo*" (so to speak) the Triple Crown. Countless Bishops, Archbishops, Cardinals and Popes have sprung from the humblest origins—however nature may impose its limitations on the completely free application of the principle. The sins of the parents are visited upon the children even unto the fourth generation. This is one of nature's most stringent laws limiting the application of the principle. So also, the possession of a certain independence of means and of "family" is an advantage which can never be denied; nor is it desirable that it should be denied. To come of a well-to-do and refined stock produces qualities which could not be produced otherwise. Nor is it possible to eliminate the advantages given by other accidents of birth. A parish priest of China, for instance, must necessarily, from a point of view of promotion, be at a disadvantage in comparison with a parish priest of, say, Rome.

Nevertheless the equal opportunity of advancement afforded within the Church is as near perfection as is possible and desirable, and this practical sense of the ideal is an undying Latin tradition, dating from ancient Roman republican times. Even under the Empire, however in practice the ideal was discounted, as a theory it was never abandoned. The principle of an hereditary Emperor was never juridically admitted. The highest post in the Empire was always theoretically reserved to the Roman citizen who held the most apt combination of qualities; and when the Roman Empire became Christian, to be a Christian, to be a Catholic (the terms were then identical) was merged in the conception of citizenship.

Fascism, which is nothing if not traditional, is wholly at one, then, with this practical ideal of equal opportunity. So it is wholly democratic in tendency in this sense also; and if it departs from this principle in any particular, as, for instance, in favouring an hereditary Monarchy, it is for reason of utility. The advantages of an hereditary Monarchy are numerous. By it, above all, is insured the continuity of the State at all times; and though some form of Republic, like the Venetian Republic, having a president or Doge, elected for life, or rather selected, by some elaborate method calculated to result in the choice of a man truly representative and belonging to no particular Party to fulfil the highest post in the State, is an alternative form of Government to that of a limited hereditary Monarchy, with much to recommend it, the balance of advantages, under present circumstances, in most modern States, remains, I dare say, with the latter. In any case, it is not a matter on which to dogmatise.

Thirdly, there is another meaning to the word "Democracy" with which Fascism accords. I mean that "Demophily" such as is recommended by the Popes.[69] Here Democracy merely means a special zeal to give the labouring classes, who are oppressed in the modern world as scarcely ever they have been before, those humane conditions of life which not only Charity, but Justice dictates.[70]

Apart from the above meanings, however, Fascism is very much opposed to Democracy. We have already dealt with Democracy in the sense that Rousseau gives it or in some other sense by which the "general will" is made the sole legitimate authority. In these senses I will refer to it as "Democratism"— that religious myth of Democracy, which has nothing directly to do with the advocacy of Democracy in the sense of a Polity, as above described. "Democratism" is a dogma, not a policy. It is the dogma of the Sovereign People, the falsity of which I have already and exhaustively exposed, the dogma which would make us bow down inexorably to the "general will" and make us all the slaves of mere number. It is a form of political Pantheism, of "Naturalism," which would make of the State a very God. It is not necessary for us to discuss it again here.[71]

So now we come to the last meaning of the word "Democracy," the meaning which really, and justly so, is confounded with that perverted type of Polity which Aristotle condemns— "mob rule." From this principle Fascism turns away in disgust.

But there is a contingent side to this point. Does modern parliamentary Government, coupled with a wide franchise, necessarily identify itself with "mob rule"? The answer is: *not necessarily*—that is, if we mean by parliamentary Government

---

[69] *Cf.* Leo XIII., Encyclical, *Rerum Novarum*, 1888.

[70] *Cf.* Jacques Maritain, *Charles Maurras et le devoir des Catholiques* (Librairie Plon, Paris, 1926).

[71] *Ibid.*

merely some form of popular and elective Government. The mixed type of Polity which Fascism favours is not an unpopular form of Government. But Fascism would certainly say that a form of Government whereby the people at large do, in fact, elect a practically supreme Parliament, is bound to tend towards mob rule, even where "Democratism" is not the order of the day. It is all a question here of degree, of machinery, of the presence or absence of constitutional checks, of the presence or absence of other checks, such as a *de facto* governing class, of habits, sound traditions, etc.

If we have a wide electorate and a practically supreme popularly elected Parliament, and if, at the same time, homage is widely shown to "Democratism," the plunge towards mob rule will be rapid and difficult to retrieve without Revolution. If, on the other hand, "Democratism" is repudiated by those who speak for the State; if a healthy tradition, dating from a time when "Democratism" had not developed into a popularly accepted Gospel, remains powerful among the people; if theoretical constitutional checks still remain on the Statute Book, however seldom invoked; if, in fact, there exist a governing Aristocracy firmly entrenched in the State bureaucracy, then no great harm need be feared from such a form of Government. In given circumstances it may even have a balance of recommendations in its favour. This is how Fascism would judge the matter.

When we come to look at the Constitutions of France, say, or of Great Britain, or of Italy before the fascist Revolution, the question enters the realm of practical politics. That Italy was drifting rapidly towards mob rule during the generation preceding the fascist Revolution, few will gainsay. That the condition of France, whose spokesmen openly preach "Democratism," appears to be very similar to that of the old Italy, there seems no reason at all to doubt. The case of Great Britain, however, is not so clear. There "Democratism" is not so explicitly avowed as in France. Nevertheless, it is very generally avowed and often implicitly avowed in the speeches of responsible English states-men. This alone constitutes a great danger. On the other hand, in England the bureaucracy is still largely in the hands of the public-school man, who, with all his faults, holds steadily to a number of sound traditions. This is undoubtedly the most pow-erful check extant in Great Britain against the degeneration of the State into a condition of mob rule. But the public-school sys-tem has also its dangers, in that it has resulted in a cleavage of English social life into a rigid caste system. However deferential and kindly disposed the "Toff" may be to the "Bloke," the Bloke is made to feel his inferiority and he resents it. In France and Italy no such caste system exists. Fascist Italy is far more dem-ocratic in this sense than England. Nevertheless, the existence of the Toff in England is certainly a bulwark against mob rule; so, too, is the existence of certain, however weak, constitutional checks. The whole tendency, however, appears to my judgment decidedly bad. The caste system, as well as the cleavage between economic classes (in Great Britain particularly marked, in that Capitalism has there developed in Europe as nowhere else), is generating explosive material. "Democratism" in one form or another is already widely regarded as Gospel truth among the ill-instructed masses. The public-school man is not so power-fully entrenched as he was. The popularly elected Parliament is subject, in practice, to fewer and fewer checks. I should say, therefore, that Great Britain has been for some time sauntering down the path that leads eventually to the abyss and has now reached a turning where the gradient has become suddenly much steeper. France, on the other hand, has already gained a dangerous momentum further down. Both have meantime lost the companionship of Italy, who has turned round and is labo-riously trudging in the opposite direction; and both are begin-ning to wonder if Italy is not right.

That is, roughly, how I would diagnose the situation. But we may conclude, in any case, that there is nothing in parliamen-tary Government, as usually understood, inherently pernicious. Nevertheless, coupled with whatever advantages it may possess as a practical system, it is open to many objections. In expounding a few of these objections, further below, I shall not be referring to those who would idolise the "general will." Such people are past praying for; and I can only refer them back to Chapter II, with the gentle reminder that, whatever may be said for their idol, parliamentary Government is no mouthpiece of it, because, as I have already pointed out:

(I) The sum of individual wills, even if unanimous, is not the same as the "general will."

(II) Where are you to draw the line as to the enfranchised and disenfranchised? For, if you leave out any class, with any claims to being reasonable, you make the result still less approximate to the "general will."

These, of course, are no arguments against parliamentary Government. They are, however, absolutely damning arguments against the idea that parliamentary Government follows as a logical consequence of setting up the idol of the "general will." Those who believe in the "general will" have not only to scrap Rousseau and fall back on a more brutal, more materialistic Philosophy still in order to justify their God, but invent a new method of consulting him. It would be interesting to hear what method they would now put forward.

As for a justification of majority Government, apart from this absurd attempt to harness it to the chariot of the idol of the "general will," it generally rests on the idea of force: *e.g.*, that what the majority wishes cannot be avoided because the majority possesses the force; and that, therefore, it is better to count heads than to break them.

This notion is an absolute fallacy. The majority of any body of opinion is always (except in moments of intense excitement and in conditions when the result is practically a foregone conclusion) led by a minority. In the first place, therefore, you create the force before which you must bow down—in other words, by advocating majority Government on the above plea, you are making yourself, not the slave of the majority, in the abstract, as you suppose, but the slave of a system which would create for you your majority. Secondly, quite apart from this point, if you really wanted to give power to those who held the preponderance of force on their side, you would not be so illogical as to enfranchise women and old men. More logically you would limit the franchise to the Army, or, still more logically, to the Artillery, the Air Force and the Tank Corps only. Thirdly, you would, in any case, have to make voting obligatory and insist on clear majorities in every constituency by means of some electoral device or other. For at present few parliamentary Governments are backed by a majority of votes. On the Continent, where there are many parties in the field, where frequently some system of proportional representation maintains, this is almost unknown. In England it only occurs by coincidence. The present Conservative Government, for instance, in spite of its overwhelming parliamentary majority, is actually returned on a minority vote. On the Continent again, or in Ireland, under a system of many Parties or of proportional representation, the Government shifts continuously, not in accordance with the will of the majority of the electorate, but in accordance with the various manœuvres of groups inside Parliament scheming for a turn of office. Moreover, though in a sense Government does and must rest on force, the greatest of all forces is, in the long run, Reason. Is there any cause to show why a majority, if it is not a majority among qualified judges or among a body of persons sitting in deliberation and very equal in their status of education (when we may, as a general rule, justly conclude that *pars major præsumitur sanior*), must necessarily possess the better Reason? None whatever. And this leads us to the consideration of one of the great objections to parliamentary Government, with or without a majority behind it. Does it make for reasonable Government? Is it a system tending to throw up an Aristocracy of intelligence and morality?

As a matter of fact, the system puts a premium on men with a gift for speech, rather than on men with a gift for cool judgment. We know that not one-tenth of the members of the House of Commons are fitted to hold the rank of Cabinet Ministers.

Most of those who reach that rank would, even as it is, be lost, were it not for the permanent official behind them with his technical knowledge. The choice of competent Cabinet Ministers and Under Secretaries of State, under a parliamentary system, is extremely restricted, as all Prime Ministers know. Under a parliamentary system, as generally understood, we are giving full play to the tendency of allowing ourselves to be governed by a host of amateurs in politics, generally with little to their credit but the gift of the gab, unless it be some slight administrative experience to be compared with that of a Club Secretary—amateurs, too, who make, not politics, but a political career their profession for the sake of the publicity it gives them, which they so love. Nor does the system put a premium on morality to compensate for the premium it sets on mediocre intelligence. On the contrary, that man has the advantage who is unscrupulous in his promises and sly in getting out of them; who is not ashamed of beating up voters with a big drum; pandering to the gusts of public sentiment; exploiting the ignorance and even the misery of the common man.

No joint-stock company, in spite of the fact that here the shareholders have a definite and defined right to have a direct say in the management of their affairs by vote, would dream of adopting such a system. Any such company that did so would soon be in the hands of the receiver. Imagine Mr. Derrick and Lord Seepage, whose turn it is to retire from the Board of the Down-our-way Petroleum Company, but are both eligible for re-election, circularising the shareholders before the next annual general meeting, with a "Vote for Derrick and big dividends," and a "Vote for Seepage and safety, with a big bonus to follow," at the head of their respective pamphlets. Would any of us, before such a spectacle, invest our savings in such a company? Never for a minute. Yet the far more technical and complex business of running a State competently we allow thoughtlessly to be carried on under a system that, if suggested for any other kind of business, would be ridiculed out of court.[72]

---

[72] In England, as we have seen, for special reasons the system works

better than in most places, though none too well. The removal, therefore, of some of its worse features might prevent the breakdown which otherwise, given a few decades, looks inevitable. With some such limited programme in mind, I would suggest the following constitutional reforms:

(1) Make the family (the real social cell) instead of the individual the basis for the suffrage (see below).

(2) Give the elector the right to vote against anyone or all *en bloc* of the parliamentary candidates in a given constituency as an alternative to voting in favour of any one of them—in other words, give him the right freely to refuse altogether the choices made by the Party machines, thus compelling, if necessary, new elections with new candidates.

(3) Institute second elections in order to insure that no member be returned without securing his quota of votes, which must be at least equal to the total number of votes cast, divided by the number of candidates. Thus, if there were three candidates and 10,000 votes recorded, no candidate could be elected unless he secured 3,334 votes, *after deducting any adverse votes.*

(4) Make voting obligatory.

(5) Cut down the total membership of Parliament to not more than 10 members per 1,000,000 habitants.

(6) Contrive to make (and to set up machinery for the purpose of revising and maintaining) the constituencies—all of which should be single member constituencies—roughly equal in population.

(7) Insist on the public auditing of Party funds, together with the periodical publication of the names of all contributors.

(8) Restore the powers of the House of Lords to equal those *in every respect* enjoyed by the House of Commons, but contemporaneously make of the House of Lords a true House of Faculties, composed, that is to say, of:

(a) Only a very restricted hereditary element.

(b) A large number of *ex-officio* life appointments (a proportion of the Bishops of the Established Church, certain high dignitaries of other Christian Churches, Presidents of the Royal Society and similar bodies, retired Chief Permanent Secretaries of the more important Ministries, retired Ambassadors, ex-Viceroys and ex-Governors of Dominions, Chiefs of the Imperial General Staff, First Sea Lords, Admirals of the Fleet, Field and Air Marshals, the Lord High Chancellor and the Lords of Appeal in ordinary, the Lord

Chief Justice, the Master of the Rolls, the President of the Probate, Divorce and Admiralty Division, the Lord President of the High Court of Scotland, the Lord Justice Clerk of the Scottish Judiciary, and the Chief Justice of Northern Ireland).

(c) Life representatives appointed by the Councils of certain recognised professional Associations (Doctors of Medicine, Surgeons, Engineers and Architects, University Professors, etc.), and

(d) A limited number of life appointments selected from among Privy Counsellors of at least one year's seniority, not already entitled to sit by virtue of some other qualification.

The hereditary element I would suggest restricting to:

(a) Princes and Princesses by blood closely related to the King.

(b) Peers and Peeresses in their own right of England, Scotland and Northern Ireland, whose title to sit dates from the reign of James I, who have reached the age of 40.

(c) Representative Peers (or Peeresses in their own right) of England, Scotland and Northern Ireland elected severally by their peers in the proportion of 1 to 25.

With regard to the suggested family vote, the idea is a very simple and logical one. Theoretically you enfranchise everybody indiscriminately—men, women and children; but you restrict the right to exercise the vote to:

(a) Married men and women.

(b) Men and women who have reached the age of, say 30, but you give an extra vote to the father or male guardian of a family for every child or ward who has not attained the right to vote—or, alternatively, to the mother or female guardian of a family, if the father be dead or absent in some qualified sense. The father or mother, as the case may be, would also have the power to enfranchise their children or wards at any time within their own discretion. Such a law would confer absolutely equal rights on men and women, except the prior right of the father to exercise the additional votes. Thus the male vote would predominate. So, likewise, would the vote of those bearing the greater responsibilities. Finally, the system would place the centre of gravity of power between the responsible but vigorous ages of 35 and 55.

(9) Reduction by concentration of portfolios in the number of Cabinet Ministers.

(10) Drastic local Government reform under three headings:

Again, who in his senses imagines that an electorate, even if confined to persons of education, is capable of deciding any important technical issue with any justice—Free Trade *versus* Tariff Reform, for instance—a valuable opinion in regard to which requires the possession of a special knowledge of the Science of Economics and an enormous amount of technical and statistical data to which this knowledge must then be applied. Finally, no Party, under the ordinary parliamentary system, dares put forward a measure, however good, if it runs the risk of unpopularity. What Government, for instance, resting on a parliamentary majority, would have stayed in office a week in any country, with such a Bill as the Gentile Education Reform Bill on the table of the House? On its main provisions hardly an expert in Italy disagreed as to its merits. It was a wonderful measure, but it meant that every household would be affected in the sense that it would immediately become more difficult for the young members of the family to pass their examinations and acquire those much-sought-after diplomas, which, on the Continent, mean a great deal towards obtaining so-called respectable "black-coated" employment. Moreover, the measure wrenched the whole teaching profession out of their rut and put them, so to speak, "back to school," to their great personal inconvenience. The consequence was a howl of protest, wherein the voices of countless disappointed fathers mingled with those

---

(a) Simplification and reduction in number of the various and multifarious types of local authority, with the object of introducing economy and greater administrative efficiency, the elimination of overlapping, etc.

(b) Much further decentralisation in the technical and administrative sense; centralisation, on the other hand, in the political sense.

(c) Introduction of the Corporative system on the Italian model, but adapted to English needs, as the basis on which local authorities should be constructed.

(11) Ministers to have the right of speaking, but not of voting, in both Houses. This provision is rendered necessary by the institution of a non-Party House of Lords.

(12) The office of Lord Chancellor to be made a life appointment.

of injured vested interests. Only a form of Government, which protects the Government from the consequences of unpopularity, would ever have enabled such a Bill to become Law. Who knows, indeed, how many useful measures have never even been contemplated under parliamentary *régimes*, merely because they would have meant governmental suicide? The truth is that the parliamentary system makes Government the panderer to popularity, on the one hand—gives power to the masses to decide innumerable issues about which they cannot possibly have the knowledge required in order to exercise a sound judgment—and for the rest it is only too often a game, which flatters the masses into thinking they are the masters, but in reality is played by a limited number of wire pullers.

This might be tolerable, if the result were happier or the players of the game somewhat more respectable. As it is, we have little to comfort us, and the question arises, why do we acquiesce in this state of affairs? Because there is no alternative system? Nonsense. There are countless examples of political institutions in history, many of them eminently successful, to copy or to adapt. As many more could be drafted by any body of constitutional lawyers. Why then? Because, I believe, we have drifted; and because our minds have been poisoned. We have drifted from an older type of Constitution, which was inherently sound under different conditions, into an evolution of the same in a wrong direction under the influence of the false ideas which the French Revolution and various other materialist schools of political Philosophy disseminated during the eighteenth and nineteenth centuries.

Fascism, in freeing opinion from the hypnotism of these false ideas, has made it possible in Italy to look at the parliamentary system, as it is generally developed, for the first time objectively. What are its practical advantages? What are its disadvantages? In the light of an unprejudiced examination, under Italian conditions at any rate, there is so little to be said for it, that, even among the opponents of the present *régime* in Italy, it has few defenders outside the dispossessed clique of professional politicians. If the same problem could be examined elsewhere, with equal absence of prejudice, on the sole criterion of advantages *versus* disadvantages, I wonder how the system would fare, say, in France or in England. I believe very little better. Fascism in this has shown itself a great emancipating movement. It is like a breath of fresh air in a stifling room.

CHAPTER V

FASCISM AND EMPIRE

I REFER the reader back to Chapter I for the definition of Empire. An Empire is a particular form of State; and, as I have already shown in Chapter II, it comes into being naturally like any other form of State, according to circumstances. Generally speaking, it is a form of State that succeeds historically the city or tribal State, but precedes the national State. For, as I have reiterated more than once, the vitality, and so the very justification, of an Empire is exhibited in its power of assimilation, that is, its power of welding into a single national State its various heterogeneous elements by creating within its limits a single national or super-national sentiment—and thus ensuring political progress.

Nor, as I have shown, is there anything inherently wrong, aggressive or unstable in the imperial State. We have, therefore, to ask: Why is it that Imperialism has come to enjoy to-day such a poor reputation? We find it denounced everywhere, in every class of society, and used by many almost as a term of abuse. In every country we meet, indeed, a handful of self-styled Imperialists, proud of the appellation; and there are, of course, the statesmen of imperial States, who naturally defend the Empire, for whose destinies they are responsible, in act and speech, while the Empires themselves, where vital, of their own momentum carry on. But even among the statesmen of these Empires, in their speeches it is not hard to detect, very commonly, an apologetic note, an effort not to emphasise the imperial character of the State overmuch; and a vein, which smacks of hypocrisy in their mouths, where they speak of the Empire as a burden, a burden for the fastening of which on the people's backs, it seems, the rapacity of past generations of less mild men must be held responsible, which they cannot, however, in duty bound renounce without doing more harm than good.

The reason for this doubt lies in the history of Europe since the Pagan Renaissance, when Religion decayed and lust for power became the order of the day. It is, alas, true that modern Imperialism has exhibited the ugly side, not so much of Imperialism, as of human nature. Out of the lust for power and wealth, by the rapacity, indeed, of past generations of less mild men, the foundations of the modern Empires of the world have been largely built. So, too, in part were built the Roman Empire and many other ancient Empires. But the fact remains, as the edifices arose, in many cases at least, the ideal of a vast political progress arose with them, so that the original idea of domination for the sake of power and pelf gave way to the idea of assimilation for the sake of political progress and a higher civilisation. And, if, under the humaner lights of the spirit of the day, the imperial States would now examine their consciences, they need have no cause to be ashamed of themselves if they would only face their task henceforth with a right intention and according to those right principles, which every State should, indiscriminately, follow if it would accomplish the purposes for which it is divinely instituted. An Empire may be a burden, if you like, but it is also an opportunity and a privilege—an opportunity for carrying a great part of the world a step further along the road of political progress, a privilege by which the best of a particular tradition may be spread for the advantage of others.

Unfortunately many of those who are proud to call themselves Imperialists are of the very type which merits our reprobation, Militarists and adventurers, men without an idea in their heads beyond themselves, men without religion, greedy financiers, hunters of wealth for wealth's sake, men with the eyes of fish. But there are some, many of whom are or have been simple soldiers and sailors, who have learnt to think imperially in the way they should. It is for these to leaven the rest.

So, too, in spite of the humaner spirit of the day, the world is still suffering from the greedy atmosphere it has breathed during the past few centuries. There is much in this humaner spirit which springs rather from exhaustion than from a change of heart. Men have become more nervously sensitive, not more morally sensitive—or so it seems. The final justification of the Empires of to-day can only be accomplished with a truly positive change of heart.

But do not let us exaggerate. The Empires of to-day, no less than the Empires of yesterday, have not by any means been all built up on avarice and lust. Empires exhibit natural growth. The conditions of the world are not static. Empires grow, filling up by divine right the voids created by States in dissolution, by anarchy intervening. The State which is strong, that carries its head high, as every State should, whose citizens are loyal and enterprising and sane and healthy and prolific, the State that has much to give the world, will inevitably grow under favourable geographical conditions, expand, become an Empire, assimilate her parts, become a greater national State, expand again. This is the real way in which Empires are built even in the worst periods. The lust and the avarice of private individuals and of statesmen, which, in all times, in varying degrees (fallen human nature being what it is), have characterised the growth of States, are, almost invariably, if we examine the phenomena carefully but broadly, episodical compared with nature's thrust of life, which, hating a void, imposes expansion, in the dynamic conditions of the world, on those States in whose veins life runs strong and generously.

This, in the first place, is the fascist view of Empire. Therein, in a sense, in the Biblical sense, it takes no thought of the morrow. Rome was not built in a day. And if fascist Italy again becomes worthy of an Empire, inevitably an Empire shall she possess. Without any aggressive intent, without any militarism, her Empire will grow, the work of God rather than of man.

The struggle for existence is another matter. It has nothing to do with Empire, though out of it, Empire may grow. A State has a right to fight for its life. This is a law of life, from which none of us can withdraw. The world is not one State yet, meting out justice for all; and in this world of comparative anarchy, the unprepared State will succumb. A sense of this reality is not incompatible with the highest ideals. On the contrary, the greatest idealists are the greatest realists. Idealism, in this sense (not the philosophical sense) is contrasted with materialism, not realism. The average Englishman, whose logical sense, under his present dispensation, has been left deplorably untrained, is apt to confuse materialism with realism, idealism with ideology; and thereby, owing to his practical talents operating perspicaciously despite his confusion of thought, he has, not altogether undeservedly, earned the name of humbug.

The struggle for existence in a world of comparative anarchy as between States may inevitably lead to further wars. Not so the ideal of Empire, as Fascism would interpret it. And if the world at large, if the big Empires that to-day control the raw materials and the empty spaces fit for colonisation, hem in a vital and prolific nation, not naturally enjoying the possession of abundant raw materials and empty spaces for her sons to settle in, and prevent, thereby, that Nation from maintaining a proper standard of life for her sons, by closing their doors to colonisation and exacting a monopoly toll for the raw materials on which her industry may thrive, it is they who will be responsible for any wars that break out in consequence of such a Nation's right to live and to enjoy a better life.

The chief hope here for accommodating matters, lies, perhaps, in the work of the League of Nations. If the League succeeds in not rendering itself sterile in the futile aim of maintaining, for the sake of an illusory peace, static conditions in a world which is necessarily dynamic, the League will justify its existence. Otherwise, it will be the cause of war, rather than of peace, like one who invites an explosion by the bottling up of steam in a confined space.

Italian Fascism at first looked askance at the League. It hoped little of a League, founded under the auspices of an ideologist like Wilson, a League that looked like the fulfilment of a prophecy by such a false prophet as Rousseau, planted in the fatherland of Rousseau and Calvin, and engendered in the cynical atmosphere of the Paris conference, a League whose assemblies have been characterised by the worst examples of fulsome, demagogic, hypocritical oratory and by political manœuvres recalling the worst features of parliamentary log-rolling, a League, too, whose most enthusiastic supporters spring from the ranks of just that sort of political sentimentalists with whom Italy at home will have nothing more to do.

But Mussolini's idealism, his realism, his capacity for piercing the veil of mere appearances, has gradually brought his followers round to a rather different view of the League. From an attitude of doubt and disapproval, an attitude of cautious hope has arisen, coupled with a determination to make use of the League as an instrument to promote justice and equity, as between States, rather than peace at any price. Fascists never disputed that the League was capable of doing much good, in any case, in a minor way by uniting and concentrating within itself, with a view to better efficiency, the many international organs required to serve the international life of States, and by providing a new and useful weapon for diplomacy by conference together with machinery for conciliation, arbitration and the judicial settlement of disputes, etc. But Fascists consider that, in order really to serve humanity, the spirit of the League must be transformed in a more objective sense, aim at justice rather than peace-at-any-price, and come to be moulded by the legal mind rather than by that of the politician. They hold it to be more important to build up International Law by the gradual process of working from precedent to precedent, and to define principles of equity in accordance with the doctrine of objective rights based on the functional value of States, than to extend the

League's role as an international gendarme in this stage of its career.[73] This is now Italy's attitude towards the League.

But to return to the question of Empire, there is another point, embodying the fascist conception of Empire, other than what has been described already, requiring to be elucidated. I have shown the task of Empire to be assimilation as a means to higher, more integrated political unities; and the power of assimilation depends on good, strong Government, just laws and the influence of what the Germans call *Kultur*, which is best rendered into English, albeit sounding a little affected, by the quite literal translation into "culture." [74] A Nation can, of course, have a worthy culture, or an unworthy one; but in any case, the influence of culture in the task of assimilation shares with Law the major place, and may even be said to include Law. It is, in effect, all that a Nation spiritually stands for. It is the concrete expression of a Nation's tradition, the genius, one might say, of the Nation, that which Religion and Philosophy, more than anything else, determine in the long run.

Empire, therefore, is indissolubly connected with a culture, an idea, a type of civilisation, a way of approaching the problems of life. Hence there is a sense in the word Empire which transcends its territorial sense; and this is its spiritual sense, its really more important sense, in that its territorial sense is but a ready-made receptacle to receive the spirit. But the spirit may, after filling the receptacle, be defused beyond it. A powerful

---

[73] *Cf.* Ramiro de Maeztu *Authority, Liberty and Function* (Allen & Unwin, London, 1916): "An International Law based exclusively on Treaties would make present frontiers eternal. . . . War itself is more violent but less unjust than such an abominable aspiration." The attempt to do so is largely responsible for the failure of the Hague Conferences, and may yet account for the failure of the League of Nations.
[74] Unfortunately the word *Kultur* has earned an evil savour, because the German *Kultur*, so widely advertised before and during the War, happened to be impregnated with the false Idealism of the leading German philosophers.

national State, respected among other States, with a great civilisation, a great culture, will exercise inevitably a powerful attraction beyond its frontiers. It will influence the culture of other Nations. It will have an assimilating effect beyond what is strictly its own province; and this influence in itself is a kind of Empire-building. It is, in fact, the finest form of Empire-building, for it conquers without destroying life, that is, by the sincere flattery of imitation, so to speak, only.

Fascism would create for Italy also an Empire such as this. And it will inevitably do so, if Italy has anything of real importance to give the world. And if, besides the importance of its gift, that gift be truly good, those who might thus become spiritually influenced by Italy would never have anything to regret. All-conquering Rome was in many ways spiritually conquered by little Greece and proudly handed on the culture of Greece, blended with her own, to the world at large. Italy appears, indeed, to have a genius for conquest of this sort. It was largely by Italian agency that Rome in the person of the Church spiritually conquered Europe again and created the great European civilisation of the Middle Ages, on the foundation of ancient Roman Law. The culture of the Italy of the Renaissance, yet a third time, mixed blessing as it turned out to be, made something of a universal conquest in a later age. And now we have the fourth Italy, with a new universal message, a culture in the making, which is a balanced synthesis and direct development of her own and Europe's traditional past, anxiously claiming to be heard. This book gives some indication of what this message is and what it means. Italian Fascists hope, nay believe, it will, for one thing, mean—slowly, slowly, in the course of many generations, but inevitably—the free reunion of Europe, of Christendom, under the leadership again of the dual Rome, that of the Pope and that of the Emperor. When Italians speak of Empire, it is of this that they are chiefly thinking. It is of this that the new Italy is fondly dreaming and preparing herself to achieve. But the chief means that Italy intends to employ to this end is just this, very simply: to give the world in herself an example of a new and perfectly balanced social equilibrium within the unity of a strong and vigorous national State acknowledging the moral supremacy of the Catholic Church. She would thus show the world, which is hankering after such an equilibrium, the way to achieve it, and would invite all and sundry to follow her and join with her in the making of a new and better political and social synthesis, built on the old traditions.

But if this ideal be a worthy one and represent truly the right road for all to follow, the sooner others, besides Italy, take to it, the better; and if anyone can, in friendly rivalry, there take the lead from Italy, to him the greater glory. All on this road are welcomed as equals; but God will assign to the most vigorous and zealous, to the one who can achieve most perfectly the task of harmonising her own interests with those of the world at large in accordance with principles of universal justice, the honour of *primus inter pares*. The Roman idea has no restrictions of place or person.[75] In the pursuit of this ideal, because of its universality, there can be no exclusiveness. There is room for all. If pride keeps anyone away, so much the worse for him.

---

[75] *Cf.* James Bryce, *The Holy Roman Empire*, Chap. VII, "The Theory of the Mediæval Empire" (Macmillan & Co., London, 1932, revised edition).

CHAPTER VI

THE *WELTANSCHAUUNG* OF FASCISM

THE present *Weltanschauung* of Fascism may be summed up in one word: *Youth*. Fascism would have men look at the world with the eyes of a well-knit young man, the Knight Chivalrous; and if I were asked to choose an appropriate motto for Fascism, it would be "*ανδρίζεσθε*," "*Quit ye like men.*" I remember this was the motto of my old school, St. Aubyns, Rottingdean; and maybe the ideals that were instigated in me there have contributed to my enthusiasm for Fascism now. Rottingdean, in those days, was also the home of Kipling, and it was then, if I remember rightly, or very shortly afterwards, he wrote that extraordinarily stirring little poem "If," which sums up all that is best in Kipling's ideal Imperialist, all that is best in the English public-school spirit. I will quote it in full, for it conveys the sentiment of one half of the *Weltanschauung* of Fascism:

"If you can keep your head when all about you
    Are losing theirs and blaming it on you;
If you can trust yourself when all men doubt you,
    But make allowance for their doubting too;
If you can wait and not be tired by waiting,
    Or being lied about, don't deal in lies,
Or being hated, don't give way to hating,
    And yet don't look too good, nor talk too wise:

"If you can dream—and not make dreams your master;
    If you can think—and not make thoughts your aim;

If you can meet with Triumph and Disaster
    And treat those two impostors just the same;
If you can bear to hear the truth you've spoken
    Twisted by knaves to make a trap for fools,
Or watch the things you gave your life to, broken,
    And stoop and build 'em up with worn-out tools:

"If you can make one heap of all your winnings
    And risk it on one turn of Pitch-and-toss,
And lose, and start again at your beginnings
    And never breathe a word about your loss;
If you can force your heart and nerve and sinew
    To serve your turn long after they are gone,
And so hold on when there is nothing in you
    Except the Will which says to them: 'Hold on!'

"If you can talk with crowds and keep your virtue,
    Or walk with Kings—nor lose the common touch,
If neither foes nor loving friends can hurt you,
    If all men count with you, but none too much,
If you can fill the unforgiving minute
    With sixty seconds' worth of distance run,
Yours is the Earth and everything that's in it,
    And—which is more—you'll be a Man, my son!"

The poem expressing the other half of Fascism's *Weltan-schauung* has still to be written, that which would make Kipling's man complete—a right religious sense, a delicate sensibility, all that Christianity added, in fact, to perfect what was best in the ancient world, the Greek spirit of enquiry, the steadier Roman virtues of *Gravitas* and *Pietas*.

It may be objected that the modern Italian does not conspicuously shine for his modesty or discipline; but it is precisely for this reason that Fascism in Italy is laying particular stress upon these virtues. Sober the modern Italian already is, enterprising and hard-working, and exceedingly pious in the Latin sense of the word, which implies the reciprocal devotion between parents and their offspring. But he has a long way to go yet to acquire, nationally speaking, the whole gamut of fascist virtues. So have we all. But if we move about to-day among Italy's young men and women, especially of the upper middle classes, the nobility outside the international cliques, the sons and daughters of the professional classes and of the peasant, the signs are extraordinarily encouraging. These young modern Italians seem to be set on combining the sporting, fair-play, chivalrous qualities of the public-school class in England, with greater intelligence, greater alertness, far greater consciousness of responsibility, a more genuine sense of Religion and artistic sensibility. The children of the new generation, the born-after-the-War, are a veritable joy to behold. They are already immeasurably superior to the children I remember in the days before the War—and this of all classes. They are healthier in their bodies, better fed, healthier in their minds, better educated. They have learnt to make thought and action one, to do what they say, to say what they do, to stand up for their own opinions, to be courageously sincere and sincerely courageous. To hear them singing their fascist songs as they go marching out of a Sunday, little boys and little girls in their most attractive "*Balilla*" uniforms,[76] is both touching and inspiring. The seed is well sown and it will ripen gloriously. Of this I have not the shadow of doubt; and I cannot believe anyone can doubt it, who knows Italy profoundly, as I do. The difficulty in Italy (and this may prove to be the same elsewhere) is not with the very young, nor yet any longer with the young men between the ages of 18 and 25, who, under fascist discipline, have been amazingly transformed during the past few years. All the faroucheness, the vulgarity, the "exhibitionism" so often apparent during the first period, have been ground out of these. But the middle generation, the men between 30 and 45, represent a more difficult

---

[76] The fascist Boy Scout and Girl Guide organisation is known as the "*Balilla*," named after a Genoese boy hero, who started the revolt against the French occupation by throwing a stone at the foreign soldiery in 1746.

proposition; and I doubt if they can, as a whole, be transformed into the complete Fascist.

This generation is born of one when it was the fashion to suppose that the discoveries of Science were in hopeless contrast with the truths of Religion, an illusion now, happily, completely dissipated. Their parents gave them either too little religious instruction or unintelligent, over-conventionalised instruction, and they fell easy victims to the *Zeitgeist*. Their eyes are now, indeed, opened, but the religious void in them remains; for they were already whole men when the breath of Fascism caught them up—and it is difficult for any but those with some flair of genius, or else for the exceptionally thoughtful, without some special Grace, to fill up this void, created during their school days. The average man, especially in Italy, where competition for the better jobs is particularly severe, where there are few with the means to afford the leisure required for reading and reflection, cannot easily make a complete conversion. The War, nevertheless, redeemed this generation. The War, more than anything else, as any impressive experience, hardship and suffering usually do, opened their eyes to the curse that attaches to Materialism. Intensely patriotic, made deeply conscious of the truth that a Nation is worthless unless imbued with the spirit of discipline and self-sacrifice, they at least acquired the merit of allowing themselves to be led by the better ones among them and by Mussolini, who is a generation ahead of his own. But they are too many of them stamped by the defects of their up-bringing—too many boasters, too many self-opinionated, too many over-fond of rhetoric and of making, at all costs, a *"bella figura,"* as they call it: cutting a fine figure—anything to be able to show off as just one better than their companions. Most of the troubles of Fascism in Italy are owing to the breaking out of these defects of this generation, which, though it made Fascism, cannot aspire to be its fulfilment.

The speeches of Mussolini and of the Secretary to the Fascist Party, Signor A. Turati, have only to be read and it will be realised how hard the leaders of Fascism hammer the rank and file, who will not or cannot live the fascist ideal. But the process is undoubtedly telling and the result is a new generation growing up, who promise to make a governing class really worthy of the ideal. And in connection with the bringing up of these younger men and women, nothing has struck me more forcibly to the credit of Fascism than the manner in which it has saved them from that wave of unchastity and irresponsibility which elsewhere has proved one of the most serious consequences of the War. The plea which young men are apt to put forward to excuse or sanction periodical acts of immorality—the plea that it is good for health—is now ridiculed as the hypocritical homage that self-indulgence pays to virtue. That barbarous snobbery which parades immorality and the capacity for hard drinking as a token of virility is now at a discount. Young Fascists are taught to realise, not by lectures, but by experience, that when we keep our bodies fittest, our desires turn least to immorality; that one form of more easily controlled self-indulgence, such as an over-indulgence in food or drink, leads to others; that creative work of any kind—work to which we can give ourselves with passion—or the healthy excitement that sport and civic responsibilities afford us are as easy a means, and a far more satisfactory and a more pleasureful means, besides the only right means, of working off our surplus psychic energy. Any other means, after all, is a waste of life; and waste is sin. The *Weltanschauung* of Fascism, in putting a premium on creative and recreative activities, has gained for Italy a notable victory for the cause of chastity and sobriety. The knight chivalrous that Fascism exalts is, indeed, the very antithesis of the gay Don Juan. The latter type, in fact, is one of those that Fascism will not tolerate in any disguise or at any price.

The Italian knight chivalrous, however, is perhaps not quite the same person as the one associated with the term in the romantic North. He is anything but a Parsifal, that curious invention that would make an ideal type of the innocent fool, nor yet does he share the more humane simplicity of a Sir Galahad. If I were to choose a real historical figure which responds most nearly to this Italian ideal, I would mention Federico da Montefeltro, first duke of Urbino, the greatest captain of his age, astonishingly humane in a century distinguished by its callousness, brave, normal-minded, sincerely religious, robust and virile, yet combining with all these soldierly virtues, a culture and subtlety of mind only rivalled by his contemporary, Lorenzo. For myself, I endorse this Italian ideal. To my mind there is no more attractive type of man than the intellectual and cultivated soldier; and this may be said to be the very type of the knight chivalrous of Fascism. As the Fascist refrain goes *Libro e Moschetto*, *Fascista perfetto*, that is, Service and Understanding, wherein a sound, practical, realistic sense is mated to a balanced, artistic and speculative intelligence.

But the complete knight chivalrous must indeed be also a true follower of Christ. Above all, he must forget himself to find himself. He must remember that we are all members of one another. He must learn to love greatly. He must transcend his own self to assert it through the very negation of its empirical nature, to use a form of expression, consecrated by Gentile, which may be more intelligible to some modern minds than the simpler Biblical text. Moreover, a man can lose himself thus only in one way—and this is the secret of Youth—in *activity*, whether it be practical or intellectual, an activity which is also a creative passion and therefore born of love for his fellow-men. As the most typical of Italian philosophers and by far the greatest of them all, St. Thomas Aquinas, said, so simply and yet so adequately: *Unumquodque . . . secundum naturam hoc ipsum quod est, alterius est,*[77] and again: *Pars habet inclinationem principalem ad actionem communem utilitate totius.*[78]

---

[77] St. Thomas Aquinas, *Summa Theol.* 1ª, q. 60, art. 5.
[78] *Ibid.*, 2ª, 2ᵃᵉ, q. 26, art. 3.

PART II

GENERAL REMARKS

I PROPOSE to give, in this second part, which is intended a kind of Appendix to Part I, a summary description of a few of the more important applications of fascist doctrine in Italy. As I pointed out in the Introduction, the constitution, public institutions and laws suitable to the conditions of one country may be quite unsuitable to another. Though a political Philosophy, to have any validity, must indeed have a universal application, its actual application must necessarily vary in different circumstances. Nevertheless all the civilised States of the world to-day have a great deal in common; and inasmuch as this is so, any successful applications of a doctrine in one civilised State may be usefully examined by others with a view to adaptation, if not to exact reproduction.

The time is not yet ripe for a detailed description or for a final criticism of the concrete applications of fascist doctrine in Italy. The present situation in Italy is transitional. The new constitution, the new public institutions and laws are in course of being brought into being. The process is as yet by no means complete. I am accordingly confining myself here to a summary description with the special purposes in view of illustrating the foregoing thesis and of arousing interest in the various measures already adopted, or foreshadowed, measures well worthy of attention and study by all who claim to be practical politicians and aim at finding a happy solution to our present discontents.

To this end, and in order to understand the full significance of this legislation, the student should perhaps particularly bear in mind the following principles, which are continually, if only implicitly as a rule, being referred to in the text of the fascist laws.

1. Fascism regards it as the duty of the individual so to contrive his life that the pursuit of his interests coincides with those of the community. The State is and can be the only impartial judge as to whether the individual is doing this or not. If he is not, the State has the right and duty to interfere.

2. Private initiative in the field of production is considered as a general rule the most efficacious and most useful instrument in the interest of the community (*cf.* Art. 7 of the Labour Charter, section VI); and thus the institution of private property is sanctioned as a natural right, whereby the family tie, the most important and fundamental of all ties, is strengthened; which makes, more than anything else, when widely distributed, for true Liberty.

3. Private property, however, is also a public trust. If a man's subjective rights to private property are abused, if he fails to exercise his rights in a manner which corresponds with a sense of responsibility to the community at large, he becomes liable to having his rights curtailed or even abrogated altogether—that is, not in general, but in the particular department where his sense of duty has failed him.

4. We may say, indeed, that Fascism sanctions an objective, "functional" theory of rights.[79] Similarly, this sense of responsibility, which a true sense of Religion, which family affection, which patriotism and a consciousness of nationality provide, is the only true basis of citizenship, that is, the eligibility to assume responsibilities in the Government of the country. In other words, only those persons with a public conscience are fit to exercise public responsibilities and are therefore entitled to political rights.

---

[79] *Cf.* Ramiro de Maeztu, *Authority, Liberty and Function* (Allen & Unwin, London, 1916).

5. Consequently the State cannot tolerate the propaganda of ideas which may reasonably be said to undermine Religion, the Family and the State; and not only is it, therefore, the duty of the State to censure the propaganda of such ideas, but to prosecute individuals who, by disrespectful word or action, bring Religion, the institution of the Family and the main institutions of the State (the King, the Prime Minister, as responsible head of the Executive, Parliament and the Law Courts) into contempt.

6. Furthermore, it is the duty of the State to do what is possible so to construct society that it becomes easy for the individual, in the pursuit of his private interests, to make his interests coincide with those of the community; and its duty is to do everything in its power to raise the moral standards of the people and to encourage their sense of communal responsibility and self-discipline.

7. Individuals cannot serve two masters. They cannot own allegiance to a political body outside the State, such as a political *Internationale*, as well as to their own country's Government. They must choose; and if they prefer the former, they must be and deserve to be treated as foreigners.

8. Co-operation for the good of the whole must be the order of the day. Consequently those in charge of local Government or of autonomous public institutions must not be permitted to pull at variance with the general aims of the central Government. Hence, whatever measure of administrative decentralisation may be deemed advisable, political centralisation is essential. So likewise only those class associations who admit the principle of class interdependence and the paramount interests of the community as a whole, whose constitution, moreover, is a guarantee of their *bona fides* in these respects, can be recognised by the State and be granted the right of representing their class economically. Here we have in a nutshell the idea of the unitary State, so often referred to by fascist writers. Hence the State must aim at becoming one organic whole, in which the

individuals composing it, by organising their collective activities, are integrated with the State institutions, so that all may pull together towards a common goal.

9. Class warfare may, in certain circumstances, be a fact; but it is not a necessity. Those who would have class warfare are agents for dividing the country against itself, and a house divided against itself will not stand. Hence such persons must be classed with those who deserve to be deprived of political rights. But, in saying this, it is important to make a distinction. Class warfare must not be confounded with that individual competition, given the dynamic conditions of life, for the better posts and a higher social status, which makes it possible to classify broadly into categories those who may be said to be pressing to rise and those who may be said to be resisting the pressure. This, which Fascists call the "struggle of capacities," and not class warfare, is, of course, an eternal social fact. In other words, the auto-defence of individuals, categories of workers and classes must give way to the State's justice.

10. The State, whose only interest and duty it is to promote the general good, is the only power capable of taking an impartial view in the interests of the whole between individuals or individual groups, whose interests come into conflict. Hence, if any such conflicts fail to be settled in the first instance by friendly discussion between the parties it is the duty of the State, by means of a constitutionally appointed Court, to settle the dispute and enforce the settlement (cf. Art. 5 of the Labour Charter, section VI).

11. Party Government is not a necessity in the Government of a country any more than it is a necessity in the management of a business. Constructive and effective criticism is necessary on the other hand for proper Government. But constructive and effective criticism may be provided by other means than by opposing Parties, just as it is provided (and in abundance) within the constitution of public companies.

12. Government must in any case not be in a position to have to court popularity. Popularity is no measure of good Government. Similarly, a majority is no sanction for a Government measure, unless it can be shown that the view of the majority is the better view. What is required of Government is that as few mistakes should be made as possible in the public interest. Whatever machinery of Government results, therefore, in the fewest mistakes, is the better machinery. The specific sanction of a Government is its power, its ultimate sanction, however, is its reasonableness. Any Government, whether resting on a majority or otherwise, will, if it has the power to enforce its laws, exact obedience. The ultimate legitimacy of the laws enforced does not depend on the number of persons in favour of them, but on their justice and reasonableness; and unless it can be shown that majority Government is, taken as a whole, absolutely the best means that experience has devised to insure reasonable Government, it has no claims for pre-eminence. Since, moreover, there is no conclusive evidence that this is so, the claims of majority Government must be judged objectively without prejudice in its favour in accordance with the circumstances of the case.

13. Means, too, must be devised, as we have seen, by which the central Government may be kept in touch with the needs of the indefinite number of parts which make up the whole community, like a good nervous system in a living body. Consequently some kind of representative system must be devised. But the precise nature of such representative system is a matter of objective contrivance.

14. The executive power should be strong and capable of acting swiftly. It is expedient, therefore, that, as in the American Constitution, it should be in many respects independent of the Legislature.

15. The complexity of modern life, the great interdependence in a modern State between the parts, the swiftness of communications, etc., require the modern State to shoulder an ever-increasing burden of responsibilities and to engage in evermore manifold activities.

This fact must be faced and the State adapt itself positively to the task, not lag behind it reluctantly until circumstances force it to take action in accordance with the old Liberal principle. The dogmas of *laissez-faire* and a *minimum* of Government control are dead.

HETEROGENEOUS LEGISLATION

THE accumulation of fascist legislation in Italy is truly colossal. There exists scarcely a department of public life that has not been touched. A whole and ample treatise deserves to be written to demonstrate the value of the work accomplished, a value which can hardly be exaggerated. Four great pieces of legislation, however, stand out as landmarks characteristically fascist, namely, the Law on the attributions and prerogatives of the Prime Minister; the Law defining the powers of the Executive; the Law of the Corporations; and the Labour Charter. A section will be devoted to each of these laws and a fifth section to the general question of parliamentary representation, the final form of which has not yet been decided on, but can be foreshadowed. The present section will, after giving some idea of the remaining legislation already passed, deal a little more fully with the Reform of the Administration and the creation of the "After-Work" Institution.

The greater part of what is dealt with in this section is scarcely controversial, unless we except the Local Government reforms. The remainder may be said to be what other previous Governments talked of doing and aspired to do, but only the fascist Government has been able to carry into effect.

We have already referred to Gentile's great Education Act, which stiffened the standard of examinations; made it more difficult for unnecessary numbers of boys and girls to obtain the required qualifications at the expense of the State in order to compete for "black-coated" employment; canalised those unable to pass examinations, entitling them to pursue their studies at the classical and literary higher schools, into technical schools; put the teachers themselves back to school during the whole of their career, thus forcing them to keep abreast with new knowledge and methods; encouraged private schools by the institution of the State examination; reduced the number of State-aided universities; restored religious teaching in the elementary schools and provided for it at all State schools, etc., etc., etc.

Then we have the financial reforms and achievements: the unification of the three State issue banks; the conversion of the State budget deficit of 3,029,000,000 lire for the year 1922-1923 into the handsome surplus of 1,155,000 lire by the year 1926-1927. Similarly the State Railways budget's enormous deficit has been converted into a surplus. The same applies to the Post and Telegraphs budget (the telephone service was handed back to private enterprise, which has resulted in a great improvement and in the introduction of the automatic telephone). These results have been brought about, moreover, without increasing taxation and without resorting to inflation or loans (with the exception of the "*Littorio*" loan [1927] raised for the main purpose of converting short-time treasury bonds). At the same time the internal national debt has been reduced by 7,634,000,000 lire; the international debt questions have been satisfactorily settled with Great Britain and America; the instalments on these debts have been regularly paid (the first instalment to America, be it said, by private and voluntary subscriptions); money has been found for electrifying considerable sections of the railways and for largely renewing the rolling stock and improving the services, so that the trains now run punctually, provide second-class sleepers, and are clean. Further, no less than 6,000,000,000 lire has been spent between the years 1922-1926 on public works, housing, road and railway construction, while an immense project for land reclamation has since been prepared and financed. This will be carried out during the next five years, together with a most comprehensive road improvement scheme. Then the amount of paper money issued on account of the Government has been halved and the value of the lira brought up from 110 in 1922-1923 to approximately 93 to the pound sterling, at which point it has been stabilised. Lastly, no less than 12,000,000,000 lire have been expended on rehabilitating the war-damaged districts.

Altogether, for a country that is reckoned from 20 to 40 times poorer than Great Britain and is peculiarly deficient in raw materials, possesses insignificant colonies and a congested population which increases by 470,000 souls annually,[80] these results seem almost miraculous. They have been achieved solely by sound principles of finance, by a fearless economy (for example, the number of State employees has been reduced by 80,000; the number of railway employees per axle-kilometre from 62 to 32), by a vigorous enforcement of taxation and a complete overhauling and readjustment of the incidence of taxation, which has brought with it at the same time greater justice for the poorer man.[81]

Next, there has been accomplished a complete reform of the Army on the principle of quality rather than quantity. The Navy, too, has been reorganised and an Air Force created, where before there was none worthy of the name. But the actual expenditure on the Army and Navy in comparison with the amounts spent before the War (after taking into account the fall in the value of the lira and of the purchasing power of gold) has been reduced.

Then we have the conclusion of over forty treaties with foreign powers, many of a solely commercial nature, others of friendship, others embodying the principle of arbitration (for example with Switzerland, Albania, Germany and Spain). A law has been passed, moreover, to provide for the mobilisation and organisation of the civil population in time of war.

---

[80] The figure for 1925. In 1926 the figure had dropped to 420,000.

[81] It should be noted that death duties for the first and second degrees of inheritance have been abolished.

Again, the Judiciary has been reformed, procedure speeded up and the various High Courts of Appeal unified. The police have also been reorganised.

But it would be superfluous here to extend the list, although a somewhat more complete list would deserve to contain examples of many important minor measures passed into law, such as the unification of the Mining Laws, and the important and original Law protecting authors' rights, besides the many temporary measures adopted for the defence of the realm, the new Press Law[82] and the suppression of secret and subversive organisations. So let us conclude our general survey by mentioning the drastic reform and re-codification of the Commercial, Civil and Penal Codes (not yet complete),[83] the creation of a number of new autonomous State institutions, such as the National Militia, the National Balilla (Boy Scout) Institution, the National After-Work Institution (see below), the Royal Academy, the *Patronato Nazionale* (see below), the A.G.I.P. (the National Petroleum Company), the Central Statistical Institute,

---

[82] There is nothing that calls for special comment in the Press Law except the one clause that makes a newspaper liable to confiscation should anything be published considered likely to result in a disturbance of the public peace. This clause may be interpreted arbitrarily and so may result in restrictions of the liberty of the Press beyond what many may consider expedient. It is justified, however, in the circumstances, given the revolutionary conditions still existing in Italy, the inflammability of the Italian character and the previous licentiousness of the Italian Press. The remaining clauses merely extend the list of Press offences to include specific appeals to violence and the disruption of the State, contempt of the State's institutions, deliberate untruths and obscenities—offences which make the newspaper liable to prosecution.

[83] The draft of the new Penal Code has recently been published and has been given an especially warm welcome in Catholic circles, in that it is based on the theory of individual responsibility and not on the modern "positive" theory of Law. Its sanctions are particularly severe with regard to matters touching public morality.

and the National Institution for the Protection of and Assistance to Mothers and Children.

The latter, together with the National Balilla Institution, forms part of the magnificent work accomplished for promoting the physical and moral welfare of the race. These measures are supplemented by a number of others dealing with juvenile courts, the white slave traffic, prostitution, alcoholism, smoking by the young, hygiene, provisions to combat malaria, tuberculosis, venereal diseases and other "white plagues," the control of indecent films and theatrical representations, the prevention of the sale of pornographical literature and artificial birth-control propaganda, workmen's insurance against old age, invalidity, accidents, sickness and unemployment. Most of these reforms bring up the standard of social legislation in Italy to equal the best in other countries and some of them may be said to constitute important advances.

The Reform of the Administration has resulted, as we have seen, in a reduction of the swollen bureaucracy by no less than 80,000 persons, although at the same time the work of the State administration has been largely increased. This is accounted for by the independence of the Executive (see below), who have thus been given a free hand to reorganise, by better organisation, by large administrative decentralisation and by the concentration or unification of many of the Ministries. Thus the Ministry of Finance and the Treasury have been amalgamated, a Ministry of Communications and a Ministry of National Economy created, in which are now grouped governmental departments that were formerly separate, often with a Minister of their own (such as the Ministry of Agriculture, which is now absorbed by the Ministry of National Economy). Steps have been taken, too, to prepare the way for the creation of a Ministry of National Defence, absorbing the three Ministries of War, Marine and Aeronautics. A Chief of the General Staff, with a department, has, for instance, already been organised to co-ordinate the three arms, while Mussolini himself has for some time been in charge of all three Ministries.

The most fascist, however, of the administrative reforms apply to local government. Here, as we have seen, the principle lies in administrative decentralisation, political centralisation. To this end Sub-Prefectures have been abolished, the Prefectures increased and the system of Mayors has been abolished. In the small towns the supreme direction of local affairs is now carried out by an officer nominated by the Crown, called by the mediæval title of *Podestà*, assisted by a communal secretary and in most cases by a small advisory *junta*, one-third of which is appointed by the Provincial Prefect, two-thirds appointed by the local trade and professional organisations. In the larger towns, besides the *Podestà*, one or two Vice-*Podestàs* are similarly nominated; but in this case he is assisted by a Council of between ten and forty members nominated by the Prefect from a list (of three times the number of seats to be filled) prepared by the local industrial and professional corporations, and possessing wide powers of control. In Rome a Governor takes the place of the *Podestà* and in Naples, for the present, a High Commissioner, both with extended powers. This scheme has certainly resulted in higher efficiency and better co-ordination. The *Podestàs* are administratively responsible to the Prefect, whose approval is required for all local bye-laws; they are unpaid (save in very special circumstances) and they must possess certain educational qualifications for their appointment.

The Prefect of the Province, who is the supreme governmental magistrate in local affairs, is responsible for the maintenance of public order and for co-ordinating the administration of his Province. He also is assisted by a small council, and acts as President of the provincial Economic Council, composed of the representatives of the employers and employed of all the chief industries of the Province. This Council takes the place of the old Chamber of Commerce and, among other duties it concerns itself with the regulation of prices. The Prefect's powers are very wide and he is responsible directly to the Ministry of the Interior, which has instituted a permanent service of inspection to report on local conditions and on the efficiency of the administration with a special view to the economical expenditure of local public funds.

The whole administration of the country has thus come to be organised as a hierarchy of powers. Public servants are divided into three classes, namely, secretarial, accountancy and what in England corresponds to the second-division clerks and employees. The salaries paid are equalised according to rank throughout the administration, including the fighting forces and judiciary, the highest-paid officials at the summit of the hierarchy being the President of the High Court of Appeal and Field-Marshals.

Perhaps the most notable of the new autonomous State Institutions founded by the fascist Government is the After-Work Institution. Its object is to provide interesting, physically healthy, mentally and morally uplifting activities for the working classes after their hours of labour. It may be described as a central clearing-house and co-ordinator of institutions like the Y.M.C.A., the Men's and Women's Institutes, etc., the Playground Recreation Association, the Carnegie Trust, in England or America or, better, all these things and similar things rolled into one.

The executive and central administration are assisted by two permanent Commissions, one known as the "*Liaison*" Commission, which keeps itself in touch with the various kinds of workers and their peculiar needs. This work of *liaison* has been made all the more effective since the organisation of the Corporations of Labour. The second Commission is technical and is subdivided into a number of Committees, each dealing with a particular activity, as follows:

1. Cinematograph.
2. Radiotelegraphy.
3. Music.
4. The Theatre.
5. General culture.
6. Professional technical instruction.

7. Woman's work at home (needlework, lace-making, embroidery, etc.).
8. Home nursing and medicine.
9. Folk-lore.
10. Domestic economy.
11. After-work industries, including home-crofts.
12. Hygiene.
13. Housing.
14. Furnishing.
15. Excursions into the country, to the mountains, sea-side, etc.
16. Touring.
17. Sport.

Each Province has a similar organisation, which allows for decentralisation and provides for peculiar local needs. The bulk of the money is found by the workers themselves through the Trade Union (Syndicate) rates. Strike funds no longer being required, large sums are now available for social work.

The work already accomplished by this Institution is positively remarkable. Besides the money found by the workers themselves, voluntary subscriptions and assistance by private persons and firms have literally poured in, while the State itself contributes to maintain the purely administrative side. It is impossible, however, to give a full account here of the Institution's activities. Those readers who would care to pursue the subject further may be referred to one of the Institution's publications, *I Primi Due Anni di Attività dell'Opera Nazionale Dopolavoro*, 1927, obtainable from the Institution's headquarters in Rome (*Opera Nazionale Dopolavoro, Via in Lucina* 17).

I will accordingly confine myself to noting a few points that have struck me personally in the course of a short tour of inspection undertaken during 1927 in Central Italy.

I was particularly struck by the fine buildings placed at the disposal of the Institution in large and small towns alike, the excellence of some of the lending libraries and reading rooms

(where the principal newspapers and reviews, besides those published by the Institution itself, are to be found), and the variety
of opportunities for sport which the Institution provides, rang-
ing from tennis and football to bowls and billiards, from skiing
and roller-skating to dancing, athletics and cycling. Everywhere
I found great enthusiasm among the organisers and the workers.
In Florence I noticed there were eighty railway-men spending
several evenings a week in attending English classes, which
include, for the higher standards, lectures (with slides) in English on a variety of interesting subjects. At a small town near
Florence I came in for a theatrical show, most creditably performed by the operatives of a straw-hat factory. Some of the
firms in North Italy have built well-equipped, small theatres for
their work-people, and all the great actors and actresses, on the
invitation of the Duke of Aosta, who was first President of the
Institution, have volunteered to give up so many days of the
year in acting gratuitously to the work-people in their own halls
and in coaching and teaching them for their parts and giving
them hints for the production of their plays. I ran across a couple
of professional actors in the course of doing this in a small, out-
of-the-way town in Umbria. I found thousands of work-people,
too, taking advantage of the facilities granted by the Institution,
with the assistance of greatly reduced fares on the State Railways, to make holiday excursions into the country from the
towns and *vice versa*. The special arrangements also to promote
opportunities for the work-people to travel greatly impressed
me. To any worker, on demand, a policy is issued for a given
tour, together with full instructions with regard to routes, lodg-
ing and board, and the sights to be seen. The worker then subscribes weekly by the purchase of special stamps affixed to the
policy until the sum required for the chosen tour is covered.
Armed then with his policy, he is free to make his tour without
any further expenses—and, of course, the arrangements of the
Institution enable this to be done at an absolutely minimum
cost. But these are details which could be multiplied indefinitely. For instance, a free insurance policy is issued to each

member to cover all accidents befalling him in the course of his recreative activities; special reductions are accorded to members, not only with regard to travelling tickets, but also for theatres, cinemas, sporting shows, medicines, and in certain general supply stores. Facilities are accorded to members for obtaining protection for original intellectual work (authors' rights) and for the poorer members with regard to education. All members, moreover, have the right of free entry into the museums and picture galleries belonging to the State. Suffice it to say, in conclusion, that the Institution has covered the whole country with a network of organisation, which is by no means a paper organisation, but one that is fulfilling the hopes of its promoters far beyond what was originally expected. It is, in fact, accomplishing a truly marvellous piece of social work, which will undoubtedly bear, in the course of time, precious fruits for civilisation in Italy.

THE LAW ON THE ATTRIBUTIONS AND PREROGATIVES OF THE PRIME MINISTER

IT is not necessary for my purpose to give a translation of the law in English. The burden of it can be summed up very briefly. It certifies the King as head of the Executive and the Prime Minister as head of the Government. The Ministers are responsible to the Prime Minister for their particular departments, and through him to the King. The Prime Minister accordingly ceases to be *primus inter pares* with respect to the other members of the Cabinet, but its veritable chief. The King exercises his position as head of the Government through his responsible Ministers; and the Prime Minister is responsible to the King for the proper Government of the country and not to Parliament. The Prime Minister is *ex-officio* a member of the Regency Council, in the event of a minor ascending the throne; he takes precedence of all save members of the Royal Family; and anyone committing an act against the life, the integrity and liberty of the Prime Minister is liable to heavy punishment. Lastly, no motion in either House may be proposed without the consent of the Prime Minister; and if a bill be rejected by one House, it may be re-presented after a term of three months to be voted upon by secret ballot, after any proposed amendments have been discussed and adopted.

The law thus establishes the independence of the Executive of the Legislature. The Legislature nevertheless has ample opportunities of criticising the Administration on the occasions when the departmental Budgets are submitted; and these have to be submitted each year regularly.

For a Parliament, when Party Government is not in accordance with constitutional practice (refer Section VI), there is no earthly reason why the Executive should not thus be independent of the Legislature. It is for the Prime Minister to adapt himself to the general attitude of the two Houses of Parliament or, if he also fails to lead them, his Government will have all their legislation blocked and their supplies eventually cut off. So the power of the Prime Minister is by no means unlimited. So also, if there arose a conflict between the King and Parliament over the Government, the King, sooner rather than later, would have to give way and charge somebody else with the formation of the Government.

In the absence of Party Government, moreover, little greater burden of responsibility is placed on the King than there is where the usual form of parliamentary Government prevails. The King's choice cannot fall on the leader of a minority party, where no organised parties exist. He would call the man who seems to him best fitted to form and conduct his Government, just as he does at present within the majority Party in the form of Parliament to which we are accustomed. Thus, in the event of the sudden death of Mr. Baldwin, for instance, the King would summon one of the Cabinet to form the Government, but it cannot be foretold for certain whom he would summon. He exercises his own judgment in such cases, as he did when he summoned Mr. Asquith and not Mr. Morley (who was equally in the running for the appointment) on the death of Mr. Campbell-Bannerman.

THE LAW DEFINING THE POWERS OF THE EXECUTIVE

IN the Italian [constitution][84], the law is described as the right of the Executive to issue rules having the binding force of Law.

These rules, which may be effected by Royal Decree, after having received Cabinet approval and after consultation with the Council of State (which corresponds roughly to His Majesty's Privy Council, one section of which is a purely legal body) are such as appertain to:

(a) The execution of the laws of the land—that is, laws very frequently require detailed regulations to enable them to be explained (*cf.* King's Regulations with respect to Military Law).

(b) The interpretation of laws or of customs having virtually the force of Law; *e.g.*, conditions may arise when the interpretation of a law becomes necessary or a custom may require definition and so be given definitely the force of Law.

(c) The organisation and working of the administrative machine. In other words, the Executive is solely responsible for the administration and its organisation, and for the Government officials who are, so to speak, the employees of the Government. Thus an amalgamation of Ministries, the creation of a new Ministry, the suppression of a Ministry, the conditions of

---

[84] Word missing in the original text. [Editor's note]

employment of Government officials, etc., etc., are the sole concern of the Executive. Parliament accordingly ceases to have legislative rights in this respect; although, as we have seen, the presentation of the annual departmental Budget affords opportunities for criticism and control.

The law also defines and limits the power of the Executive to promulgate Royal Decree Laws by Orders in Council. Such laws are declared to lapse if Parliament fails to approve of them within two years. On the other hand Parliament is bound to be given the opportunity of considering them not later than the third session from the date of their promulgation.

Hence the powers given by this law to the Executive are definitely limited, so that the independence of the Executive can in no sense be described as exaggerated. In fact, a very even balance of powers has now been created in Italy between the King, the Government and the Legislature, comparable to that existing between those of the President of the United States and Congress. Nor has the written Statute of the Kingdom of Italy been in any way altered by the changes in constitutional practice authorised by this law or by the law described in section III.

THE LAW OF THE CORPORATIONS

THE Law of the Corporations, passed on 3rd April, 1926, together with a number of explanatory regulations having the force of law, which have since been authorised, is a lengthy document occupying 36 closely-packed pages in the edition in my possession. Consequently a general description is all that I intend to attempt here.[85]

The general aim of the law is the organisation of the productive forces of the country within the orbit of the State, so that private interests may be more easily made to coincide with the interests of the community; to put an end to class warfare, to promote co-operation between the various factors of production; to substitute the justice of the State for wasteful strikes and lock-outs as the means by which industrial disputes maybe settled, to make productive labour and a sense of responsibility to the Nation as a whole the basis of citizenship.

To this end only those "professional associations" (by which term are included both workers' and employers' unions) are recognised juridically, which subscribe to the following requisites:

(1) Each professional association must represent one category and one category only of employers or workers (*e.g.*, mixed unions would not be recognised). The idea here is that each professional association is a class organisation created to protect the

---

[85] *Cf.* Carlo Costamagna, *Diritto Corporativo Italiano* (Unione Tipografico Editrice Torinese, Turin, 1927).

interests of that class; and since, if two or more classes were represented in a single association, such an association might become divided in its interests, the unity of the association might be threatened with a collapse and its members thereby lose the advantage of collective bargaining.

(2) There must be only one association of members of a particular category in any one territorial circumscription (district). The main reason for this proviso is the same as for (1). Associations, however, may be organised by Commune, by Province, by Region or nationally; and associations of the same category in different Communes, Provinces or Regions are grouped to form federations of provincial or national extent, according to the peculiar circumstances of the particular trade. Such associations of the same category—single and federal—are classed, in accordance with their territorial extent, as associations of the first and superior degree.

(3) No employers' association may be juridically recognised unless the members represented employ at least *one tenth* of the number of workers engaged in a particular category of work within its district.

Similarly no workers' association may be recognised unless the members represent at least *one tenth* of the number of workers within its district engaged in a particular category of work.

The object of this proviso is obvious. Organisations insignificant in numbers in relation to the whole number of persons engaged in a particular category of work could hardly be considered sufficiently representative of that category to deserve recognition, if, as will be seen further on, they are to be the only organisations with a legal right to represent that category. A figure larger than one-tenth might have been chosen; but there are parts of Italy where the proportion of organised workers is small, and one of the objects of the Act is to extend the benefits of collective bargaining to all workers. It is important to bear this in mind, for anti-fascists have attempted to make out that this proviso implies that the fascist associations represent so few employers or workers that it was necessary to put the minimum proportion as low as one-tenth; or rise very few of the fascist organisations could be recognised. They even try to make out that by this proviso the mass of employers and workers are in fact controlled by a fascist oligarchy representing only one-tenth of the whole! The facts are quite the reverse. The fascist organisations are out of all proportion stronger throughout Italy than any of the other organisations.

(4) No association whatever may be juridically recognised unless, in accordance with their Articles of Association, they include among their objects, not only the general furthering of the economic and moral interests of their members, but also the taking of an active part in the technical instruction, religious, moral and national education of their members and the support of charitable foundations open to their members.

No association, moreover, may be juridically recognised unless the directors of the association, together with the association's staff of employees, can provide guarantees of capacity, morality and a firm national faith.

Here, of course, those anti-fascists, who reject the fascist doctrine to the effect that only those who have a national consciousness and a sense of responsibility to the community as a whole possess a right to have a hand in the Government of the community, may be allowed to complain. Here we are up against a question of principle. It is not a question, as some would make out, of securing power indefinitely to the Fascist Party—it is a question of securing power indefinitely to those of high moral character, intelligence and patriotism. Indeed, through this proviso the fascist revolution realises one of its greatest ideas, namely, the reconciliation of Democracy in the sense of *une carrière ouverte aux talents* and of Aristocracy in the exact meaning of the term.

So only those professional associations that subscribe to the above requisites may be juridically recognised. Other associations may be freely formed, and may be recognised *de facto*, but not *de jure*.

The juridically recognised associations possess the monopoly of legal representation for the whole class of employers or workers of their particular category within their district, including those employers or workers belonging to the same category, who are not members. The collective labour contracts made under their auspices apply equally to members and non-members of the same category.

They have a right to levy (a maximum rate is fixed both for employers' and workers' associations) contributions not only from their own members but from the whole category of employers or workers whom they represent. But non-members equally share in the benefits secured through any action of the association.

Each association is bound to set aside a certain percentage of its revenue to form a guarantee fund; and after providing for the costs of its organisation and for the various forms of welfare work, which it is bound to undertake on behalf of its members, it must subscribe a definite percentage in support of the National After-Work Institution, the National Balilla (Boy Scouts) Institution, the National Institution for the Protection of and Assistance of Mothers and Children, the *"Patronato Nazionale"* (an Institution the object of which is to provide the worker with legal advice, assistance with regard to any claims he may have respecting insurance, assistance with regard to emigration and a host of similar services), and the corporation of which it forms part.[86]

Individuals who pursue more than one regular calling may belong to two or more associations. A juridically recognised association may have no members below the age of 18; but women have the same rights of membership as men.

Associations are juridically recognised by the Minister of Corporations after fulfilling certain formalities.

---

[86] The corporations in turn pay over a proportion of their funds, thus provided by the professional associations, for defraying the cost of the Ministry of Corporations itself. The latter accordingly is not a charge upon the fruits of ordinary taxation.

The associations of employers and the associations of workers engaged in the same industry are grouped together to form a corporation. This is a State organ and, beyond the representatives of the associations composing it, the State provides for the cost of its administration by means of the quota reserved to it from the associations' receipts.

Its duties include the supervision of its associations to the end that they answer to the requirements of the law and fulfil their duties according to the law and their Articles of Association; the establishment of labour exchanges and the keeping of statistics of the employed and unemployed; the co-ordination, encouragement and subsidising of the welfare work of the associations; and the conciliation by means of their good offices, when seized with the task by the parties concerned, of any labour dispute.

Professional associations of the liberal professions (doctors, engineers, artists, etc.) though in other respects they resemble the other associations, form part of the corporations in so far as they may be considered an essential part of a given industry. On the other hand, co-operative societies (including guilds) have their special status.

Employers of labour, whether they belong to juridically organised associations or otherwise, are bound to make a return to the government department concerned of the numbers of their employees or workers.

The Minister of the Corporations, after fulfilling certain formalities, has, in circumstances of mismanagement, fraud or the violation of the law and regulations, the faculty of delegating plenary powers to the Secretary of the association, or, for a period, to a government commissioner, or even, according to the gravity of the case, of dissolving the association.

The associations of government and local government servants do not come within the scope of the Act, but are provided for otherwise.

If the conciliatory machinery provided by the corporations fails to settle a labour dispute, the question goes for final settlement before one of the sixteen ordinary Appeal Courts of the

Realm. The judge in such cases is aided by two assessors, chosen by the judge, from a list of expert on the particular matter under dispute. Lists of these experts are compiled by the Courts and revised every two years. They are chosen from among ordinary citizens and are divided into groups and sub-group according to the subject of their expert knowledge.

The Court decides on the interpretation of existing contracts in accordance with the law of the land and the regulations regarding the interpretation of collective contracts.

The Court also decides the conditions of new collective contracts in accordance with principle of equity and with those laid down in the Labour Charter (*q.v.*, Section VI).

Strikes and lock-outs are severely forbidden and liable to very heavy penalties.

Strikes and lock-outs are classified under three heads: those having a political object or with the object of putting pressure on the State; those concerned with the working of public services (a schedule of what constitutes a public service is annexed to the Act); and those having an ordinary economic object concerned with industries not scheduled as constituting a public service.

The degree of penalties varies in severity with the nature of the strike or lock-out as classified. Each class of strike and lock-out is defined. I will give here the definitions of those that come under Class III:

(a) Employers of labour, who, without justifiable motives and with the sole object of obtaining from their employees (or workers) a modification of the conditions of the actual collective contracts in force, suspend work in their factories, businesses or offices.

(b) Employees or workmen who, numbering three or more and by previously concerted action, abandon work or do their work in such a way as to disturb its continuity or regularity, with the object of obtaining different contracts of labour than those actually in force.

Thus the professional associations are the foundations on which the corporative State is being built. The local professional association of employers of the same category are grouped into federations and then re-grouped to form six great national confederations, as follows:

1. Agriculture.
2. Industry.
3. Banking.
4. Commerce.
5. Transport by sea and air.
6. Land transport and internal waterways.

The professional associations of workers are likewise grouped into six great national confederations, each corresponding to the six confederations of employers. Likewise the associations of professional men (artists, doctors, etc.) are grouped into a national confederation.

In all, therefore, there are thirteen great national confederations, without counting the separate national organisation of the co-operative societies or guilds, who are grouped together in the *Ente Nazionale Cooperativo* (National Co-operative Institute). The whole are co-ordinated through the organisation of the Corporations, which, as I have stated, are organs of the State, under the supreme direction of the Ministry of Corporations, which keeps also in direct touch with the individual needs and aspirations of the various categories of production by means of a Council, on which the various Confederations are represented.

It proved a long and difficult task to classify all these activities, to constitute the various professional associations and to complete the hierarchical organisation. Subject to certain modifications that may yet be introduced, the edifice is by now sufficiently advanced to have allowed the Government to prepare the scheme on its basis for the new Parliamentary representation, which is dealt with elsewhere.

Things, indeed, are now beginning to work fairly smoothly; and with this I think there is only one more point in connection with this vast and revolutionary ordering of society that need be mentioned here. The members of the professional associations have no need to belong to the Fascist Party, nor indeed to call themselves expressly fascists. Nobody is pressed to join the juridically recognised or, if one prefers to call them the fascist associations. At the same time nobody is refused who applies to join, provided he or she has nothing against him morally, and is not known as a public agitator in favour of class warfare and other ideologies expressly condemned by law. He or she is not required to sign any undertaking. As a member he or she may be regarded as at least acquiescing in the scheme, and that is all that is required. The guarantees required with respect to the Secretary of the association, etc., and the very nature of the organisation itself are its own safeguard against the objects of the scheme being defeated. The benefits which the scheme is affording both employers and workers are daily turning doubters and the half-hearted into enthusiastic members and supporters. As Rossoni, one of the principal authors of the scheme has said: "We are in no hurry to get everybody within our ranks. We have abundant numbers to enable the scheme to be worked without the introduction of all the country's workers. It is better that these should come in gradually as they become convinced of its merits. Meantime those who remain outside are no great losers, for they participate equally in all the essential benefits."

THE LABOUR CHARTER

Text

1. The Italian Nation is an organism having ends, a life and means superior in power and duration to the single individuals or groups of individuals that compose it. It is a moral, political and economic unity, which collectively realises itself in the fascist State.

2. Work in all its forms, whether intellectual, technical or manual, is a social duty. On this score, and only on this score, is it protected by the State.

The whole body of production must be considered as a united effort from the national point of view; it has a common object which may be summarised as the well-being of the single individuals or groups of individuals composing the Nation and the development of the national strength.

3. Trade Union (Syndical) or, in other words, professional organisation is free. But only the Trade Union which is juridically recognised and placed under the control of the State has the right legally to represent the entire category of employers and employees (workers of all kinds) for which it is constituted; to protect its interests *vis-à-vis* the State and other professional associations; to stipulate collective contracts of labour binding on all persons belonging to the category; to levy contributions from them and to carry out as delegates on their behalf functions of public interest.

4. In labour contracts the solidarity between the various factors of production finds its expression through the conciliation of the opposing interests of employers and employed and their subordination to the superior interests of production.

5. The Magistrature of Labour is the organ whereby the State shall intervene to regulate labour controversies, whether with reference to the observance of pacts or other existing regulations, or with reference to the determination of new labour conditions.

6. The professional associations which have juridical recognition shall be the means by which the equality before the law of employers and employees (workers) is to be assured, by which discipline in the effort of production and labour is to be maintained, and by which production and labour may be improved.

The Corporations shall constitute the joint organisations of the forces of production and represent collectively the interests of production.

In view of this collective representation, the interests of production being national interests, the Corporations are juridically recognised as organs of the State (referred to sometimes as the "corporative organs").

As representatives of the collective interests of production, the Corporations may dictate binding regulations with regard to conditions of labour and to the co-ordination of production, whenever they receive the required powers from the respective associations composing them.

7. The corporative State considers that private initiative in the field of production is the most efficacious and most useful instrument in the interests of the Nation.

The private organisation of production being a function, however, of national interest, the organiser of any economic undertaking shall be responsible to the State for the direction given to production. Collaboration between the factors of production, moreover, results in a reciprocity of rights and duties. The hired worker, whether intellectual, technical or manual, is an active collaborator in any economic undertaking, the management of which, however, belongs to the employer who is responsible for its proper working.

8. The professional associations of employers shall be obliged to promote in every way possible an increase of, and improvement in, the methods of production and a reduction in costs. The duty of the representatives of those who exercise a liberal profession or an art and of the associations of public servants is to promote the interests of art, science and letters, to improve productive methods and to see that the moral ends of the corporative organisation of society are energetically pursued.

9. Intervention by the State in economic production should take place only when private initiative is lacking, or is insufficient, or when the political interests of the State are involved. Such intervention may assume the form of supervision, assistance or direct management.

10. In labour disputes, judicial action may not be undertaken until the corporative organ has failed to bring about a settlement by conciliatory means.

In controversies concerning individuals respecting the interpretation or application of labour contracts, the professional association may offer their good offices with a view to settlement by conciliation.

Competency in such controversies devolves in the last resort on the ordinary Magistrature with the addition of assessors nominated by the interested professional associations. (Thus is constituted the Magistrature of Labour.)

11. The professional associations shall be obliged to regulate, by means of collective contracts, the conditions of labour between the categories of employers and employees (workers) which they respectively represent.

These collective contracts shall be stipulated between associations of the first degree (*e.g.*, the simple members of a given Corporation), under the control and guidance of the Corporation. In certain cases, however, in accordance with the provisions established by Law and the approved regulations contained in an association's Articles, the collective contracts may be stipulated between associations of a superior degree (*e.g.*, the federation of associations representing a particular category).

Every collective labour contract, under penalty of nullification, must contain precise regulations on disciplinary matters, on the period of trial (before employees, that is, any kind of hired worker, are confirmed in their contract), on the amount and conditions of salaries and on the hours of labour.

12. The activity of the Trade Unions, the work of conciliation of the Corporations, and the decisions of the Magistrature of Labour shall guarantee the approximation of salaries to the normal conditions of life, to the possibilities of production and to the earning power of labour.

The actual determination of salaries shall not, however, be controlled by any general rule, but entrusted to agreements between the parties through collective contracts.

13. The statistics collected by the Departments of State, by the Central Statistical Institute and by the professional associations which are juridically recognised with respect to the conditions of production and of labour, the condition of the money market, the variations in the standard of living of those who hire out their labour, duly co-ordinated and elaborated by the Ministry of Corporations, shall provide a criterion for reconciling the interests of the various categories and classes, and the interests of the latter with the superior interests of production.

14. Salaries should take the form best suited to the requirements of the employee (worker) and of the undertaking.

When payment is made by piecework, and the piecework accounts are settled over periods longer than a fortnight, adequate accounts must be made up weekly or fortnightly.

Night-work is not included in the regular periodical periods of labour, and must be payable at higher rates than day-work.

When labour is paid by piecework, payment must be determined so that the industrious worker with a normal capacity for labour shall be able to attain small earnings above his basic pay.

15. Those who hire out their labour have the right to a weekly rest on Sundays.

Collective contracts shall apply this principle, taking into account the existing legal regulations and the technical requirements of an undertaking, and within these limits shall insure respect for civil and religious holidays according to local traditions. Employees (workers) must scrupulously observe working hours.

16. After a year of uninterrupted service in an undertaking requiring continuous work an employee (worker) shall have the right to an annual paid holiday.

17. In undertakings requiring continuous work, an employee (worker) shall have the right, in the event of his being discharged through no fault of his own, to an indemnity proportionate to the number of years of his service. Such an indemnity shall likewise be due in the event of his death.

18. The passing of any undertaking requiring continuous work into new hands shall not affect the labour contract, and the employees (workers) shall preserve all their rights under the new management. Similarly, the illness of an employee (worker) not exceeding a determined period shall not terminate his labour contract. A call to arms or service in the national Militia shall not be a reason for the discharge of an employee (worker).

19. Infractions of discipline and acts which disturb the normal working of an undertaking, committed by employees (workers), shall be punished according to their gravity by fine, suspension of work, or immediate discharge without indemnity. A description of the cases to which such penalties are applicable shall be specified (in the labour contracts).

20. New employees (workers newly taken on) shall be subject to a period of trial during which the right of terminating the contract is reciprocal, with payment only for the time of actual work.

21. The obligation to make collective labour contracts extends, together with the benefits such contracts secure and the discipline they exact, to home workers also. Special regulations shall in due course be issued by the State for policing home-work and securing hygienic conditions in the homes where such work is carried on.

22. The State shall ascertain and control the phenomenon of employment and unemployment of workers, the figures for which form an index of the conditions of production and of labour.

23. The labour exchanges shall accordingly be under the control of the Corporations (which are organs of the State) and so based on the various categories of employment. Employers shall be obliged to engage workers through the medium of these exchanges, with freedom of choice between the whole number of names inscribed on the rolls except that, other things being equal, preference must be given to members of the Fascist Party or of the juridically recognised Trade Unions in the order of seniority of their enrolment.

24. Professional associations of workers must carry out selective action among their members with the object of bringing about a continual increase in their technical capacity and moral worth.

25. The Corporations shall have the duty of seeing that the laws relating to accidents and the policing of labour conditions are observed by the individuals who are members of the associations composing them (and representing their category).

26. Insurance is an excellent example of the spirit of collaboration between classes. Both employer and employee must proportionately contribute to the costs. It shall be the duty of the State through the Corporations and professional associations to co-ordinate and unify, as far as this may be practicable, the systems of insurance and the insurance Institutes.

27. The fascist State proposes to bring about, first, the improvement of insurance against accidents; secondly, the improvement and extension of maternity insurance; thirdly,

compulsory insurance against occupational illnesses and tuber-culosis, as a first step towards compulsory insurance against all illness;[87] fourthly, the improvement of unemployment insur-ance; and fifthly, the adoption of a special marriage endowment insurance for young workers.

28. It is the duty of the workers' associations to protect their members administratively and legally regarding accidents and social insurance. Wherever practicable, the creation of a Provi-dent Fund for sick workers, shall be made part of the collective labour contracts, such fund to be fed by contributions from both the employers and employees, and to be administered by offic-ers appointed by both parties under the control of the Corpora-tion.

29. Welfare-work organisations must in all cases form part of the programme of the professional associations, on behalf of both members and non-members of the same category. The pro-fessional associations must carry out these duties directly through their own organs. They must not delegate them to other organisations or institutes except for general reasons arising out of the fact that a particular welfare-work organisation goes beyond the particular category of producers represented.

30. Education and instruction, especially professional instruction, shall constitute one of the principal duties of the professional associations towards both members and non-mem-bers. They shall support the work of the After-Work Institution and other national educative movements.

The above, I think, read in conjunction with the last section, needs no explanation. I have added in brackets here and there, some explanations of the use of a word or of a phrase, where otherwise a misunderstanding appeared to be possible. In trying to render, too, my translation into intelligible English, it has been necessary, in order to make certain of reproducing the sense, to do some slight violence to the text.

---

[87] Insurance against tuberculosis has since become obligatory (Oct., 1927).

The text which I have taken as my model is the official one reproduced in a small volume by His Excellency Giuseppe Bottai, Under-Secretary of State for the Corporations (*La Carta del Lavoro*, published under the auspices of the Ministry of the Corporations, 1927). Those who can read Italian would do well to study this little volume, which contains a running commentary, clause by clause, of the Charter by one of its principal authors; for Messrs. Rossoni (Head of the Federation of Workers' Trade Unions), Benni (Head of the Federation of the Employers' Unions), Bottai and Mussolini himself may be regarded as the principal authors of this exceedingly important document.

Its publication on 21st April, 1927, was widely commented on all over the world as the most remarkable attempt in social legislation to protect the worker from capitalist exploitation, the capitalist from ca'canny and to subordinate both capital and labour to the paramount interests of the Nation.

It signifies the codification of the guarantees of the workers, conferring, as it does, on all workers the advantage of collective bargaining and providing the type for the collective contract.

The Labour Charter, however, is not a law. It is a manifesto prepared and issued by the central fascist revolutionary organisation (The Fascist Grand Council). Nevertheless, portions of it have already been translated into Law, others into regulations having the force of laws—and orders have been issued to the Prefects that its terms must be respected and form the base of all collective labour contracts. Similarly the Law Courts are to take it as the criterion on which to base their decisions with respect to any disputes with which they may be seized.

The sixteen ordinary provincial Courts of Appeal, which are bound to prove more impartial (given the high tradition of justice which Italian Courts enjoy) than specially constituted tribunals, are now working everywhere as the Magistrature of Labour. Such Courts are accustomed to assessing damages and settling cases on pleas of equity, so that, aided by the expert assessors provided by the Corporations Act, they may be regarded as eminently suited to try trade disputes. In Italy, where there is no caste distinction between the "Toff" and the "Bloke", as there is in England, there has never been any question of the working man not having complete confidence in the impartiality of the country's judges. For one thing, the legal profession is much more democratically recruited than in England, and the Italian, having a good deal more imagination than the average Englishman, is far more capable of seeing another man's or another class's point of view than we are. These facts, taken together with the more elaborate, albeit more fussy, rules of evidence in Italian Law, are the chief reasons accounting for this fortunate condition of affairs, which no doubt has largely contributed to the enthusiastic acceptance of the whole scheme by the working classes. It was among the employers rather than among the working classes that grave doubts were at first expressed and where a lack of enthusiasm is still evident.

Only one important case involving trade disputes has, up to the time of going to Press, been referred for legal decision. In this case the workers' association won their plea. The main work of the Corporations to date has consisted in arranging by agreement new collective bargains and revising the old ones. There were more than 1,000 such transactions in 1926, and in these the working man has in nearly every case bettered his position, sometimes to a marked extent. But several years must, indeed, elapse before we can pronounce judgment with any real confidence on the working of the corporative State; yet this much we may say: the Labour Charter is one of those things which cannot easily be gone back upon, for it represents a genuine social conquest.

THE NEW ITALIAN PARLIAMENT

THE Italian Parliament is composed of two Houses, a Senate and a House of Commons (Deputies) having equal powers. The idea of the fascist Government is to transform the latter into a House of Representatives of the organised productive forces in the country and to maintain the former, more or less as at present composed—that is, of members nominated by the Crown on the advice of the Prime Minister.

To be exact, the Senate is composed of the Royal Princes closely related to the King and an unlimited number of life members eligible should they qualify as persons of national eminence in any one of a series of categories—such as distinguished members of the fighting forces, civil servants, scientists, professors, lawyers, writers, politicians, etc., and those who pay a certain minimum sum in direct taxes. All members except the Royal Princes must have reached the age of forty and the Senate has the right to reject nominations effected under any of the categories save the last named.

Probably for the present no change will be made in the composition of the Senate, the fascist idea being that it already fulfils very adequately the fascist ideal of what a Senate should be, namely, a House of Faculties and of the most distinguished men among those who have conspicuously served their country.

Nevertheless it is felt that the Senate could be improved, and the following questions are under debate:

(1) That the numbers should be limited—that is, each category limited—beyond certain *ex-officio* members, such as those who have held the appointment of Chief of the General Staff, President of the High Court of Appeal, Chief Secretary of the great Departments of State, besides ex-Prime Ministers, Field-Marshals, etc., and possibly Presidents of the Royal Academy (which, by the way, is a new body created by the fascist Government and composed of the more eminent writers, artists, scientists, etc., of the land—rather like our own Royal Society, but extended to include men of letters and artists having special social functions to perform).

(2) That the last category, at present composed of rich men, should also be limited and be changed to one of a general character with no money qualification; and that the Senate should be given the right to reject the nominations, as with other categories.

(3) That the various professional organisations, such as doctors and surgeons, engineers and architects, journalists, university professors, lawyers, etc., should have direct representation in the Upper House rather than in the Lower House, each representative serving for a specified number of years, but re-eligible.

Whether any of these reforms will be passed into Law is, however, at present doubtful. In any case, the question is not one of urgency and will no doubt be deferred until a later date.

The reform of the Lower House, on the other hand, has been definitely decided on, though the new law is only regarded as provisional, pending the complete organisation of the corporations, on which the eventual system of national representation will be mainly based, with the idea that the House of Commons should become the corporation of the corporations through which the variously organised particularised interests in the country may be reconciled in the interests of the whole Nation.

Meanwhile, the present law will provide Members of Parliament representative of the confederations of employers, employees, professional orders, co-operatives and associations performing work of national importance. The candidates shall be proposed by the above bodies in excess of the number of seats available in the new Parliament (four hundred), while the Grand Fascist Council, which has now been recognised juridically as a constitutional organ of the State with a number of privileges and advisory powers, will reduce the number of candidates to the required number of seats and submit the final selected list in the form of a plebiscite to the general body of electors. Quite a different type of Member of Parliament should consequently be thrown up, a type who, while capable of voicing to good purpose the interests of the body he represents, will not need to be an orator and is not likely to be a demagogue. The level of ability, too, should be greatly enhanced, for the interest of the body represented will be to send up its best, most experienced, most expert members; for the representative must be a member himself of the body he represents—and, practically speaking, the representative will be personally known to the vast majority of the members of the body he represents.

Thus there will be no organised Parties represented at all in either House. Members of the Lower House will not be elected or selected on a political programme, but according to his ability to represent the various bodies' interests. And the Upper House, just as it is, being a House of Faculties and of persons who have risen to it on account of the eminent services they have rendered the country, will also represent no Party organisations. So any legislative measure proposed by the Government will be debated on its own merits. Members, as at present in the Senate, may vote for the Government one day, against it the next. Criticism will be no less severe and the fate of legislation will be not only entirely in the hands of the members, but to a considerably greater degree than under a system of Party Government, when a Government, having secured a majority at an election, possesses the practically unchecked power to pass any measure it pleases into Law. The only check in fact under a system of Party

Government, to a Government's omnipotence, is the fear of unpopularity at the next election, unless, of course, the tables are reversed with regard to a Party organisation in the Upper House.[88]

The system of Party Government, as Mussolini once humorously remarked, is indeed a game invented by England, like cricket and football. It is scarcely serious; and this, curiously enough, appears to be its sole justification. When neither Party, as in England, profoundly minds whether it is in or out, though preferring to be in, little harm is done. Under 18th-century conditions, when practically speaking only the landed interests were represented, heated as feeling sometimes ran, the heat was of the keenness of the game. Each side respected the other and gave it a sporting chance. Both sides obeyed the rules. Victory came to the side which excelled in clever debate, telling invective, cunning tactics (or even smartness, like the organising of a snap division) and, one might add, the art of gulling, if not of bribing, the electorate. Both sides knew that, whoever was in power, the safety of property and of England would not be imperilled.

With the Victorian era a change came about gradually. But it was a period of piping peace and growing prosperity, which postponed the day of reckoning. The gentleman-born still practically held the monopoly of the seats and each one knew that, in or out, neither his class nor his country would be let down.

---

[88] As this edition goes to press (November, 1927), the Fascist Grand Council have passed a number of resolutions laying down the principles on which the new representation is to be based. These principles are in perfect agreement with my forecast, except that it is provided that the next legislature (1929-1934) will mark an intervening stage before the whole reform comes to be completed. The next legislature will represent the professional associations, but these representatives will not be freely elected. In the following legislature, on the other hand (when, it is hoped, the revolutionary period will have subsided and the corporative organisation of the State will have shot its roots and be working normally), the representatives will come to be freely elected by the professional associations.

They were all public-school men, generally public-spirited, who knew what a game was and how to play it. Only gradually did the new man, who had not the same public-school, play-the-game traditions, begin to invade the sacred precincts of Westminster. Representatives of theories undermining to the traditions of the country, some of them dangerous for its safety, began to show formidable numbers. Representatives of oppressed and exploited classes, crying out bitterly and profoundly for justice, began to make their voices heard. Simultaneously the growth of business in the conditions of a modern State became nearly overwhelming. The "premier club of the land" ceased to be the busy *rendez-vous* for the nimble-minded and intellectual sons of the upper classes. It became a house of work. Politics became a serious matter, and to play them as a game became, as a matter of fact, an anachronism. Yet still we persist in playing it! But the idea of politics as a game, such as the Party system provides, is incomprehensible to the foreigner and to the working man. It matters little to us, it is true, if the foreigner, who has always taken politics seriously, fails to understand it; but it is fatal to the foreigner, who, in his blindness, has copied our system. For if he cannot play the game and adhere to the rules, the game breaks down, as it has broken down hopelessly in nearly every case on the Continent. For one thing, the game is made for two. It is dangerous to play it with three. It is fatal to play it with an indefinite number, and this is how the foreigner (and the Irishman) plays it, who is so serious about politics that he will with difficulty compromise on his paper programmes, with the result that an indefinite number of Parties come to be formed, so that none hold a majority and one of the worst forms of Government corruption—log-rolling—creeps in.

On the other hand, it matters very much to us that this sporting attitude of the English gentleman towards politics exasperates the working man, who would give his life to improve the conditions of his class. For him politics is the only constitutional hope, and so to him is a deadly serious matter. No wonder, in the face of the persistence of the game-spirit, he nurtures dreams of revolution!

Italy on fascist principles, taking also, as she does, politics very seriously, has swept the game away; and she is making arrangements to provide a new kind of Parliament, which will be equally in touch with all parts of the country, equally in touch with all sections of the population, equally capable of bringing constructive and effective criticism to bear upon the Government, equally master of the country's legislation, equally capable of voicing the needs and grievances of all classes, but insures, at the same time, that criticism shall be constructive (not absent on one side out of Party loyalty or captious and opportunistic on the other for tactical reasons); that Governments should be stable and not be at the mercy of gusts of unpopularity; that the Executive should be unhampered within prescribed limits, having regard to the colossal modern responsibilities with which it is shouldered; that the Member of Parliament should be independent, not fearing for his popularity, not of the type that spells demagogue, an able exponent of the interests he represents and an expert in his particular department. Italy, moreover, is setting up a Parliament that will be an expression of the true idea of national solidarity instead of the false individualistic conception of the State which has led to the adoption, all the world over, of a pernicious individualistically organised electoral system. It secures representation only to those persons, corporatively organised, with equal rights for men and women, who possess national consciousness, a social sense, a sense of duty to the community, as guaranteed by the juridically recognised associations that accept the postulate of class inter-dependence within the supreme interests of the Nation.

It is a great experiment, if you please (for all such things take after the nature of experiments), but it is also a great idea founded on a sound theory. It deserves, indeed, to be watched and studied with the very greatest sympathy and open-mindedness.

EPILOGUE

I AM very conscious that what I have written might have been better written. My work has been done in my spare moments from other pressing occupations. If I could give myself the time to rewrite this book, I am aware that I could greatly improve it. Chapter No. III is too long. There are too many repetitions. These repetitions are the result of my striking, in the course of my work, new material, and of new ways of expressing much the same thing striking me as possibly illuminating to certain readers. I only trust that this excuse will prove their justification.

In any case, I believe I have succeeded in giving an accurate and, on the whole, a clear account of the doctrines and *Weltanschauung* of Fascism. Such an account is urgently required in England and, for all I know, in America too. Fascism to-day has been woefully misrepresented in England, is strangely misunderstood. And this, I think, is chiefly due to a conspiracy of circumstances. Conservatives have made public for the purposes of their own propaganda only those aspects of Fascism which result from a strong and efficient Government. This is, however, only half the truth, which reactionaries have seized upon to justify coercion; while Liberals and Socialists, who consider themselves the progressive Parties and resent the intrusion of a rival altogether opposed to their respective ideologies, are concerned in allowing Fascism to pass as reactionary. Hence there has resulted a kind of conspiracy of silence and of subdued tones on all sides. Moreover, the independent commercialised Press has helped to give a wrong impression of the facts; for very naturally they find current news, especially if it is of a sensational character, better selling matter than ideas. So the British public, who largely rely on these newspapers for their instruction, have obtained their notions of Fascism from the accidental incidents of the Revolution in Italy.[89]

We need not seek for further reasons, although it is unquestionably true that the more unscrupulous supporters of those against whom Fascism is fighting its battle, have also indulged in a campaign of violent calumny. It is impossible to attribute all the misrepresentations that have appeared in the liberal and socialist Press to ignorance only.

The object of this book, however, is to give an accurate exposition of fascist doctrine, as endorsed by the creators and leaders of the movement in Italy; and the doctrine has nothing whatever to do with the question whether or not Italians are or are not applying the doctrine wisely, or realising it too precipitously, that is, at too great a cost in human values. The doctrine remains the same in either case, and must be judged on its merits. Those who come to approve of the doctrine must take their own steps to realise it in accordance with the conditions of the country of which they are members; and in an old country like Great Britain, with a long national history and tradition, the constitutional path is undoubtedly the right one for these people to take. The coming of Fascism in England, we hope, need not be accompanied, as in Italy, by violent Revolution, so that English men and women must above all begin by learning to dissociate in their minds Fascism and the various violent and dictatorial accompaniments that happen to be associated with it in Italy.

And it is on a point closely connected with this that I would like to conclude. Fascists in each country must make Fascism their own national movement, adopting symbols and tactics which conform to the traditions, psychology and tastes of their own land. Do not seize on the accidentals of the movement or

---

[89] The above was written before I received Mussolini's Preface.

you will be in danger of missing the essentials. Remember that, though truth is universal, its acceptance need never make the world the same colour, for in its application to the individual case is born variety. It is only falsehood that is drab. The infinite variety of the Universe is in reality a perpetual testimony to its essential unity, a chorus of harmony in praise of its Maker, One God in three Persons.

INDEX

FASCISM

To
MY WIFE

TABLE OF CONTENTS

CHAPTER I

INTRODUCTORY

FASCISM may be described as the ripening fruit of a world-wide movement of ideas, which for various historical and psychological reasons have first emerged in Italy into something sufficiently definite for the student with an acute sense of history to appraise, and sufficiently universal in appeal to enable him to realize the importance of the part they may be destined to play in the history of the world during the coming generations.

There is, of course, a purely Italian side to fascism, because every movement of ideas receives its particular outward expression in accordance with particular circumstances; and although the term itself "fascism" is no more than an adaptation of the Italian word *"fascismo"*—similar adaptations have entered the vocabulary of every language—we should be ill-advised to restrict its use to denoting only those phenomena which reflect actual Italian conditions. For the word has already acquired a universal import; and, if its use were restricted to the forms the movement has assumed in Italy, we should be at a loss for a word denoting its wider and more general aspects. On the other hand, its wider meaning includes the narrower.

Italian fascism is still fascism in its wider sense, while the contrary proposition would not be true. Nevertheless, for the simple reason that the movement has as yet assumed a definite expression in Italy and through Italy alone, it is Italy that has become the fountain-head of the movement; it is to Italy we must turn in order to understand its true significance; it is by

Italy that we must consent to be taught if we hope to profit by any lessons that fascism may contain. So much for the present; and for the same reason we need feel no resentment in acknowledging our debt to Italy for the addition to our language of a new word, which, though a rose by any other name might smell as sweet, is convenient, etymologically apt and already well sanctioned by popular usage.

The derivation of the word "fascism" is certainly both apt and interesting. In ancient Rome the symbol of the State, borne by the lictors before the chief magistrates, was a bundle of rods and an axe. This device has been adopted by the fascists in Italy, has become part-emblem of the Italian State and is likely to be adopted by the adherents of fascism wherever this movement may spread; for it is a visible sign of the movement's most elementary, most easily grasped, most central political and social principles. Moreover its political and social aspects, though not necessarily the more important, are as yet the more outwardly evident, and of course they in turn reflect the spirit which created them; and, if the significance of the device's Roman origin is obviously great for Italy, it should not be forgotten that the whole of the civilized world, not Italy only, should properly be considered in various degrees Rome's heir. Had it not been indeed for the Roman Empire it is doubtful whether western civilization, which now dominates the world, would have grown beyond the constitution of large States on the oriental despotic model on the one hand, or beyond federations of city States on the Greek model on the other. Some of these States might have produced great civilizations, in so far as civilization may be identified with a high degree of order and culture. But they would in all probability have differed from the civilized States of to-day as profoundly as the conditions of Czarist Russia, for instance, differed from that of Great Britain or the constitution of the Hanseatic League from that of modern Germany—nay, more so, because both Czarist Russia and the Hanseatic League were also strongly influenced by Roman tradition.

The symbolism is twofold. In the first place the axe is the symbol of State authority, of the importance, nay necessity, of the authority of the State to any well-ordered society, recalling the Roman tradition of authority and of the reign of law and order which was Rome. Secondly, the bundle of rods invokes the idea that in unity we discover strength. Whereas a child would be able to break each rod, taken singly, over his puny knee, a bundle bound together is capable of resisting the force of the strongest man. So the idea of authority is here blended with the idea of co-operation, of the need of co-operation as well as of authority in any well-ordered society. Hence the *fasces* borne before the Roman magistrates were likewise held in ancient Rome to symbolize the Commonwealth, the society to which each citizen belongs, bound together with the symbol of the State's authority, justification of which lies in its capacity to promote—in the temporal order—the highest collective good, which in turn is conditioned by the degree in which individuals prove their ability to develop a spirit of solidarity and to allow their social instincts to override their egoisms.

In other respects *fascio* is a common word in Italy that had been adopted before the advent of fascism by various revolutionary bodies whose organization consisted of small local bands of persons under a central guiding authority. In 1914 Mussolini himself organized such bands under the name of *Fasci d'Azione Rivoluzionaria* with a view to bringing about Italy's participation in the war on the side of the allies. In 1919 these bands were reconstituted by him under the name of *Fasci di Combattimento* to fight communism and prepare the way for the triumph of his revolutionary programme, which was destined quickly to develop into the "fascist" movement. This sidelight, however, on the manner in which the word "fascism" was evolved to denote what the Germans admirably call a *Weltanschauung*—a way of looking out upon the problems of life—need not detain us. The purpose of this book is not to furnish a chronicle of events, but to explain the ideas for which fascism

stands. To this end it is more important to grasp the simple symbolism underlying the word, which led to the choice of the bundle of rods and the axe as the emblem of the movement; for
therein we have a key-notion of its meaning: *authority* and *co-
operation*.

It is an all too common, though for that matter a very under-
standable, mistake, however, to regard fascism as a purely
political and social phenomenon. Its political and social
achievements, especially the former, have had a very wide
advertisement, whereas its precise aim and its *Weltanschauung*
or what may be called its *temper*, are still relatively unfelt outside
Italy. The truth is that the political and social revolution which
has occurred in Italy: the new constitution, the fascist syndical
and corporative institutions, the new Italian penal code, the new
press laws, the great after-work and maternity and infant welfare
institutions and so-forth—*in fine*, the various concrete political
and social achievements to date of Mussolini's government—
are merely the expression under Italian conditions of the fascist
temper, which is really the essence of fascism and requires before
all else to be explained. This will constitute the primary object
of this book. And if accordingly fascism is not merely a political
or a social system, neither, it should be noted, is it a complete
philosophy of life or a religion. Attempts have been made inside
and outside Italy to identify fascism with a particular philosophy or with a particular religion, or to treat it as if it were a complete philosophy of life or a religion by itself. This, in my view,
is a mistake. What, on the other hand, can be accomplished and,
in course of time, will no doubt be accomplished with greater
and greater precision, is the task of rationalizing fascism: its
reduction in other words to a set of interdependent principles
co-ordinated to form a system touching all manner of human
activities: an intellectual digest, a syllabus of the movement.
Such a system would be required to be justified in the light of
philosophy and it may very well turn out to have some strict
relationship to a particular religion. No doubt, too, there will be

numbers of attempts by different methods to justify it philosophically; but a reasoned course of revealing the significance of a given movement through the intermediary of a number of carefully explained principles to which the mind may cling as to so many points of support and thereby obtain a steadier and more convincing intuitive vision of the whole idea or ideas which the movement suggests, does not, cannot constitute a philosophy by itself in any full sense of the word. All the same, such a rationalized system as a syllabus presents, still more when philosophy provides an apology for the principles enumerated, satisfies a human need. We all need, in different degrees, to think our beliefs, our ways of resolving the problems of life in the form of abstract propositions as well as to perceive them intuitively. But no abstract thinking can ever take the place of comprehensive intuitions; for such thinking is the result of a cold analytical process which is apt to destroy the unity of the emotion-provoking intuitive vision of any complex event, although, indeed, it may actually help us to obtain a wider intuitive vision of any complex event than we had before, when thereafter we allow ourselves again to approach the subject with the eyes of the artist, who alone can provide us with the necessary synthesis.

Such a synthesis, taking account of innumerable *imponderabilia*, may be compared to the perfection of a circle in contradistinction to a many-sided equilateral figure, laboriously constructed on the basis of known commensurable data (*e.g.*, the process of abstract reasoning upon elementary self-evident truths and presuppositions) and representing, as the number of sides is increased, a progressive approximation to the circle. The equilateral figure, however, can never coincide with the circle until the number of sides becomes infinite. Short of infinity it will always be possible theoretically to superimpose upon that figure other figures of exactly the same number of sides of the same length in such a way that each side of the first figure intersects one of another, so that, although the figures actually fail to coincide, any one represents an equally close approximation to the circle. This illustrates the manner in which abstract reasoning, though it may fix a number of important truths, leads constantly to paradox: two or more systems equally proximate to the truth, yet apparently contradictory. The intuitive vision (the circle) alone resolves the paradoxes. On the other hand, abstract reasoning (to continue the simile) leads frequently to the construction of similar equilateral figures beyond the radius of the original circle, thus carrying us—by daring speculation, so to speak—into new fields of knowledge, the full significance of which, however, will not become apparent until intuition steps in again to describe the wider circle.

Nobody, indeed, I feel sure—to pass from the above mathematical simile to a concrete instance—could be brought to grasp the meaning of Christianity by reading a catalogue of its dogmas, however well they may be explained, however well justified in the light of philosophy. A syllabus of Christianity, accompanied by an able apologetic, may very well convince the reader of the essential reasonableness of Christianity, of its compatibility with science, of its pragmatic excellence. Such a syllabus, in these and other days of intellectual controversy, may even be regarded as indispensable for the educated Christian as a means of attack and of defence and as a refuge in moments of clouded vision or of doubt. But to understand Christianity intimately (apart from the question of belief, which depends on grace) one surely requires to be touched with the spirit of Christ Himself, *by an intuition of His word in its completeness*, consequent on coming in contact with Him through the story of His life, His recorded parables and His poetic images, through the writings of those who knew and loved Him and of those who later believed and do believe, and through the spirit diffused by His Church in its rites, its arts and its perennial charity.

Similarly a syllabus of fascism would be altogether inadequate as a means of conveying its intimate significance. A few chapters containing an argued statement of the more important fascist principles may be usefully included in a work of this kind, so that the reader may be possessed of a number of useful land-marks, of so many intellectual points of support. But such chapters should properly be preceded by a description of the fascist temper; and in order to be able to do this with any effect the writer must try to raise himself into something of an artist, so that he may present a picture to the reader which is a united whole, a synthesis of the thing he must describe: in other words, something of a work of art. Otherwise the reader will be led to lose himself in a labyrinth of detail; he will fail to see the wood for the trees. For fascism, being a movement of ideas, is characterized by what at first sight appears to be innumerable contradictory interpretations. But the business of the artist is to reach beyond the jostle of opinions, to select what appears to him as chiefly significant of the reality behind the ever-shifting forms, to compose a work expressing his intuitive vision (even though it may be a narrow one) of the whole object, such as the reader through the exercise of his artistic sensibility may be brought to share.

If we cast our imaginations back for a while to, let us say, Florence at the beginning of the fifteenth century, we shall obtain a notion of the *kind* of thing fascism is; and this exercise will help us to understand why it is that those who are caught up by the movement are so filled with a strange excitement. Fifteenth-century Florence was stirred by what we now call the Renaissance. Here we have an historical example, one with which we are well familiar, of a movement of ideas. The Renaissance represents no particular philosophy, though it gave birth to many, though it gave a new direction to philosophy in general. Similarly the Renaissance cannot be identified with any particular religion, though it weakened the authority of the Catholic Church and gave birth to Protestantism and led to a widely spread agnosticism and to a cult of pagan ideals. Again it represents no particular political system. On the contrary its first results in this field were to destroy the mediæval democracies, substituting for them the personal rule of tyrants; and later, on the ruins of the tyrannies, class government developed, first that of the nobility and then of the bourgeoisie. If the direct consequences of the movement have by now almost worked themselves out, nobody would wish to deny their prodigious importance or the permanent value of the experience. And when people first began to be caught up by its spirit, it is difficult to exaggerate the excitement that it caused. A new world, filled with infinite possibilities, was dawning. No one dreamt of the final consequences; but a new hope had entered into people's lives, creating a new and marvellous vigour, stimulating the spirit to its loftiest flights.

If we turn to the introductory chapter of Miss Edith Sichel's little book on the Renaissance, belonging to this series[90], we cannot fail to catch some of the enthusiasm which pervaded those wonderful budding days of our modern era. "It was a movement," she says, "a revival of men's powers, a reawakening of the consciousness of himself and of the universe. . . . Like other movements it had forerunners, but, unlike other movements, it was circumvented by no particular aim, and the fertilizing wave that passed over Italy, Germany, France, England, and, in a much fainter degree, over Spain, to leave a fresh-world behind it, seems more like a phenomenon of nature than a current of history—rather an atmosphere surrounding men than a distinct course before them. The new birth was the result of a universal impulse, and that impulse was preceded by something like a revelation, a revelation of intellect and of the possibilities in man. . . . Beauty was manifested to man afresh—beauty and joy. . . . Rabelais's giant baby, Prince Gargantua born in the open air, in the midst of a festival, waking to life parched with thirst and calling loudly for drink, must have been a conscious symbol of the child of the Renaissance."

Fascism presents a quite analogous phenomenon. There is, moreover, another reason why I have selected the Renaissance as a parallel event: there is a close historical connection between the two movements. The Renaissance, in fact, we can now see,

---

[90] This book was part of the collection "Home University library of modern knowledge." [Editor's note]

was a spiritual movement, which, though it looked back to ancient Rome, reacted against the unbroken continuity of the Christianized Roman tradition of the Middle Ages and looked back, beyond Rome, with still more eager eyes to ancient Greece. It provoked the re-birth of Greek speculative thought. Like fascism it matured first in Italy. "Italy," in the words of Miss Sichel, "was the well-spring from which other countries drew life." Out of it grew the modern world as we have come to know it, the modern world which, though still in many respects institutionally Roman, and Roman in many more practical ways still than we are apt to realize, is conspicuously an expression of the triumph of the Greek spirit of speculation, rationalism, individualism and, paradoxically, of uniformity of types in contrast with the Roman spirit of practical common sense, respect for tradition, social solidarity and individual personality. I should, perhaps, add here that I am using the terms "Roman" and "Greek" in a wide sense as typifying two extreme, contrasting, but not necessarily contradictory mental attitudes. Bearing this in mind we may say accordingly with perfect truth that since the time of the Renaissance the Greek spirit has more and more, in spite of many reactionary attempts to check its growth, prevailed over the Roman, until at last it has become a positive danger to society and to morality. It flowered like an overblown rose under the influence of a too hot sun after rain. It ran to excess. God was dethroned and man placed in his stead as Lord of the Universe. God became the creation of man, instead of the Creator; and the Greek spirit unchecked by the synthetic philosophy of the Church which had degenerated since the time of the great St. Thomas into a game of subtle dialectics, precipitated the world into a run of tremendous riot. For the Greek spirit unchecked seems to lead to a dissolution of the body and to moral chaos, just as the Roman spirit unchecked seems to lead to a rigid crystallization of the mind and of institutions, spelling death no less assuredly, albeit in another language. So we now find ourselves living in a world of mental chaos and physical strife, in a world where institutions are threatening on all sides to crumble, where the minds of men have no longer any secure points of reference, where scepticism is rampant, where nation is pitted against nation, class against class, individual against individual, in a seeming death struggle, made all the more hideous by the drab uniformity of almost everything that surrounds us, which promises life only to the strongest and the most ruthless.

Now fascism is a reaction against this excess; but it is more than this, as I shall attempt to show. For it would be wrong to describe fascism as merely a "Roman reaction." Such a description would be partly true only, and for this very reason the most dangerous form of falsehood. Nobody in his senses would be so foolish as to deny—the modern fascisticized Italian certainly would not—the exquisite life-giving quality of the Greek spirit, the inestimable value of its contribution to civilization in the domain of knowledge, whether intuitive or scientific. The age of Pericles, the height of the Italian Renaissance, and the modern era of science and invention, stand irrefutable witness. Nobody in his senses, on the other hand, would surely wish to call in question the fundamental importance for civilization of the staider, but more essential, Roman spirit. With respect to an ideal State, the latter might be held to represent the foundation and framework, the former the superstructure and decoration. Man, regarded in the abstract as an isolated individual, draws his life-blood from the Greek spirit; and man, regarded equally in the abstract as a social animal, does likewise from the Roman. But man, as he exists in reality, at once a self-regarding and a social animal, needs to be compounded of both spirits, just as he needs, in order to be in harmony with his essentially dual nature, to conciliate his personal interests with those of the social group to which he belongs.

To produce a civilization which would be a harmony of the Greek and Roman spirits, between speculation and common sense, between novelty and tradition, between freedom and law, between religion and science, appears to have been the actual hope of the more thoughtful leaders of the Renaissance itself. There are documents that go to prove that the Church of St. Peter in Rome was designed to symbolize this harmony.

Pope Julius II strove to achieve it. But the world was drunk with its newly found freedom. There was no stopping the riot; and only now that we have lived and experienced the consequences of this riot, the bitter aftermath, do we realize how much better it would have been if the erstwhile enthusiasm had been contained. Now the world, if we survey it widely, appears tired and bored. But there are, and have been for some time, many signs of a coming revival. These signs have spoken with innumerable discordant voices. Some are voices of reaction, others are those of sick men who have lost touch with reality and have nothing to offer us but impossible dreams. Others again have taken the form of patient diagnoses and partial remedies, little and less little steps in a constructive direction, the beginnings of the foundation of a new high road, clever devices for building the required bridges and parapets, things that in themselves are of small avail but may come to serve later on as an inspiration for minds partaking of a maturer atmosphere. And then, suddenly out of that ever-miraculous soil that is Italy—Italy that for sixteen solid centuries (people are apt to forget this fact!) from 250 B.C. to A.D. 1550 led and dominated the culture of the Western world, except for a comparatively short period during the Dark Ages when Byzantium became the focus of art and thought—fascism burst into the light of day amid circumstances that confused the issue, flavoured by an Italian aroma that smacked of something alien to foreign national palates, fiercely opposed and traduced by the representatives of the old order, misunderstood as much by friends as by foes. Gradually it has fixed the attention of a curious world as a constructive force, as a phenomenon capable for good or for evil of filling the souls of men of diverse nationality, of enflaming a whole nation, of exacting supreme sacrifices. In Italy itself the movement has resulted in a violent social and political revolution; and social and political reformers all the world over are beginning to examine the consequences with a view to seeing whether they may not provide lessons for the resolving of present discontents among other peoples. Few, however, outside Italy have as yet any adequate, wholly conscious notion of the fascist temper of which the fascist reforms are the peculiar Italian expression. Fewer still appear to realize that the movement, unlike that of the Renaissance, possesses a quite definite and conscious aim. Nevertheless, to the close observer there can be no doubt whatever that such an aim exists and that it is no less than the gradual construction of a new world-civilization, which would be the reflection of a synthesis of the Greek and Roman spirits, a conciliation of the ideals of the modern era with those of the old.

The ideals of fascism indeed correspond closely with the hopes of the early Renaissance; and as Italy occupies the unique position in Europe as the country whose traditions represent the longest and the most varied experience, a veritable melting-pot of all that is both old and new, it would not be surprising if in her newly found vigour and unity she succeeded at last in accomplishing, under the more favourable political circumstances of today, what perhaps she only just failed to accomplish for mankind in the fifteenth century.

CHAPTER II

THE SPIRITUAL INTERPRETATION OF HISTORY

VARIOUS attempts have been made since the latter half of the eighteenth century to escape from the excessive individualism which developed as a consequence of the Renaissance. Although the fundamentally individualistic outlook remained unaffected, the need for curbing individual excesses was realized and philosophy reacted to this need. Some of the philosophers of the age, like the utilitarians and hedonists of the nineteenth century, sought to prove under the influence of the prevailing, and—as it seems to us now—an astonishingly misplaced optimism, that the sum of individual interests in the widest conditions of liberty would in fact in the long run promote the greatest possible collective interest. Similarly Rousseau's theory of the social contract was invented as a mythical hypothesis (mythical, because few people ever believed that it corresponded to historical fact) to justify the sinking of the rights of the individual in the abstract conception of the general will of the society to which he belonged. On the other hand, Comte, the founder of positivism—of which Herbert Spencer may be considered later on the leading English exponent, Ardigò the leading Italian—attempted to substitute for the prevailing individualism the "religion of humanity"; while the German idealistic school of philosophy, headed by Hegel, broke definitely from the individualist and utilitarian idea of society, and taught that a people is not an accumulation of separate individuals artificially united by conscious agreement for their mutual advantage, as Locke and the French philosophers had affirmed, but a spiritual unity for which and by which its members exist.

It would be out of place here, however, to follow in detail the trend of philosophic thought during the past two centuries since the genuine spirit of the Renaissance itself dried up. It will be sufficient to register the fact that the attempts to limit the excess of individualism, ushered in by the Renaissance, have one and all dismally failed. The utilitarian theses have been proved under the stress of actual experience to be at variance with demonstrable fact, and have since been completely abandoned. Rousseau's theory was substituted in practice by the idea of majority rule, as representing what was thought to be the nearest approach to a determination of the general will, since it was found that the general will had no precise articulate means of expressing itself, except possibly by violent popular outbursts—by no means desirable—in moments of extreme crisis and excitement; and majority rule, in turn, turned out to be the very contrary of Rousseau's ideal, since it rendered the State at best but an unstable equilibrium of contending individual forces and government the servant of party and class interests. The positivism of Comte and his successors, again, has fallen into discredit, partly because no sufficient reason was forth-coming on the basis of their philosophy to justify in the eyes of the more active and self-confident members of society the altruistic ideals which were advocated. Consequently it tended to give way to the ideas of some of the more extreme members of Nietzsche's school which divided humanity into those animated by servile herd instincts and those others, born aristocrats and leaders, who were a law unto themselves: the cult of the super-man, the very apotheosis of individualism. Lastly, the German idealistic school merely succeeded in sublimating the egoistic impulses of the individual into a racial and national egoism, by which the State became deified, with the result that the excessive individualism of the age was merely carried on to a higher and even more dangerous plane.

Lately people have begun to realize therefore the impossibility of scotching the prevailing excessive individualism so long as the individual was made the starting-point of philosophy; for it may be affirmed that nearly all the various systems of philosophy from Descartes onwards may be described as fundamentally individualistic in the sense that nearly all of them either reject, tacitly or positively, or neglect the dual character of the universe based on a transcendent idea. Finally attempts have been made to escape from the antimony of rejecting individualism without rejecting its fundamental presuppositions, by abandoning any attempt to find a system capable of justifying an altruistic life and by falling back on purely empirical action; and this attitude led to the rise of the philosophy of pragmatism, which taught that a shifting relative truth—relative, that is, to the actual, evident needs of life, individual and collective—constitutes the only kind of truth available to us; and that consequently what is useful may be regarded as true. Parallel with pragmatism there arose modernism, which, in the form condemned by the Catholic Church, is in reality a particular form of pragmatism applied to Christian dogmas, which were to be regarded henceforth in the light of splendid myths, useful to life and representing mysterious truths hidden somewhere below the surface of scientific reality. The philosophic bases, however, of these systems were extremely tenuous. They satisfied few people, though many actually act in accordance with them in default of a livelier faith. The dead hand of materialism, in fact, which is one of the most widespread consequences of an unbalanced individualism, has so fastened itself upon the age that countless people find it difficult now to believe in anything at all. They live, so to speak, from hand to mouth, the more ruthless and the more emancipated from custom indulging in an unfeigned egoism, the remainder living on the residue of the moral capital—by force of habit so to speak—bequeathed to them by former generations of "believers." But on every side efforts are being made nevertheless to escape from this slough of despond. On the one hand there is evident a marked revival of Catholicism. On the other, spiritualism, Christian Science, even the grossest forms of latter-day superstition are all symptomatic of the same trend away from abject materialism. So too that vague irrational idealism, which is to be met with nowadays on all sides—the morbid refuge from the materialism of the age of the super-sensitive being, who, like the ostrich, burying its head in the sand, imagines thereby he has escaped from the reality which his inability to believe in a universal moral idea causes him to abhor—testifies to the beginnings of a general revival of faith. And this process is being abetted by the progress of modern science, which at length has abandoned its attitude of hostility towards revealed religion. We appear indeed to be on the verge of a new age of faith; and it is fascism which appears to have definitely ushered this new age in.

The basic idea of fascism indeed is the spiritual interpretation of history. Fascism is a definite revolt against materialism, that is, against all forms of interpreting the universe from a purely naturalistic or purely individualistic standpoint. If all fascists are not as yet fervent believers in a Divine transcendent Providence, all fascists have at least a will, a thirst to believe in such a One; all fascists have a reverence for the supernatural and are resolved that the new generations shall be brought up in a religious atmosphere and be protected from the dissolving poisons of materialism in all its forms. This is the paramount reason of fascist intransigeance in Italy now, of fascist intolerance, if you will: for fascism is resolved to build up a generation of believers, as the only means of reaching out of the present chaos, cost what it may. Italy may, in this respect, be compared to a nursery garden of young saplings, which have to be protected from the wind and from frost (from the demoralizing influences of contemporary scepticism and of almost sadistical indulgence in destructive criticism) until such time as they become sufficiently grown to withstand alone the inclemencies of the weather.

To grasp this fact about fascism is to hold the key to the understanding of the whole movement; for it explains how fascism started without any definite theoretical ideas; for the spirit of the anti-materialist revolt was already well abroad in Italy when circumstances forced it to express itself in action before it

had reached sufficient maturity to explain itself to itself by sys-
tematic thought, to render itself completely coherent—a process
which marks invariably a subsequent stage in the development
of a spiritual idea. It explains, moreover, its fury against everything representative of the old *régime*, of the old materialistic
mentality, whether considered in relation to the former theories
in vogue or as its logical expression in political and social institutions; it explains Mussolini's character as both an idealist and
as a man of action with his medium-like gift of interpreting the
traditional transcendental spirit of the Italian common people
as it gradually emerged out of the experiences of the war and its
aftermath, when for the first time Italians as a whole clearly
realized a sense of unity and the mass of the people, mostly peasants, among whom the old Renaissance and pre-Renaissance
traditions had never withered, acquired a consciousness of their
spiritual needs. It explains all the differences of opinion among
those who would attempt to rationalize the movement; and at
the same time it explains their unanimity in action, their desire
to be disciplined and led, and to acquiesce in the loss of certain
liberties and even in mistakes of leadership rather than have no
leadership, provided the spirit of the movement be maintained.
It explains, amid many similarities, the essential difference
between fascist nationalism and other forms of nationalism
based fundamentally on individualism, whether this be invested
with the form of eighteenth-century French rationalism or of
nineteenth-century German idealism. It explains the fundamental divergence of outlook and aim, despite a number of parallel
forms respecting practical institutions, between fascism and bolshevism, which fascists regard as lying still under the spell of
Victorian science (which pitted itself against religion) and under
the tyranny of abstract thought.

Yet fascism is not exactly, on this account, the antithesis of
our modern era. It realizes that no heresies would ever have had
a chance of capturing the minds of an age, if they did not contain
a certain deposit of important truth; that the essence of a
heresy—of a wrong view of life—lies in their being one-sided

views of truth, taken as fundamental by abstract thinkers or by inexperienced or imbalanced enthusiasts at particular junctures of history, whenever a reaction happened to be called for against the danger of a crystallization of the forms of life. Thus Marx's materialistic interpretation of history, which is the lever of the bolshevist creed, is not rejected by fascism except it be regarded as representing the whole or, at least, a fundamental truth. On the contrary, the materialistic interpretation of history is regarded by fascists as one of many interpretations of history, the result of a particular process of analysis—consequently a one-sided interpretation, useful only if supplemented, or rather complemented by—nay, welded together with—other interpretations. In positing, rather, as fundamental the spiritual interpretation of history, fascists do not accordingly deny the influence on life of material conditions. They would rather place such influences in their proper place and seek to preserve a true proportion in accordance with their transcendental, dualistic outlook, claiming, however, that in the long run it is man's spiritual outlook on life, his spiritual values, that determine within the bounds set by the irreducible facts of reality and of natural existence, the exterior institutional and economic forms of human life.

Thus the attitude of fascism may be described as eminently synthetic, intuitive. It is anxious to preserve everything of value in the thought of our modern era; and for this reason, though it rejects the typically materialistic bases of modern thought, though it insists on the picking up, as it were, of the old early Renaissance and pre-Renaissance traditions and puts a heavy premium on the value of tradition itself, it sets its face resolutely against what may be termed reaction. Its outlook and its aim are positive not negative. In a traditionally Catholic country like Italy, it looks to itself as the movement, for instance, prophesied by Gioberti, that will enable the Church, which since the sixteenth century, despite its perennial vitality, may be regarded as having been a beleaguered city shut in by widely triumphant antagonistic forces, to assimilate modern culture, relinquish its timid attitude towards modern speculative thought, belie the accusation still often made against it of obscurantism, come out into the open and once more assume the leadership of the world of culture. Similarly, in re-establishing the idea of authority in the State, in aiming at the creation of a governing aristocracy, fascism in no way seeks to go back upon such conquests of the French Revolution as the equality of all citizens before the law, the abolition of the closed caste system, democracy in the sense of a career open to talent or of a constitution broadly based upon the people. And if we traced the attitude of fascism towards the various philosophic movements of our modern era, we would find it ready to acknowledge a debt to them all, to Hegel, to Comte, to Henry James, to Nietzsche, to Bergson—even to Bentham and Marx.

Fascism indeed would reject nothing *a priori* of the result of modern "progress," claiming only that what vitiated the value of so much that has been accomplished since culture ceased to have its roots in revealed religion was its materialistic and super-individualistic bias; that to remove this bias, to substitute for it a spiritual, dualistic and transcendental outlook on life will enable the gold to be separated rapidly from the dross and cause every modern conquest of value to fall into its proper place in a new cultural synthesis such as the world has not known since the height of the Middle Ages.

To this end fascism is determined to educate the new generation into one of believers in a Divine Providence, the heralds of an age of faith, to make of the new generation one of heroes who know no fear because of their faith, who would exalt the spirit of sacrifice, gladly fly in the face of any danger run in a worthy cause and welcome martyrdom with a smile. This is no exaggeration. This is the root of the fascist revolution. God is to become once more the central principle of our conscious life, with an objective, didactic moral law, founded on reason, recognized as paramount, not accordingly running counter to the natural quasi-normative laws of organic life, such as the laws of conservation, integration and growth, but transcending them; a law that sums up and harmonizes all our loyalties, dethrones the individual or the State from the position they would usurp from God, yet renders the self-regarding sentiment of self-respect or patriotic feeling capable of receiving a divine extension. The success of fascism accordingly depends on the extent to which the new generation growing up in Italy, or wherever fascism may catch on, will be capable of making this transcendental outlook on life part of its very being. Those who have faith are aware that no death for an ideal is ultimately unfruitful, that even if all we love appears to perish in one supreme heroic sacrifice, we shall be inevitably sowing the seeds for an eventual and glorious harvest of our heart's desire; and it is this spirit which fascism would wish to see leavening the world again, the best spirit of the Crusaders. If this could be done, fascism claims that the rest would come of itself: our present economic and social conditions would be transformed into something less vulgar, into something less servile for the masses, into something less futile for the privileged few. Not that fascism would hold out any Utopian promises. Death, destitution and suffering are the wages of sin and the conditions of our natural existence. But there are eras of social equilibrium and eras of social unrest, eras of beauty and eras of ugliness, eras of courage and character and eras of despair and neurasthenia. What fascism claims to promise, if its spirit be laid hold of in the manner it would wish it to be until it becomes the dominating spirit of the age, is the gradual unfolding of an era of social equilibrium, of beauty and of firmness of character wherein the inevitable trials of life may find compensation in spiritual comforts.

We may now accordingly amend our definition of the aim of fascism given towards the end of the introductory chapter as follows: fascism would bring about the gradual construction of a new world-civilization, which would in effect be the reflection of a synthesis of the Greek and Roman spirits, a conciliation of the ideals of the modern era with those of the old; but it would insist that such a civilization can only be built up upon the root and main trunk, so to speak, of the old pre-Renaissance, transcendental, dualistic view of life, of a spiritual interpretation of the universe, to which basic standpoint modern culture must be assimilated—grafted, so to speak, on the ancient tree just in so far as it may be possible to do so without risking the latter's vitality. So fascism is essentially conservative if we define conservatism, as conservatives themselves would have it, as the aiming at the preservation and creation of values worth preserving. It is progressive in the same order of thought, in the sense that it is open to every new idea or attitude compatible with those things which history and experience have sanctioned as, at once, both socially and individually useful. It rejects the new that is not a development of—or, alternatively, that cannot be grafted on to—the old proven values which it deems worthy of preservation. And in this fascism is fundamentally Roman. But it would have men to be scientific husbandmen, anointed by the Greek spirit of restless curiosity, capable of cultivating—provided the principle of organic development be never lost sight of—by fearless application, research and experiment, new and more glorious flowers and fruit than that which nature, left to herself, would be able to produce.

CHAPTER III

THE *WELTANSCHAUUNG* OF FASCISM

THE class which in Italy, as in certain other countries, has preserved intact the dualistic and transcendental outlook on life, the moral qualities, the mentality and the traditions of the early and pre-Renaissance era is the peasant. This fact is due to a number of historical, economic and political causes. During the sixteenth century Italy, though she continued to contribute conspicuously to the cultural life of the world, ceased to be the world's cultural centre. The sceptre passed from her to other nations, especially to France. Her soil gave every appearance of exhaustion and for three centuries Italy became, metaphorically speaking, fallow land. She slept. Only with the nineteenth century was she destined to re-awaken. The discovery of the Cape route to the East and of America had sapped her commercial vitality; the new age of coal and iron—materials she scarcely possesses—contributed to making her an economic bye-water. The strength of her Roman traditions of universality, civil as well as ecclesiastical, militated against her forming a national unity, such as many other nations had assumed at an early date, so that she became politically weak and the prey to foreign conquests, with all the demoralizing evils attendant thereon. Modern culture, as we have seen, ceased to have its roots in revealed religion or even in a spiritual conception of the universe; and the Catholic Church, which remained powerful in Italy, sought to preserve the traditions of Catholic thought by a policy which in many of its practical effects tended to exclude Italy from participating in the modern cultural life of the world. The enemies of the Catholic Church will call this a policy of obscurantism, its friends a policy of patience: for faithful to the idea of its eternal mission and thinking in terms of centuries rather than in terms of decades, the Catholic Church preferred to say, "Wait, the time will come when modern culture will cease to present a danger to Catholic faith; then will come the time—and never too late if the alternative choice is loss of faith—to assimilate its conquests." In any case, whatever interpretations may be placed on them, these and other reasons have brought it about that the peasant class in Italy to-day has maintained its early and pre-Renaissance, *Weltanschauung*, grounded on the solid Roman spirit.

The same is only partly true of the other classes. Portions of the nobility, and, to a great extent, the artisan classes have also maintained it. But the middle classes and the urban proletariat, which grew greatly in strength and numbers during the nineteenth century, are in varying degrees more modern than ancient in outlook. Their education since Italy became a united Kingdom has been religious and positivist; their traditions, since the Napoleonic invasions, liberal rather than conservative; their mentality neo-European.

Broadly speaking, we may say that the peasants and the artisans especially, and in a less degree those other classes who are vocationally employed, who, in other words, pursue a calling by choice rather than by necessity—the landed nobility, the professional classes, the small independent workers and shopkeepers who own their own means of production, the co-operators, etc.—represent the older traditions, the rest the new. But the former represent a considerable majority of the Italian population; and it was therefore inevitable that as soon as the peasants, who in turn form the largest class within this class, began to possess a definite self-consciousness as a class and to appreciate their position as an active element in the life of united Italy, the older traditions should gain in influence at the expense of the new. This tendency was already apparent before the world war and was a herald of the advent of fascism. The War itself, which gave a sense of unity to the country, such as had never been experienced before, accentuated this tendency; but I prefer to reserve for another chapter some account of the various movements which preceded and eventually led to the development of fascism. The point I wish to emphasize here is that the old traditions and mentality are native to the majority of Italians; and since fascism would wish to make these old traditions and mentality the basis of its spiritual renovation, since it is determined that the new generation of all classes shall be rooted in them, a description of the essential characteristics of the peasant class in Italy will afford the best possible insight into fascism's *Weltanschauung*, although to this description something more will then have to be added in order to make the picture quite complete.

It is not necessary to insist on the dualistic and transcendental outlook of the Italian peasant. He is eminently a God-fearing man and his whole nature is alien to interpreting the ways of the universe from a naturalistic standpoint. Many of his most pronounced characteristics, on which fascism lays great stress in its very comprehensive educational programme, have only, too, to be stated in order to be understood; he is sober, hard-working, thrifty and sparing, well disciplined and exceedingly respectful of authority. Above all he is profoundly pious in the Latin sense of the word which implies a reciprocal devotion and respect between parents and their offspring. The family feeling, which is very strong in Italy, fascism desires to see accentuated in contrast to the dissolving processes at work in so many other countries and among certain classes in Italy herself. The peasant, besides, presents a strongly marked sex differentiation; the men are manly, the women womanly, the former exceedingly robust, full of a healthy animal, combative spirit, loyal, generous and fearless—the latter, mothers in instinct before all else, with an appealing tenderness and power of sympathy, a love of home and of domestic pursuits. If the peasant moreover is attached to the institutions of the religion in which he has been brought up, he is by no means priest-ridden. On the contrary, he has much self-assertive personality and, with all his respect for authority, is as resentful of interference by the priesthood, should the latter incline to overstep what he would consider the proper limits of his purely religious activities, as he is resentful of any attempt to undermine his economic independence. The Italian peasant indeed has a strong proprietary instinct which is wedded to his family feeling. If he is not a small working proprietor, co-operating with his fellows by means of well-organized co-operative societies, he is either a half-share working farmer, with proprietary rights strongly sanctioned by custom, or else a small working tenant farmer whose rents are fixed at a very fair rate through the operation of a system of collective bargaining embracing wide districts. On the other hand, entrenched though he may be behind his property rights, his mentality is anti-capitalist, because he produces more for consumption than for profit. Secured, in varying degrees of his house, his corn, his fruit, his vegetables, his milk products, his poultry, his eggs, his wine, his oil and his fuel, etc., he lives largely on what he produces, selling only a comparatively small percentage of his annual production, wherewith to buy his surplus necessaries— with the result that he is rendered comparatively independent of price fluctuations. If he is in certain provinces—notably in southern Italy—grossly superstitious, this is due to lack of instruction; but his superstition does not interfere with his acute sense of reality; and if he is comparatively ignorant, his common sense and above all his intuitive sense are highly developed. On the whole he exhibits an extraordinarily vital rhythm and balance, in contrast with the modern town-dweller, owing to his contact with nature; while the rich memories of his racial experiences, extending back for centuries, are preserved and renewed in his incomparable folk-lore.

It is with these qualities—minus, of course, the superstition and the ignorance—that fascism is determined to leaven the whole country. Some of these qualities are already widely diffused among all classes, notably the proprietary instinct, the family feeling, sobriety, a high degree of common sense and of reality, which goes hand in hand in Italy with a sense of the ideal. Realism and idealism are not opposite qualities but, rather, complementary; and there is perhaps nothing so striking in the Italian character as the manner in which these two things may be seen to balance each other. It constitutes a good example of the kind of mentality and of the kind of approach to the problems of life issuing from it, upon which all good fascists lay particular stress. For their view of life is eminently synthetic, arising from the habit of thinking intuitively rather than in terms of abstract propositions.

To apprehend things synthetically implies the combination into an indivisible unity of a number of heterogeneous elements, which, related separately, offer a paradoxical appearance. Life itself, under a process of abstract analysis is bewilderingly paradoxical. Only when viewed synthetically with the intuitive vision of an artist are the paradoxes resolved. There has been a pronounced tendency during recent centuries, a habit of mind engendered by the vulgarization of methods of thought required for scientific purposes, towards applying a process of abstract ratiocination to the problems of life, of practical activity. But life, which expresses itself in action and is at the mercy of innumerable contingent circumstances, invariably eludes the results. Abstract principles are of course extremely useful, nay, necessary, landmarks, fixing certain eternal truths and preserving them from corruption. Often, too, they are the salvation of the mystic who is in danger of becoming misty, or, as far as conduct is concerned, they serve as a rule of thumb for the disequilibrated, for those who have been uprooted from their natural environment and have lost their bearings. Or again they may enshrine ideals of perfection, which only too frequently, however, have to give way before a practical choice of evils. They would then be the exterior expression of an internal light; but example and the magic of a concrete experience made communicable to others by a work of art or a poetic image, as, for example, in the language used by the Christ, are able to convey

very much more of this light than the most exacting intellectu-
alistic definition. It is impossible to turn life into a system. Life
is an art and should be conceived as a work of art, which is the
expression of an intuition. Intuition, in point of fact—the appre-
hension of all we consciously experience as a series of unities
moving from the simpler to the more and more complex, to
something ever more synthetic—is the very basis as well as the
very highest form of knowledge. In this sense truth is no less
than beauty; and art, the exterior expression of all our spiritual
experiences, including our very daily lives in action, is the language by which we exchange the results of the continual efforts
of each one of us to reach out to the highest apprehensions of
truth within our ken.

So each one of us in analytical introspection is a chaos of
warring personalities and motives. In order to be able to act with
any consistency, to achieve a consistent personality, we must
contrive to bring all these warring elements within ourselves
into a harmony; and in order to be able to live at peace with our
fellows we must contrive to harmonize ourselves with the social
conditions under which we are destined to live. We must contrive, in other words, to make a synthesis of ourselves with
regard to both our interior and exterior lives. We must make of
ourselves artists, whose selves are our own masterpieces; and in
order to be able to do this we must develop our æsthetic sensi-
bilities, learn to relegate logical and analytical processes to their
proper sphere as means and not as ends, means to the achievement of ever vaster intuitive perceptions, of ever more complex,
but no less unitary, synthetic visions of life. The significance of
life will then emerge as an active principle of continual creation
and re-creation in the ceaseless pursuit of ever higher harmo-
nies, wherein thought and action are perfectly reconciled,
implying the existence of a final and infinite harmony in the act
of an infinite Creator and, likewise, a faith in the existence of a
Creator as the needed cement whereby we may integrate our
various disparate experiences in the art of building up ourselves
into as completely balanced men and women as possible.

This intuitive outlook, typical of the Italian peasant, represents indeed the *central active principle of the fascist Weltanschauung, in contrast to the rationalistic and analytical temper of the centuries that have just flown by.* Fascism would thus teach us principally what might be called the *art of integral living*, to use an expression of Aldous Huxley's, the art of making ourselves as completely balanced men and women as in the power of each one of us to make, to which relative balance only a highly developed æsthetic sensibility, in the widest sense of the term, can lead us. It would break down the modern tendency towards over-specialization and would free us from the tyranny of abstract thought, which places us out of touch in our practical lives with concrete reality and renders our ideas lop-sided. It would by no means on that account ask us to despise reason, but it would remind us of what the rationalist is apt to forget, namely, that reason goes far beyond mere logic.

This ideal of the completely balanced man and woman in the fascist idea may be said to include the perfectly normal man and woman, who is well adjusted to his or her environment. This, however, would not exclude the exceptional in the sense of the exceptionally endowed, or the original in the sense of a creative artist. It would exclude only the abnormal in the sense of the mentally deformed, stunted and disequilibrated, the unilateral, the over-specialized, the logic-ridden intellectual—those constitutionally unable to sympathize with the interests and vocations of others different from their own, those lacking in common sense and measure, incapable of spontaneous action, afraid of reality. The Italian peasant, however much he may fall short of its perfection, is nevertheless representative of this fascist ideal of the normal, balanced personality such as I have attempted to describe. Mussolini, himself of peasant origin, is thoroughly representative. He is a peasant aristocrat. He is unerringly interpreting the peasant mind in the policy which he is pursuing; and in order that the new civilization should be rooted in the *Weltanschauung* of his class, formed by a life lived in contact with the soil and the sea, he is determined to make it fundamentally a rural civilization. In the following chapters I shall have occasion to allude to some of the practical measures adopted to this end. Here, before all else, I am anxious to complete the picture of the fascist *Weltanschauung*; for if the representative religious and intuitive outlook of the Italian peasant is the yeast with which fascism looks to leaven the whole of society, if his solid virtues are the basic materials out of which fascism seeks to form the character of the new generations, there are a number of elements to be added to round off the fascist ideal of the completely balanced man and woman. Although Mussolini is what the Italians call *strapaesano* (an untranslatable word denoting an almost extravagant appreciation of everything that is characteristic of rural life), although the *strapaesano* literary and journalistic movement in Italy, with its delightful sense of humour and its robust sanity, is the most typical and authentic manifestation of fascist thought and feeling, it would be an exaggeration to assert that urban life is unable to contribute anything to the ideal that fascism sets before itself.

The city is, of course, an indispensable element in any highly civilized nation's life. It is only when the cities begin to monopolize a country's life, when they become parasitic, when a vast proportion of the population on that account begins to lose touch with nature and with the natural region on which its social welfare depends, that they present an intolerable danger. The immense enveloping towns characteristic of our present type of civilization spell inevitably a biological decadence, which even the highest achievements of science and art and economic organization are powerless to avert. The city's natural role is the formation in each natural region of so many points of cultural and industrial concentration, each city being thoroughly representative of its region for the purpose of potentializing its region's natural activities. The region and the city must, of course, be mutually dependent on one another; but the city should be considered the ornament and servant of the region rather than the region the playground of the city.

The city nevertheless breeds easily certain admirable qualities which the country-side can only attain with difficulty: a refinement of manners, a more responsible civic sense, a physical and intellectual spirit of adventure, and, what at first sight appears paradoxical, the truly sporting spirit; for the sporting spirit is born out of a desire for physical recreation, which is a need felt only by a small proportion of dwellers in the country, the more leisured classes. So a refinement of manners, a more responsible civic sense, which goes beyond patriotic feeling, a physical and intellectual spirit of adventure and daring, a truly sporting instinct, the spirit of fair play—all those self-reliant, responsible, frank and chivalrous qualities which are characteristic of the public-school class in Great Britain and America, the spirit of *camaraderie* between members of both the same and opposite sexes, are required in accordance with the fascist idea to supplement the graver qualities of the peasant classes.

In the Middle Ages and during the early Renaissance the city lived by its region and was, as it should be, the potentialized microcosm of its region. It consequently threw up many notable examples of completely balanced men and women, which can serve as models of the fascist ideal of character and attainment. If accordingly I were asked to choose an historical figure which responds most nearly to the fascist ideal of manhood, I might perhaps pick out Julius II, the great warrior-pope, a man remarkably humane, considering the times, which were distinguished by much callousness and ruthlessness, brave, robust and virile, great sportsman and great patriot, normal minded, practical, endowed with a sharp sense of the reality of every situation in which he was placed—yet combining with all these soldierly virtues a deep sense of religion, an exquisite artistic sensibility and a culture and subtlety of mind only rivalled by a few of his contemporaries. This intellectual and cultivated warrior (prescinding from the question whether his character was altogether suitable for the office he adorned) may be said to be a type of the Knight Chivalrous of fascism: as the fascist refrain goes, "*Libro e moschetto, fascista perfetto*" ("Book and musket, perfect fascist")—that is, Understanding and Service, a type wherein a sound practical realistic sense is mated to a religious, artistic and speculative intelligence.

Similarly, if I were to choose a representative lady, I do not think I could do better than to allow my choice to fall upon Elizabeth of Gonzaga, Duchess of Urbino, who, besides being reputed to have been both beautiful and wise, was all that could be desired as a wife and a mother, an incomparable hostess, intelligent and accomplished, clever with her hands and an excellent housekeeper, courageous in adversity, deeply religious and a daring horse-woman to boot.

As a patron saint of fascism, St. Francis, whose capacity for universal passionate loving could sanctify all he touched and transform ordinary ugliness into beauty, has been mentioned, by several Italian writers. Mussolini himself has referred to him as the most representative of all the Italian saints. But, as the patron saint of fascism, he would not have to be the sentimentalized Francis of popular imagination, the mild-mannered doter upon animals and children, the degradingly humble, the sickeningly exasperated ascetic. It would have to be the real Francis, the very much completely balanced man: ascetic, yes, in accordance with the ideas of his age, because he insisted that his body should be his servant (nowadays he might have gone in for physical culture!); humble, yes, as one who is conscious of the infinitude of his Father's love, of His all-embracing sovereignty and of the littleness of man, but possessed of that dignity that comes of breeding and tradition, and of that assurance that comes of a consciousness of representing a worthy cause, who set his mind fearlessly and obstinately against the Pope's, and carried the victory; gentle, too, but of that gentleness that is the complement of strength and the fruit of a great love: the real Francis, supreme idealist and realist in one, one in thought and action, artist, devotee and practical organizer.

More typical, however, than Francis, perhaps, as an ideal figure embodying the virtues on which fascism puts particular store, is, in my opinion, St. Ignatius of Loyola. There was perhaps never a man who combined so well in one person learning and action; he was both philosopher and soldier, as well as mystic. He knew the value of discipline and authority. He founded the "little army of Jesus" and made it the spear-head of the Counter Reformation. It would, indeed, not be difficult to draw a parallel between him and Mussolini, different as may be the spheres of life in which the two are placed; and this something of similarity between the two characters and between the values they represent, inclines me to choose Ignatius rather than Francis as the typical saint of fascism.

The above should give the reader an idea of the values which fascism exalts, the kind of mentality which it desires to see triumph. To sum up: fascism sets before itself a definite standard of character. It insists accordingly that questions of right and wrong are matters of objective and discernible truth and that they are fundamentally concerned with questions of character; that the salvation of a race depends mainly upon the proper formation of character and that the formation of character, as well as an ultimate, practical solution of social and economic problems, depends in turn on our ability in the first place to renounce materialism in all its forms; in the second place to develop our æsthetic sensibility—not to the detriment of logic, but for its fulfilment; in the third place to correct the prevailing excess of the Greek individualistic spirit by the development of an active religious principle in our lives and of a truly Roman sense of social solidarity, made manifest and easier by a corporate organization of society, strengthened by patriotism and sanctioned by authority; and fourthly by ruralizing our civilization. All this, fascism claims, would make possible a social unification of the Western world, the emergence of a new and vital synthetic civilization compounded of the two great formative traditions of Europe, the Greek and the Roman; and it seeks to bring this result about by spreading the fire of its faith by the force of example and enthusiasm, and by bending to its purpose all the powers of authority which it can succeed in infusing with its spirit.

CHAPTER IV

THE ETHICAL STATE

I. THE AUTHORITATIVE AND UNITARY STATE

THE concluding sentence of the last chapter leads us to the consideration of what fascists call the "ethical State." There are various interpretations of this idea by fascists of different schools of philosophy. The ultra-nationalist school, the ultra-Catholic school and the neo-idealist school are continually at each other's throats on the subject. But although the polemics between these schools occupy a lot of print, all three offer extreme solutions which, in spite of the fact that the ultra-nationalist and the neo-idealist schools in particular have received and still receive considerable official support—the first on account of the need felt of emphasizing a conscious sense of nationality among Italians, such as was evidently lacking before the War, the second on account of its admirable pedagogic methods—are only partly representative of fascist opinion. Moreover the whole trend of fascist opinion is away from the extreme solutions of these three schools. What follows therefore will be an explanation of the idea as it is held by the main and what appears to me the most vital current of fascist opinion, an explanation which may be said to have the merit also of representing a common denominator of all the various currents of opinion, that on which the vast majority of fascists take their stand. It is an explanation, moreover, which may be said to be acceptable to the consciences of the vast majority of Italians who have no intention whatever of compromising their Catholic faith; and it is one which Christians of all denominations—and for that matter all religiously minded persons—can endorse.

The fascist idea of the ethical State rests on three basic principles. First, that man, besides being an individual, is by nature also a social animal, by which is implied the notion of necessary corporative existence, within which under some form of disciplinary authority (inseparable from the idea of any form of society) individuals must needs live. Secondly, that human actions are subject to the moral law, itself based upon the eternal law of God, by whose virtue all things exist, obedience to whose behests is the condition of all harmony. In other words, right and wrong involve questions incapable of solution in accordance with the various inclinations—often blind and pernicious—of individuals, but are matters of objective and discernible truth. Thirdly, each differentiated human group—of which the nation-State, in the temporal order, is the most perfect example—is a natural phenomenon which possesses an organic life embracing a series of generations of individuals composing it, possessed of a community sense and subject to natural sociological laws of conservation, integration and growth—natural laws which may be given a normative character, since they are laws of life (transcended by, but not opposed to the moral law). The third principle, indeed, in a sense summarizes the first two.

Few people will be found nowadays to dispute the proposition that societies manifest an organic character; and sociology is the science which attempts to lay bare the natural laws which govern society conceived of in the above sense as a manifestation of organic life. It attempts to establish uniformities in the ordinary scientific sense, that is, generalities having the character of successive approximations to the truth, bearing on the subject-matter. It traces cause and effect in the life of societies, informs us of the conditions favourable to the continued vitality, integration and growth of societies, of the consequences that may be expected to ensue from certain conditions, circumstances, pursuits, beliefs, policies, etc. It does not attempt to dictate to us the direction which we ought to go: but the knowledge it provides increases the hold of statesmen and social reformers over nature and so enables them to achieve more easily and with less risk of failure whatever objects they may set themselves. Or they enable us to diagnose a situation and predict certain results. It sets limits, too, to Utopian dreams, holds the statesman and social reformer within the bounds of reality and nurtures their practical faculties.

Although sociology, however, contains no categorical imperative, refrains from giving us any information on the subject of the ends which we ought to pursue, the science would lose all practical value and consequently a great deal of its interest if a great many people were not vitally concerned with the health and vigour of the societies to which they belong and with the improvement of social, economic and political conditions generally—were not anxious, in other words, to acquaint themselves with the laws discoverable by sociology for the precise purpose of making use of the knowledge thus gained to promote their community's well-being in a manner compatible, if possible, with the well-being of other communities. But what if opinions differ as to what constitutes a community's well-being? Rational progress is only possible when it is known to what end it is desired to progress. The following dilemma appears therefore unavoidable: either we must come to some definite conclusion on the meaning of good or we must leave things to work themselves out by the interplay of the blind forces of nature or of warring interests.

It might be presumed, just as I might claim for myself to be better qualified to know what constitutes my own good than anybody else, that the general will of a community, in so far as it may be ascertained, might be safely left to decide the question. If questions of right and wrong are not matters of objective and discernible truth or (even supposing it were granted that they might be so theoretically) if they are considered in practice too complicated or vague to allow of any truly valid universal moral judgments, the course dictated by the general will would indeed represent the nearest practical approximation possible to rational progress.

The whole of modern liberal and democratic practice appears in fact to be based upon this assumption. The general tendency to regard questions of right and wrong as matters, if not absolutely, at least practically subjective, in accordance with the rampant individualism of the age, points straight to this assumption as the one way of escape from the above dilemma. For thus the individual's narrow task of "self-realization" according to his private set of values might be submerged, except for those things which only concerned him personally, in the "self-realization" of his community; and this in turn might be submerged in the "self-realization" of humanity at large. So as interests tended to become universalized, a right morality—even though we might not be able exactly to define it—would be approached.

This line of argument contains many elements of truth. The most rigid moralist will admit, even though he may insist that questions of right and wrong are indeed matters of objective and discernible truth, that interests tend to be moralized in proportion as they become universalized, that in so far as an individual, whether it be a single person or a community, is capable of allowing his personal motives to be transcended by those of a concrete order of which he forms but a part, he lifts himself on to a higher moral plane. For this very reason it will be conceded by most thinkers that the moral law and the laws of life, regarded as normative in the sense above indicated, are not contradictory, and that the former may be regarded as the latter transcended to embrace a universal view.

So far so good. And we may neglect to examine the question as to whether sovereignty—ultimate human authority—must necessarily reflect the general will, because the question has now been placed beyond dispute by the most authoritative latter-day sociologists. It does *not* necessarily reflect nor arise out of the general will, except in a very special sense which will be explained later. The fact is there are innumerable kinds of sovereignty; and sovereignty arises in innumerable ways. It is the task of the historian, in diagnosing a given political situation, to pronounce judgment as to where exactly for a given community at a given moment sovereignty actually resides. And it is similarly the task of the historian to inform us how, case by case, a given sovereignty has arisen. It may arise, for instance, through natural status, as in the case of the father of a family unit, and thence develop into a patriarchal system. Or—to give another example (the examples could be multiplied indefinitely)—it may arise through conflict, resulting in some system of balanced powers through compromise or in the triumph of one party over another, the party (be it understood) being either an individual or a caste or a class or a group holding certain ideals or a community. Or, again, it may arise through the working of a system of constitutional laws or of customs having the force of law, originating in some previous more arbitrary system. The theory that sovereignty primarily originated by social contract between a number of lone, isolated individuals is as dead as mutton; though it may be presumed that when the State first arose, there existed a large measure of implicit consent among its members in favour of the original authority—the truth being that authority normally rests at once upon a measure of consent and a measure of force. For that matter, too, there may be some historical, isolated cases, when a super-authority has been created by deliberate arrangement between a number of independent sovereigns, forming thereby a new composite type of sovereignty. The League of Nations might, for example, be regarded as an attempt to create a super-national authority by some such arrangement. Sovereignty, accordingly, need not necessarily be a manifestation of the general will, in the usual meaning of the term, even though it may be a fact that a sovereign who disregards any strong manifestation of the general will (especially should such manifestation be symptomatic of a grave pathological situation with respect to the body politic) will be risking the digging of his own grave—just as the sovereign mind of a human being may bow, without abdicating its sovereignty, before the imperative need of the body undergoing an operation, however much such a decision may go against the grain, rather than risk death.

The important point to note in this connection is that sovereignty in some form is a condition of all societies. There is no society without its governing authority. If a given governing authority—the sovereign power *de jure*, for instance, of a given community—fails to assert itself, it means that it is already sharing the sovereign power with one (or more) other self-constituted *de facto* authority. In fact no *de jure* authority is really absolute. There is always in every State some kind of balance of powers, sharing between them—on occasion, at any rate—the real supreme authority. As I have already stated, authority normally rests at once on a measure of consent and on a measure of force. Fundamentally it is a question of vitality. If a given sovereign power fails to adapt itself to the requirements of changing social, political or economic conditions—if it does not, in other words, demonstrate its vitality by its adaptability—or, alternatively, if it fails to dominate its environment, its authority will in the long run inevitably pass, either by violence or gradual decay, elsewhere. If violence is to be avoided, it is well to devise a relatively flexible constitution; but, on the other hand, if a constitution be too flexible, it will mean that the centre of gravity of the sovereign power will be constantly shifting—and this in turn will mean that the ship of State will be allowed for all practical purposes to drift. Hence the devising of a constitution is a matter of very great practical importance—and of course the requirements of one community may differ very widely from those of another. But, although there may be a number of general practical principles which experience may strongly recommend for the framing of all constitutions, there is no absolute rule arising out of the inherent nature of sovereignty—*e.g.*, that sovereignty is legitimately the expression of the general will, from which alone it is derived, and that any interference with such expression is consequently illegitimate.

The fact, however, that sovereignty need not necessarily reside in or be derived from the general will, does not affect the plea of those who argue that it ought to. The assumption that we have been examining maintains that it ought to. Let us see then to what extent it can. What is the general will?

Now my task here is to expound fascism; and so I shall give to these questions, for the benefit of the reader, the fascist answers. It will be for him to judge whether they are valid. I shall then proceed to point out the consequences of accepting the fascist thesis.

The general will, in the usual meaning of the term, regarded as a phenomenal fact without reference to any basic theory, can be no more and no less than the life instinct of the herd, a reflection of its vital solidarity. But this is not apparently a rational force at all. It operates more or less strongly in proportion to the degree of a society's cohesion and sense of unity; and it also operates especially strongly in proportion to the imminence and evidence of danger; but normally it is a relatively dormant force, negative rather than positive, so that in the absence of any acute crisis it is very feebly manifested, if at all. In the presence of any acute crises, on the other hand, it tends to emerge, clamouring for a remedy, pointing very often to a particular remedy with an almost uncanny wisdom. In such cases its demands are often irresistible. Often, too, they are respectable; but because it is irrational, relatively blind and ignorant, it is nevertheless subject to error, to panic, to undue exaltation, to indulgence in ferocious violence; and sometimes it points the way, under the stimulus of fear or exasperation, to what would prove in effect to be irretrievable disaster. The fact that it is a thing to be reckoned with is a proof of the organic character of society, being the instinct for the preservation of life such as all live organisms possess; but it is an animal instinct, which, in so far as it can be supplanted by reason, should be largely discounted. And since it is strong in proportion to a society's cohesion, it must be reckoned as pre-eminently selfish. Thus the lack of cohesion in that society which we call humanity, causes it to be practically inoperative as a general human force. Similarly it is relatively inoperative as a force representing the various branches of the human race, although probably it would emerge, say, as a

European force in the face of a truly imminent and evident "yellow peril." It becomes only relatively strong as representing nations and still more national States—and it places therefore a premium on particularist national interests. It is naturally predatory. And, again, since it is relatively dormant in the absence of any acute crisis, it is very little use as a life preserver against slow insidious internal dangers, such as the harmful biological effects of over-urbanization or the demoralizing social conditions of a system producing a grossly uneven distribution of wealth. Moreover, it can only manifest itself in the form of a general psychological excitement, leading to spontaneous action in the form of monster agitations, which may have ugly and violent issues unless firmly met.

That, in a nutshell, is what fascism designates as the only meaning that can be properly attributed to the term "general will," except the very special meaning which it might be proposed to give it and is equivalent to something quite different from any of its ordinary meanings, as we shall subsequently point out. Granted that much, for the moment it is obviously not the same thing as organized public opinion, rationally voiced; because, apart from the fact that organized public opinion is seldom in practice anything more than the organized opinion of a sectional interest, the *sum of the individual wills of the members of a community is never the same thing, even if unanimous, as the general will*, for the same reason that the sum of individual interests of the members of a community does not amount to the general interest.

Now, at first sight, the assertion that the sum of the individual wills of a community is never the same thing as the general will, *even if unanimous*, appears flatly contrary to the truth; but on closer examination it can be shown that it is not so. The fact that it does indeed seem, at first sight, to be contrary to the truth affords the explanation why it has been so easily assumed that it is possible to found the government of a community on the general will. It appeared to present an easy arithmetical problem—a matter of counting heads. That the sum of individual wills amounted to the same thing as the general will constituted the principle according to which government by majority came to be considered the ideal form of government; for, although it was recognized that the will of a majority was not quite the same thing as the general will, it was taken for granted that it was an approximation to it in strict proportion to the degree in which the majority approached unanimity; and since unanimity was in practice difficult to obtain, majority rule was sanctioned as a practical proximate solution, which nobody possessed of common sense would wish to cavil at. For all intents and purposes it appears to correspond with the ideal in view. Various efforts have been made to produce arithmetical solutions which claim to render the results by counting heads more and more proximate to the general will, such as proportional representation, the referendum and initiative; and many of these more ingenious systems have been tried with relative success. But one and all are based on the fallacious assumption that the sum of individual wills represents the general will. Whether in given circumstances any of these systems produce commendable governments or the reverse is beside the point. The point is, according to the widely accepted idea under examination, that in the absence of any clearly objective criterion by which the community's good may be defined and aimed at, the general will, which can at least have no other desire than to promote the general interest, remains the only practical guide to progress; and that some form of majority rule, in the face of the practical impossibility of obtaining unanimous decisions, remains the only near approach to rule by the general will.

In the days of *laissez-faire* (when the ideas of the Manchester School were widely accepted) it was assumed by economists that the sum of individual interests pursued in conditions of the maximum economic liberty would amount to the general interest. But very soon in view of the many intolerable consequences of putting this theory into practice, economists began to discover that there existed a fallacy somewhere. Similarly as the suffrage has been extended, with a view to bringing government nearer to the general will, political scientists as well as the practical man of common sense began to observe that the results appeared to belie the purpose more and more. At first it was supposed that the contradictory results were merely due to lack of knowledge. Instruct the people better and the contradictory results will disappear—that became the cry. Gradually, however, people began to wake to the fact that there was some equivocation somewhere. Education in the sense of a wider knowledge of public affairs and of the various issues and repercussions involved in legislation was seen to be a double-edged sword: it placed the predominantly selfish in a better position to pursue their selfish aims than before, however much it placed the predominantly unselfish in a better position to pursue unselfish aims. And unfortunately the predominantly selfish remained the overwhelming majority. Only such education as was capable of developing the unselfish, disinterested side of human nature at the expense of the selfish, interested side, it began to be seen, would be of any avail. The success of the whole system was therefore seen to depend not merely on greater knowledge but on at least greater patriotism and—certainly as far as international relations were concerned—on some still higher motive. In fact a deeper religious sense was seen to be required, something capable of transcending patriotism—in other words, a higher moral purpose. Indeed the general will was seen to mean nothing at all except in the sense explained above (*e.g.* the herd instinct) *unless it were taken to mean no more nor less than a high standard of morality.* A vote cast was always a selfish vote except in so far as the voter possessed a sufficiently high moral sense to compel him to vote disinterested. Only the truly disinterested votes can thus be said to point to the *general will, because only the disinterested votes represent the social side of human nature.*

This is the meaning, alluded to above, which fascism might be prepared to give to the term "general will" (and in this sense to bow down before the general will), if it did not consider that it was to better purpose to substitute for the term "general will" the term "moral law"; for by doing so all equivocation is removed. The *vox Dei* is not thereby confused with the *vox populi*.

But to pursue our argument: The individualist never represents more than the individualist: person, class or nation. Interested voting, even if the results all go one way, simply means that the personal interests of an aggregate of individuals happen to lie in that direction. The collective interests might nevertheless lie in the opposite direction. You cannot argue from the particular to the general. It might, for example, very easily be true that in a given community the interest of each married couple, taken singly, would be to limit their family to two or three children. But statistics prove that as long as that happened the race would decline in numbers until it disappeared altogether. Or, again, if the aggregate of individuals composing a community are for one reason or another personally interested in a law permitting public gambling, and if they vote in favour of such a law because it is their personal interest to do so, the law, good or bad, will not have been passed because it was the general will, representing the collective interest, that it should pass, but because it was the will of a heterogeneous number of individuals each aiming at his purely personal advantage and relatively neglectful of the fact that the span of his life and of those he loves covers only a tiny portion of the life of his community, made up of an indefinite series of generations. The general will—the collective will—to conclude, is a question of motive and not a question of counting votes irrespective of motives; and since it is impossible to control a voter's motives, it is impossible to estimate to what extent the results of an election or of a referendum reflect the general will; or to give any value to the results with respect to the general interest. It is an operation entirely beside the point at issue; and if that be so, away goes the whole case for majority government, unless it can be justified on entirely different grounds, namely, as a mere piece of machinery calculated to result in a more efficient, a wiser and more moral government than any alternative piece of machinery that may be suggested.

This, however, brings us back to our starting-point: the question of morality mainly—the question of wisdom and efficiency in a second degree—becomes the whole and vital question. If the general will cannot be gauged by votes, as long as human nature remains as it is with its selfish interests (individual, class, national, etc.) necessarily predominant; if right and wrong are not matters of objective and discernible truth, the destiny of societies must be left in the keeping of the blind forces of nature and of warring interests and opinions. There can be no rational progress.

The whole machinery, in fact, of modern democratic governments based on an individualistically organized system of elections, despite the admirable intentions of its inventors, turns out to be little more than an admirably adapted piece of machinery by which conflicting interests and opinions may fight each other without bloodshed. The State, necessarily agnostic in the presence of this boxing match between its members, has no other task but to hold the ring and to see fair play—the limit to its agnosticism determining the rules being the degree of unanimity with regard to questions of right and wrong which happens to prevail over a given period and is voiced by organized public opinion and reflected in the laws of the land, a standard tending necessarily to shift from generation to generation, in that in such circumstances it tends to become dependent in the long run entirely on the fashion set by the actions and reactions of the successively prevailing sections, opinions and interests.

Government, accordingly, ceases to be identified with the State, which becomes merely a land of passive common denominator of opinion, but becomes an element actively concerned with the promotion of particularist—in modern conditions, mainly class—interests. Thus only two checks on tyranny exist: the passive but fluctuating common denominator of opinion represented in the State and the balance of power between the various contending egoisms. Where minorities remain strong a certain tolerable equilibrium may result which prevents the grosser forms of tyranny. But class warfare becomes the order of the day and class domination the necessary consequence of any breach in the balance of power, resulting in a tyranny precariously mitigated only by such consensus of active opinion as there happens to be as the result of national traditions and common elements of education and religion among the members of the community. An exactly similar situation is created in the international field. It becomes impossible to tell where the world may drift. Standing above the *mêlée* one would have nothing left to hope for than that the doctrine of inevitable progress were true, although it would be impossible to define what progress is. The religion of inevitable progress indeed, in favour of which—to say the best for it—there is only very slender scientific evidence, becomes under the above dispensation the very last refuge of the optimist, where all else is despair and where everything appears a chaos. The more we look at it in fact, the more untenable appears the whole assumption that we have been examining. Yet unless we can acknowledge that right and wrong involve moral values of universal validity, there is no escape from it.

Fascism takes the bull by the horns and plumps straight for this solution as the only possible one. It is part and parcel of its general rejection of materialism and of its particular aim to check the excessive individualism of the post-Renaissance period. Moreover the error, which it rejects, it claims is due to the confusion of mind resulting from the tyranny which the habit of abstract thought has extended over the minds of men during recent generations. It is, *in fine*, a solution entirely in accordance with the fascist *Weltanschauung*.

Now fascism would not deny that there are many forces, material forces, influencing the destinies of societies over which we have no control. But it would insist that to a large extent we *can* control our destiny, especially nowadays that the progress of scientific knowledge has rendered man relatively more master of the forces of nature. And this view is supported by sociology. Nor would fascism deny that a struggle of interests between individuals, classes and nations is a common fact; but it insists that there exists a universal moral law which, even though in practice it may often be overridden by the egoism of individuals, classes and nations, remains a constant and universal check on egoism—and therefore on tyranny at home and oppression abroad—through the influence of conscience—considered as the still small voice of God and not as the mere prompting of a herd instinct. It is claimed, however, that, although this voice of conscience is a constant force operating in favour of good government, it may become relatively atrophied by a habitual disregard of it or by acquiescence in the notion that it has nothing in it of the divine, or by rationalistic habits of thought resulting in the weakening of our practical intuitive judgments, or by a system of government which is designed to allow those opinions and interests to prevail which happen to be the stronger irrespective of the objective moral value represented by them.

Whereas, therefore, a belief in the subjective nature of right and wrong on the one hand, and, on the other, a belief in the view that the State cannot be other than the fluctuating resultant of various interests and opinions (since there are no means of determining the general will with respect to general interests and of therefore devising a system tending automatically to more disinterested and so to actually higher moral decisions), place our collective life at the mercy of blind force against which there can be no remedy and preclude all rational progress, a belief in the objective nature of right and wrong provides at least a possible remedy; for, however difficult it may be to prevent in practice the influence and triumph of individual egoisms, we are thereby at least driven to consider the whole question of State action and of the State's constitution from the standpoint of what may be judged likely to promote the best individual and collective life. We shall be driven to devise measures freely, without allowing, ourselves to be hypnotized *a priori* by the principle of popular sovereignty, whereby government may tend to become the prerogative of a class of *optimi*, of those persons whose egoisms are habitually overridden by their social sense, by a well-informed patriotism, by a high moral purpose, capable of transcending their patriotism, and of those persons possessing other important qualifications for government, namely, knowledge and experience of sociological and economic law's, a sense of reality and of tradition, etc. Fascism, in other words, accepts the principle of government by an aristocracy in the sense of an *élite* and makes this its aim, in contrast to the liberal principle of popular sovereignty. Similarly it rejects the idea of State agnosticism and of government by party; and insists that the whole State be identified with the active principle of government, which must consequently be an authoritative government deriving its authority from the moral law. To leave things to work themselves out by the interplay of good, bad or indifferent forces, whatever the result may be, represents to the fascist a positively shocking doctrine—a grossly immoral attitude.

In rejecting, however, the idea of popular sovereignty, fascism would not on that account necessarily exclude the people from participating in the sovereign power. The right to participate in the sovereign power should depend, so it insists, on the degree in which individuals fit themselves to participate in it by developing their moral and social sense of responsibility and other qualities. Liberty is not merely the absence of checks, still less an absolute right to live one's own life without unduly interfering with the similar right of one's neighbour, but the positive result of a conquest of self and evil. Liberty, in the absolute sense is, in the words of St. Paul, nothing more nor less than freedom from the bondage of sin. It is invariably the complement of law, whether it be moral law or civil law, the reverse side of the same medal. Hence concrete liberties may be conceded by the State, generally speaking, in proportion to the efficacy of the moral law reigning in the hearts of the people and in proportion to their knowledge of circumstances—particularly speaking, in relation to varying external conditions. As Mussolini has said: There is a liberty for times of war, another for times of peace; a liberty for times of revolution, another for normal times; a liberty for times of prosperity, another for times of stringency.

The people accordingly may participate in the sovereignty, may conquer the right to do so in proportion only as they fit themselves to do so. But there will always be some persons better fitted to govern than others and to these should be reserved proportionately the posts of greater responsibility and power. Aristocracy, with one wide alley open for new elements to stream continually upwards and another by which unworthy elements may be expelled, becomes thus the necessary ideal of government, organized in the form of a hierarchy of power and responsibility in accordance until merit, culminating in one supreme authority, with investiture from above downwards (not upwards from below; for the latter would mean selection by the less responsible elements).

This does not imply dictatorship in the sense of the personal rule of one man; on the contrary, though it implies a strict and firm system of authority, it implies a balance of power, which is shared by many in different degrees. In a nation-State, having strong traditions rooted in the people, where there exists too a high sense of moral and social responsibility, all may participate, but each in different degrees, according to the contribution he is able to make by virtue of his physical, intellectual and moral qualities to the general good. There can never be any equality in virtues, though it may be possible to attain a certain "equality of opportunity" as the phrase goes, or even a certain equality of wealth. Indeed, the fascist watchword, "Order, Discipline and Authority," seems to embody a principle having a strict relation to the necessary facts of life.

A government, moreover, founded on this principle, would, indeed, be one strictly in accordance with Roman tradition, and the government of the Roman Church affords a perfect example of such a government in being. Nor should it be beyond the powers of human ingenuity to devise a system of civil government which would correspond to this idea and tend to throw up in effect a genuine aristocracy of merit, to which better than to any other body we could leave our destiny. This is precisely what fascism is attempting to do. It is attempting likewise to reconstruct society in a manner that will tend to canalize egoistic endeavour in directions which will in effect tend to serve the collective interests; and to this end it is devising a system by which the State is built up on the basis of corporative life, working from the lower form of corporative life to the higher: the family, the trade union, the industrial corporation, the national corporative council, on the one hand, and, on the other, the communal, the provincial, the State administration—the first series integrated with the second, and the whole cemented by a powerful executive, invested with power from above, but recruited from all classes of the population. There is no reason why such a system should not succeed or should become unduly rigid. The constitution of the Roman Church has avoided the latter danger; and its success is as remarkable as its stability.

At the same time, fascism is making every effort to educate the people, not merely with a view to more widely diffused knowledge, but more particularly with the view to the formation of character, the training of intuitive judgment (hitherto widely neglected) and the development of a civic and moral sense. It sets itself definitely to encourage a conscious patriotism on the one hand and religion on the other, as the main rational foundations of civic and moral activities. It aims not merely at being a negative force having the object of preventing crime and the undue interference by one individual with the liberty of another, but at being a positive force with the object of promoting virtue. Crime it regards as any action calculated to harm the collective interests or the authority of the moral law. Hence the necessity of an authoritative government, intolerant of any form of licence, which is the liberty to do wrong. For intolerance of wrong-doing entails no loss of liberty. On the contrary, it is the guarantee of true liberty. There should be no theoretical limits to such intolerance, however great the practical limits may be, for the contingent circumstances of life are such that we are often forced to make a choice of evils, or to move slowly towards our ideals in the face of ignorance and prejudice.

Finally, authoritative government depends on leadership by competent persons. Hence, again, the necessity of government by an *élite*. The right to lay down the law on any subject exists properly only as the result of a conquest over self and of the subject-matter. So the answer to the question: "Who is to decide what is right and wrong?" is: "the competent authority." We should see to it accordingly that our State constitutions tend to select for us leaders who are competent statesmen, one of whose needed qualities is firmness of character, coupled with a refined knowledge of what constitutes good.

To conclude: fascism refuses to admit that the moral law is not an objective reality, recognizable in the heart of all but the most hardened sinner, capable of being made more and more clearly recognizable by positively concerted measures to that end, and, parallel-wise, capable of being more and better applied by a selected competent authority. It proclaims God, *in fine*, as the supreme sovereign, and the State as God's temporal vicar, responsible to God for the people's good government. This is the meaning of the fascist ethical State, which is accordingly also the authoritative and unitary State, with a definite, indivisible ethical purpose and a definite ethical justification.

THE ETHICAL STATE

II. CHURCH AND STATE

For the benefit of the reader who may have found the last chapter rather difficult reading, we may sum up the conclusions arrived at as follows: Sovereignty is implicit in the very idea of society; but it arises in various ways and is not necessarily the reflexion of the general will of a community. The general will itself must either be regarded as no more than the life instinct of the herd, that is, an entirely irrational force; and in this case, when it is manifested—though sometimes it may be irresistible and sometimes uncannily wise—it can have no right to dictate the course of events and should often be firmly resisted by the government in the interests of the community. Or, alternatively, the general will has no meaning unless it be regarded as being the equivalent of a completely disinterested manifestation of organized public opinion, that is, the will of an aggregate of individuals who have allowed their individual egoisms to be entirely transcended by their patriotic, humanitarian or religious—in other words, their social or universal selves; and since on the basis of a voting system it is impossible to tell whether the resulting expression of public opinion is or is not genuinely disinterested in the above sense, majority government or even the unanimous opinion of the whole adult population of a community, tested by means of a referendum, is not only no sure indication of the general will but, given that the force of particularist interests is, in the aggregate, almost invariably predominant, may be regarded with practical certainty as corresponding to nothing of the kind. The general will, therefore, in so far as it should be regarded as the basis on which government should rest, must either be discarded altogether or taken to mean no more than an approximate equivalent to the moral law, which every man and woman may read with at least a rough and ready accuracy by simply examining his or her conscience. And since the only alternative would be to acquiesce in the notion that the destiny of human society was completely in the hands of the blind forces of nature beyond all human control or else of conflicting individual interests and opinions, on which no objective valuation can be placed, each striving for mastery in an utterly amoral world, it is reasonable to presuppose that questions of right and wrong are indeed matters of objective and discernible truth, that goodness is the fundamental norm for all action, whether individual or collective, that tyranny means merely the triumph of evil, that liberty is no more than freedom from the bondage of sin (and is therefore the complement, the reverse side of the medal of law), that government ought to be in the hands of the best available people and therefore of a selected competent authority in order to ensure that actions should follow precept, and that in considering the merits of any proposed system of government the fundamental criteria are the degree in which authority is exercised by a strong executive composed of the best available people and the degree in which society is organized so as to provide a constitution which is neither too flexible nor too rigid, sufficiently broadly based to allow the people at large to exercise their moral right to participate in the government of their community in proportion to their social and intellectual capacities and, above all, to their moral sense of responsibility. For this reason, since there is no equality of capacities, moral, intellectual or physical, the ideal form of government is necessarily a hierarchy of authority, capable of enforcing what is right with due prudence, having regard to manifold contingent circumstances and to the irreducible facts of reality, which can be given a scientific demonstration in the form of natural, sociological and economic laws. Government, in other words, is an art, which should be reserved for statesmen—that is, to persons representative of their community's traditions and possessing a highly developed æsthetic sensibility with respect to this particular form of art, which like every other form of art requires intuitive judgment arriving at synthetic results—a fusion of the ideal and a sense of reality. Hence the task of education, above all, patriotic, æsthetic and religious, becomes a task of government of prime necessity, since together with the special task of devising an appropriate constitutional system it constitutes the major means of ensuring statesmanlike government, besides being the condition of any broadening of the basis of government and further social integration.

Government, finally, has not only the right but the positive duty, in accordance with such lights as it possesses, to aim at stamping out—even if prudence dictates that the process should be gradual—by the sanction of its laws every form of activity which is anti-social, anti-patriotic, anti-moral and anti-religious.

That, *in fine*, is the fundamental standpoint of fascism with regard to the State—a standpoint which gives the State a definite and objective ethical purpose and justification. God once more, as in the Middle Ages, is recognized as the supreme sovereign.

Granted that this standpoint is correct, the practical difficulties militating against the realization of the above principles will of course always remain. Perfection is not attainable in this world; but provided we adopt the right principles we can strive within the limitations which nature and peccable human nature impose to attain relatively good results. Although class competition and other forms of rival egoisms can never be altogether done away with, something can be done to canalize them into channels of social utility. Many forms of egoism are at bottom no more than manifestations of vitality. Methods of suppression should accordingly often and as far as possible be substituted by methods of sublimation. To this end fascism is carrying out in Italy its great economic and social experiment of the corporative organization of society, to which we have already alluded, which we shall describe in somewhat greater detail in a further chapter. Fascism in any case refuses to admit that our egoisms can be usefully made the very basis of a governmental system. Hence it repudiates both party government and any form of individualistically organized electoral system, issuing in the sovereign power. In so far as such a system might preserve a place in a constitution, it must be limited to providing an organ of opinion or of technical and constructive criticism. It must not pretend to be more than a constitutional check on an independently constituted executive composed of persons forming a carefully selected *élite*.

Before dealing, however, with the constitutional aspects of fascism, a chapter must be devoted to its economic principles. But first of all it is proposed to deal with another important question—because of its close connection with the fascist idea of the ethical State outlined in the preceding chapter—namely, the relation of the State to any particular form of religion.

Fascism claims complete autonomy for the State, that is to say, the State must shoulder the whole of its own moral responsibilities *in the application of the moral law to contingent circumstances*. No State in this field can be dictated to by an outside body, even though that outside body may represent in fact, as the Catholic Church claims to represent, a supernatural authority and an infallible guide in questions of religious and moral doctrine. At the same time fascism recognizes the independence of the Catholic Church (and, for that matter, that of any organized teaching Church) and consequently the right of the latter to take such measures as it deems fit to safeguard its interests. If therefore between two such independent bodies, Church and State, opinions differ on some point or points involving the application of the moral law to contingent circumstances, the question must be fought out. Since, however, a fascist State starts from the same basis as do the teaching Churches, namely, by the recognition of the moral law as the supreme law, there is every hope, when differences arise, of their being capable of settlement after amicable discussion. Agreement, after all, is difficult only between persons accepting differing bases for discussion. Questions of principle are then involved. But between fascism and the teaching Churches, there are no fundamental differences in principle.

In claiming this autonomy for the State, fascism appeals to the fact that the State is an organism composed of successive generations of human beings sharing common traditions, an organism which can be observed in history to possess an autonomous life of its own, with certain natural rights corresponding to those of single individuals and of families. It has the natural right to preserve its life and build up its vigour. For this reason it has the positive duty to maintain its authority among its members, to exact sacrifices from its members for the sake of the common good, to provide a patriotic and civic education for its citizens, to put down by all the means in its power forces of disruption, the preaching of doctrines which set one class against another, *in fine*, as we have observed, all anti-social, anti-patriotic, anti-moral, anti-religious activities. It has the duty to observe to the best of its ability the sociological laws of conservation, integration and growth, which not only point to the above duties but to many others, as for example the maintenance of its national traditions corresponding to its racial experiences. Traditions of course can grow and modify, but cannot be brusquely violated without endangering the health and cohesion of the body politic. The limitations of its natural rights may accordingly be said to be, on the one hand, natural morals and natural religion, and, on the other, the natural rights of individuals and of families, aiming respectively at their own vital conservation and interior spiritual freedom, within the bounds again set by natural morals and natural religion, as well as by social and civic obligations. Within the limitations which the above principles lay down and suggest, however, the State must be the judge according to such lights as it possesses. If it is not its own judge, it has no alternative but to abdicate its authority

to the body that is. Were this other body the Catholic Church—
to take a concrete case—it would mean setting up a theocracy
or else identifying the State with a particular religion to such an
extent that the logical conclusion would be, if not the coercion
of all its members to conform with a particular religion, at least
the identification of citizenship with the members of a particular
religion and the absolute prevention of any form of propaganda
by other religions. Such measures, however, would of course
tend towards a violation of individual natural rights and would
be the last thing the Catholic Church itself would desire, because
the Catholic Church itself only values a person's religion in so
far as his religion depends on convictions freely formed, and
because it would bar the Church itself from claiming any right
to develop its missions and schools in countries which happen
not to be Catholic.

Though I stand to be corrected, there is nothing as far as I
know incompatible with Catholic doctrine or Catholic claims in
this principle of State autonomy representing the fascist standpoint, as above explained—provided it be read as a set of general principles applicable to all States indiscriminately, i.e., as
including non-Catholic States.

To be sure, the Catholic Church claims more than is here
admitted in the absolute sense, or, as a practical proposition, in
relation to ideal conditions. Very briefly stated, her absolute
claims may be summarized as follows: She is the guardian of
morality and hence claims the right to decide whether any civil
law is harmful to the spiritual interests of citizens and to oblige
the State to abrogate any spiritually harmful laws or to amend
them. She claims accordingly that the Church *qua* Church is not
subject to the State, but that the State is subject to the Church in
all spiritual matters and in temporal matters as far as these affect
spiritual interests. On the other hand she recognizes that the
State is not subject to the Church in purely temporal matters,
while, as far as non-Catholic States are concerned, she is content
to limit her claims to this: that Catholics be not hindered in the
practice of their religion.

Now the practical difficulties with reference to these absolute claims are concerned with the debatable territory of what constitutes spiritual interests affected by temporal matters and with what exactly is meant by Catholic and non-Catholic States. With regard to the latter point it might be said that it is quite obvious that certain States are Catholic and certain other States non-Catholic. Italy, Bavaria, Poland, Spain, the Dominion of Ireland, might be said to be quite obviously Catholic States— Japan, Afghanistan, Greece, England, to be non-Catholic States. But what of France? France is Catholic by tradition and may be said to possess at least a large nominally Catholic majority. But a considerable proportion of this Catholic majority is non-practising, and power is largely in the hands of a definitely anti-Catholic minority. Again, there are States like Holland where the Catholic minority is so large that no Dutch government is in a position to disregard its claims. And even in obviously Catholic countries like Italy, although the Protestant and Jewish elements are weak, there exists a large body of modernists and a larger body still of non-practising Catholics. The ideal conditions from the Church standpoint may therefore, practically speaking, be considered inexistent.

In these circumstances the fascist standpoint emerges as one in which the Catholic Church is not unprepared to acquiesce. Fascism insists, as we have seen, that the State is bound in the first place as a minimum obligation to protect and promote natural morals and natural religion. By natural morals is usually meant the principles concerning good action which can be known by reason alone (i.e., abstracting from revelation). Similarly, by natural religion is meant a system of speculative principles about God and His attributes known by reason alone, abstracting also from revelation. Fascism is accordingly concerned to suppress, within the limits set by prudence, all conduct and religion which are incompatible with reason. This corresponds with the absolutely irreducible claims of the Catholic Church. Secondly, fascism sets a premium on religious instruction and is therefore in a position to come to an arrangement with the Church with regard to farther claims; and, as between one autonomous body and the other, to cut the Gordian knot involving the debatable territory outlined above, by means of a *concordat*, which will be all the more favourable to the Catholic Church in proportion to the catholicity of the State implementing the agreement. That is the manner in which fascism, in all good faith, proposes to deal with this thorny question; and as far as fascist Italy is concerned the question has been already amicably settled along these lines. Italy, as a predominantly Catholic State, has, moreover, reinstated the Catholic religion as the State religion and has shown herself prepared, in accordance with the terms of the *concordat* concluded in 1929 between herself and the Holy See, to carry out the logical implications of this reinstatement.

I have deliberately chosen to discuss this question in relation to the claims of the Catholic Church partly because fascism in Italy, as a predominantly Catholic country, has been forced to face it squarely, partly because, in asserting her claims, the Catholic Church is asserting them also on behalf of every other religion the doctrines of which do not run counter to natural morals and natural religion. This point is well illustrated by the Catholic standpoint with regard to education. The Catholic Church insists that the rights of parents should be scrupulously respected. Thus if the majority of a country is Catholic, the Church insists that the State would be violating the natural rights of parents if it did not provide for the teaching of the Catholic religion in those schools frequented by the children of Catholic parents—nay more, that such schools should definitely reflect a Catholic atmosphere. Where, as in Italy, the vast majority of the people are Catholic, this should properly mean that the State schools should be definitely Catholic schools. But this, though it may mean in practice that in certain parts of the country insignificant denominational minorities must necessarily be sacrificed, does not mean that in districts where Protestants constitute the majority, Protestant schools should not be State-provided or that Protestants and Jews should be prevented from building and maintaining their own schools wherever they need them and that these schools should, provided they maintain a sufficiently high standard of instruction and conform in other respects to the State's requirements, be placed on a footing of equality with respect to examinations, diplomas, etc., with the State schools. The parents' rights in these matters are sacrosanct; and in a country where various religious denominations flourish in large numbers, all should be treated on a footing of equality with respect to State aid. This is the Catholic claim and it corresponds with what is right and just; and it is entirely endorsed by fascism.

Fascism accordingly, in placing the moral law above the State, clearly repudiates that "deification" of the State advocated by certain forms of nationalism. At the same time, while it admits the independence and autonomy of the organized Churches and respects with a due sense of reality the latter's claim to possess the right of taking whatever measures that may seem fit to defend their interests, whenever these interests appear to be threatened, it upholds the principle of the State's autonomy and independence respecting the application of the moral law to contingent circumstances, and seeks to settle any differences of opinion arising out of its claim to autonomy and independence *vis-à-vis* the equally autonomous and independent organized Churches by means of some reciprocally satisfactory and amicable agreement in the shape of a *concordat*. The importance which it attaches, moreover, to religious education would lead it to proclaim a particular religion, wherever a particular religion might be said to occupy a predominant position in a State or might be said to be a veritable moulding influence in the formation of national traditions, as the State religion and to abide logically by the consequences, so that every act of the State may be given a pronouncedly religious aspect. It repudiates every form of agnosticism and would only be inclined to take up a neutral attitude, as distinguished from an agnostic attitude, with respect to organized religion in the event of the religion or the religious traditions of the country happening to be divided or diversely distributed. This defines the fascist attitude towards religion in marked contrast to that adopted by what might be called doctrinaire liberalism.

CHAPTER VI

THE ECONOMIC PRINCIPLES OF FASCISM

PARALLEL to the political outlook of doctrinaire liberalism, to which we have shown fascism to be so strongly opposed, there is the modern economic system which often goes by the name of capitalism—an unfortunate label (for which Karl Marx is chiefly responsible) since it suggests that those who are opposed to the system would wish to abolish capital altogether, or at least private capital. It is true that socialism advocates the abolition of *private* capital; but nobody in his senses, socialist, communist or anarchist, has ever seriously proposed that capital itself should be abolished; and, on the other hand, it is quite easy to be radically opposed to the modern economic system without wishing to abolish private capital. Fascism is a case in point. Fascism is radically opposed to the drift of phenomena which characterizes the modern economic system; but is far from being opposed to the retention of capital in private hands. It is accordingly opposed both to capitalism and to socialism. It agrees with socialism in the latter's apparent repudiation of capitalism and offers an alternative remedy. It accuses socialism, moreover, of not really offering a remedy at all, but only the final consummation of capitalism itself. But it sees in socialism—in the complete nationalization and municipalization of capital—a purely theoretical situation only, which can never be actually reached, the reverse side of the same medal as the doctrine of *laissez-faire*, advocated by the Manchester School—an equally purely theoretical situation, which, in spite of the vogue it once enjoyed in the class-room, never was reached and never could be reached. Both doctrines issue from the same type of mentality: both, fascism would say, are the child of excessive individualism, of the rejection of a dualistic and transcendental view of the universe, of the habit of abstract ratiocination—of rationalism and materialism. And the actual economic system—capitalism—is merely the practical situation lying between the two extreme theoretical situations of *laissez-faire* and socialism. Capitalism has always been a little more or a little less of both—or, rather, it has moved from a little more of *laissez-faire* and a little less of socialism to a little more of socialism and a little less of *laissez-faire*. It will probably move still further away from *laissez-faire* towards socialism; but it can never reach socialism. And there is nobody who proves this so conclusively as the socialist Bernard Shaw himself, in his *Intelligent Woman's Guide to Socialism*. So illuminating, indeed, have I found this book as a side-light on the economics of fascism that I have included it in the short bibliography[91] at the end of this volume.

As a general denunciation of the evils of capitalism, for which word Shaw proposes to substitute the more suggestive and more appropriate word "proletarianism," it is unrivalled in the English tongue; and with this denunciation fascists will be found to be in more or less complete agreement. Shaw then goes on to point out that socialism (meaning nationalized and municipalized services and an equalization of money incomes) is already within our midst, a quite indispensable contribution to modern social conditions. With this point fascism also entirely agrees. Capitalism, it would say, is necessarily socialistic—in fact tends necessarily towards socialism as itself develops: besides, if it were not socialistic, it would operate under conditions of pure *laissez-faire*, which is not only practically impossible but is a doctrine already theoretically bankrupt. The sum of individual interests operating in the widest possible con-

---

[91] Not included in this edition. [Editor's note]

ditions of economic liberty does not make up the collective interests. Few economists will dispute that fact nowadays. Moreover, in proportion as *laissez-faire* was approached in Great Britain at the commencement of the Victorian era, it resulted in such terrible abuses that the public conscience was aroused and set the country marching ever since in the opposite direction.

The opposite direction of socialism, however, leads on towards a light which is like a will o' the wisp. It has no real consistency and is for ever beyond our reach. Shaw proves this conclusively. Not only does he make exceptions for certain classes of work (his own, for instance) which lie beyond the net of the nationalizer, but he proves that either society will be brought down in ruins with a crash and cruelty such as no man of good will would ever wish to contemplate, or the process of nationalization and municipalization of capital must be so slow as to defeat any possible estimate of when it would be complete: a matter in any case of generations and generations—so far ahead as to leave the vision of the socialist's new heaven and new earth an altogether dim and nebulous imagining.

Meanwhile capitalism would continue to thrive, only in a form a little closer to the ideal of socialism. The State and municipality would be a larger employer of labour. The number of the proletariat would be in no way diminished. On the contrary, it would be increased. The number of owners of capital, who were at the same time controllers of capital, would have, on the other hand, diminished in proportion to the number of employed. And even if wealth came to be better distributed as far as money incomes were concerned, wealth would be less well distributed in the form of capital. There would be more people dependent on the few; and it is just this economic dependence of the many on the few which is one of the most characteristic results of capitalism. Under the ideal of socialism we should all be dependent on one individual—the State. We should all be proletariats. Socialism is indeed thus shown to be the very consummation of capitalism, i.e. proletarianism: the perfect proletarian State.

It might be rebutted that, under the ideal of democratic socialism, we would have a perfect co-operative society in that each adult would have an equal share in the capital and would therefore be his own employer. But the answer to this is a many-sided one. For one thing, the perfect type of co-operative society is where all the members belong to the same trade. Otherwise each single member necessarily loses all effective voice in the conduct of the business, owing to his ignorance of its various branches. Again, for an employee of a joint-stock company to possess one vote among millions as a shareholder in that company is not at all the same thing as employing himself. He is merely a cog in the wheel of a great machine; and this is another disagreeable characteristic of both capitalism and socialism (proletarianism). The only apparent way of escape by which the employee in a socialist State might be able—in a certain degree—to assert himself, would be by combining with his fellows in the same trade. This would not be guild socialism, because the trades would be nationalized. Class distinctions might be abolished, but trade distinctions, nevertheless, assuredly would not. So the government of the great State machine under democratic socialism, would become the result of a struggle between trade interests. Conditions would accordingly be very little different—even if it were granted, as socialists maintain, that on a balance, at any rate, efficiency would not suffer (a doubtful proposition, to say the least)—than in the present conditions of the liberal *régime*, where government is the result of a struggle between class interests. The struggle between rival egoisms would merely be shifted. Thus argues the fascist. Things might, conceivably, not be worse on a balance than under the liberal *régime*; but the world would have certainly become a truly drab, monotonous, grey uniformity, the State a dismal middle-class bureaucracy, in no less danger than before of an upset equilibrium of forces degenerating into a wicked tyranny. Even if socialism changed its bias and stole from fascism its faith in a universal, objective and discernible moral law and devised a system of authoritative government responsible to the moral law and not to the people at large, the drawbacks of socialism as an essentially proletarian ideal would not be removed. And that itself, to the fascist, appears immoral, for the proletarian State spells the servile State.

Meantime—having attempted to point the way by which the abstract socialist case may be disposed of—capitalism under private initiative is moving rapidly along the same lines. Joint-stock companies and corporations are more and more driving out from business the small independent capitalist. Great trusts and what is called the rationalization of industry are gradually increasing the disproportion between the givers and the takers of labour. A greater and greater proportion of young people grown to be adults have no alternative but to accept work—if they can get it at all—for which they have no calling, doomed to toil for the rest of their lives at the beck and call of others: virtual slavery. The employee, besides, is feeling himself more and more a mere cog in the wheel of so many great anonymous machines. The single shareholder in these colossal companies is similarly losing more and more his voice in their control. More and more virtual control is falling into the hands of the managerial class, which is more and more directly concerned with the satisfaction of the material claims of its employees, after feathering its own nest, than with those of the owners of the capital, who only nominally control it. Labour conditions, where this is occurring, are consequently improving. In time we may even arrive, under the capitalism of part socialism and part private initiative, at things being so well organized that the precariousness of employment becomes greatly mitigated. But man does not live by bread alone. He is purchasing his greater material comforts and greater security at the price of freedom and of his life stereotyped. Personality, independence, the beauty that comes of individual workmanship, becomes every day less and less common. To rise into the managerial class entails already, besides general capacity, the capacity of suffering boredom gladly year after year; for work is losing the gift it once had of joy. Such satisfaction as it provides is the satisfaction of the ambition to rise requited, with the reminder coming too late that the control of a machine differs very little from being controlled by it. But there is no escape; for the successful man has then become too old to acquire the capacity to take the freedom and leisure which is at last offered him. Mass production, mass ideas, culture in tabloid form, which is no culture at all, a well-oiled groove to stick in or along which to move backwards or forwards—this is our super-capitalist civilization: a machine that turns out men like sausages and does its utmost to break those that have the originality to resist.

For all this grimness, socialism appears to offer no remedy whatsoever. What socialism aims at achieving is, in the first place, what private initiative, under the influence of America's example (where conditions are more favourable than in old Europe and where capitalism is more progressive and possibly more enlightened), may very well end in achieving, with the help of the State, of its own accord, namely, a higher material standard of living for workers (higher wages and greater leisure; better sanitary conditions of work, etc.; relative security of employment; and a more rational use of machinery and scientific inventions). Socialism, on the other hand, imagines that by doing the same through the nationalization of the means of production, distribution and exchange, nobody need work for more than a few hours daily, the difference between the relative agreeableness or disagreeableness of the work to be performed being compensated not so much by higher wages as by greater leisure. For the equalization of money incomes, even if we allow for a certain graduation dependent on length of service or degree of responsibility, is part and parcel of the socialist scheme. But even if such a thing were possible, it could only be bought at the price of what would amount to practically genuine slavery or of making productive conditions relatively static. For if private initiative in business were not permitted, people might have no alternative but to spend their long leisure hours in study, self-education, hobbies and recreation (physical and intellectual); and although this might result in relieving some of the drabness of life under socialism, it would put a relative stop to the further accumulation of material wealth; for so long as people were using up only a relatively small portion of their available energy in the production of material wealth, so would the machinery for the production of material wealth be remaining, potentially, at all events, idle. If the State itself put this potentially idle machinery into motion by increasing it and holding out the necessary inducements to work it, away would go the promised leisure for all those who accepted the inducements held out to them. But this would upset the socialist scheme for equalizing wages; while, if the State failed to prevent private business, the capitalism of private initiative would still flourish alongside of socialism and there would be no ideal socialist State. On the other hand, if the State took upon itself the unheard of task of compulsorily adjusting, according to what could only be an arbitrary standard, the amount of leisure to be permitted at all (varying presumably according to the nature of the work), man would be reduced—at the best—to the condition of well-fed cattle. The double dilemma, academical as it may well be, appears incontrovertible. Fortunately, however, the question is purely academical. Pure socialism, as we have already attempted to prove, is an impracticable dream, even if it were demonstrated not to be altogether contrary to human nature. Those, on the other hand, who affirm that it is, have certainly very grave reasons to support their opinion.

Socialism (which might be called the capitalism of public initiative), to be sure, is looking to the achievement of other results besides that of improving the material conditions of the wage-earner: it is looking, in the second place, to putting an end to the appalling waste and misdirection of enterprise which takes place under the capitalism of private initiative. Where wealth is assuredly abundance, it stands aghast at the phenomenon of over-production, which is constantly recurring in present conditions. It is likewise horrified by the deliberate bringing about of scarcity in order that a comparatively few selfish persons may reap a richer reward by raising prices to an exorbitant figure. It is horrified at the rewards of capital in certain cases out of all proportion to the original risks run, bonus piled upon bonus years after the original promoters of the business are dead and buried, and after the business has amortized the whole of its original outlay and has settled down into representing perfectly gilt-edged security. It is horrified at the establishment of immense monopolies and at the impotence of the public authorities, in actual conditions, to control them effectively, to prevent monopoly prices and even the suppression of new inventions by vested interests. It is horrified at the flagrant manipulation of prices by speculators and middlemen, at the constant profiteering that goes on all around us, at the exploitation of certain classes of producers as well as of the consumer by middlemen, at the manner in which prices are regulated exclusively by the interplay of supply and demand rather than on the basis of the costs of production and, consequently, at the so frequent absence of any just price. Again, it is horrified by the creation of artificial demands for and the canalization of capital; into channels for the production of the silliest foibles and most extravagant luxuries, when there is a large potential demand for and a crying need of capital for the production of the common necessaries of life. It views with dismay the export of capital or the transference of capital from a poorer district to a richer, merely because its utilization at home or in the poorer district would fail to pay (or fail to pay as well) the private capitalist, though it might well pay the community in the long run hand over fist; and it likewise views with dismay the dividends accruing in many cases from the permission to allow capital to flow unchecked into the more remunerative channels from a private profit-making standpoint, only to result in further capital being accumulated for the production of luxuries or for expenditure on parasitical forms of employment. Finally, it is shocked to see the accumulation of wealth in the hands of a large class of idlers, who give nothing in return, who live for pleasure and avoid all responsibilities. It sees money, which is an indent on the general wealth, in the possession of those who have performed no services to the community in return for the handling of it; it sees debt accumulating on debt under a system which appears to confuse debt with wealth; it sees money issued privately for private profit in spite of the sound old maxim that the issue of money is the prerogative of the crown; the State. Usury, indeed, is rampant everywhere nowadays; and both usury and profit-making at the expense of the national interests are looked upon as an innocent game under the cloak of the old, bankrupt *laissez-faire* doctrine that the sum of individual interests makes up the national interests.

Now fascism entirely shares with socialism the horror and dismay which these practices exhibit, and points to a number of further blighting consequences and anomalies which stare us in the face under the capitalist system, such, for instance, as those caused by the increasing practice of production for profit rather than production for consumption. It sees fish unprocurable where the fish are caught until they return stale from the urban centres to which they have originally been dispatched. It sees dairy produce and other produce in the same situation. It sees fields of beautiful fresh fruit grown exclusively for the making of jams, except for a relatively small portion of it, retained at high prices for rich persons with the unabsorbed surplus hawked, before it rots, for the benefit of the poor. It sees canned goods substituted more and more for fresh goods. It sees 90 per cent of a thoroughly industrialized country like England living for the most part on relatively unhealthy substitutes. But it is not only a question of anomalies, for fascism observes also either the decay or the gradual industrialization of agriculture, with the consequent depopulation of the countryside in either case, the disappearance of the healthiest elements of the population, the progressive accumulation of the population into immense urban areas, with all the attendant evils (slums, overcrowding, lack of light and air, etc., etc., etc., or, alternatively, soul-killing suburbia) and temptations. And in the conditions of employment inseparable from capitalism—i.e. proletarianism, it observes the increasing inability of persons to sublimate their creative energies, with the consequent premium on vice or alternatively on *neuroses*, due to efforts of suppression. Lastly, and worst of all, it sees, for all but a few, the end of economic freedom, that is, the opportunity of disposing of one's work and leisure (within the limits set by the moral law) in proportions that seem best to one's own judgment and needs. Hence fascism condemns capitalism (proletarianism) root and branch and fears it. It affirms that capitalism carries within itself the seeds of a terrible decay, leading eventually, if unchecked, to the moral and biological degeneration of the race and to the ruin of civilization.

It would be easy to continue the indictment; but sufficient has now been said on the negative side to indicate the state of mind with which fascism views both the present economic system and the socialist schemes for the correcting of it. The time has come to give an idea of the remedies which fascism itself proposes. It is necessary, however, to make first a few observations of a general character. With respect to orthodox economics, fascism asserts that its conclusions are vitiated to a great extent by the fact of its original elaboration under the influence of the Manchester School. It asserts that orthodox economics represents to a great extent the economics of individualism, that is to say, it is a system of individual economics and not a system of national economics. The sum—to repeat yet again in different words what has already been said several times (I fear, *ad nauseam*)—of what is individually profitable does not necessarily amount to what is nationally profitable. Fascism admits, it is true, that the more modern economists of the orthodox school have already modified their ultra-individualist attitude, but not yet sufficiently for it to be said that a true system of national economics has been substituted. Modern orthodox economics is still more of a description of actual economic conditions than a true, universal social science. Even so, economics must always remain a very restricted science. It must be based on the abstraction of an economic man. On this assumption it may be able to formulate a number of generalizations of very great practical value. But when it comes to the consideration of real life, other factors enter into the situation, which must be allowed to modify the purely economic conclusions. For man is not merely an economic animal. If man in his social aspects is to be studied scientifically, a more synthetic science is required than economics; and it is the science of sociology, into which the purely economic factors of life enter as part of the material to be sifted along with a lot of other factors, which attempts to supply the deficiency and to provide thereby a safer guide for the statesman and social reformer than the pure science of economics by itself. It is to sociology, then, as a science to which we must turn if we are to discover the abstract principles on the bases of which remedies may be found for the evils of our present lot.

Sociology, however, is still a science in its infancy. Fascism is aware of this, as well as of the extreme difficulty of applying successfully abstract principles to concrete circumstances the complexity of which often beggar analysis; and it realizes, therefore, that we have no practical alternative but to rely on the art of statesmanship and to feel our way forward within the limits of a few basic principles of outstanding importance (capable of being gradually extended) and apparent incontrovertibility. Within these limits the fascist method is accordingly experimental—progressively experimental.

Before anything else fascism would cling to the moral law—knowing that the moral law can never mislead. It must be both the end and the acid test of every experiment. So it begins by laying down the general proposition that man's exterior life is, within the limits set by the material factors of mundane existence, a reflection of the moral values which he sincerely respects. Consequently the best way to get rid of a bad economic system is to get rid of the perverted moral outlook that is the fundamental cause of it. Hence education in moral values is the real key to the situation. Exchange our actual moral values for something better and a modification of a bad system to a better one will then grow gradually, naturally and inevitably.

With its eye still on the moral law, fascism then starts by sanctifying the possession of property; for it claims that the possession of property is the only absolute condition of economic freedom, and as such it may be said to be a natural right that a man should be secured of the opportunity of acquiring property for himself. The opportunity of acquiring property is also an opportunity for acquiring responsibility. This is as it should be, and responsibility begins at home. It is the family which holds within its limits—or should do so—the sweetest and deepest experiences of life. It is—or it should be—the expression of man's most intimate and passionate love; and such love is of God. It is right that we should be able to labour to secure not only our economic freedom, but the economic freedom of those nearest and dearest to us—to hand down the freedom we have gained to our children. So the right to acquire property and to transmit it intact are two important corner-stones of fascist economics. Besides, experience shows that the possession of private property breeds the maximum of initiative, as well as innumerable outstanding virtues.

Fascism accordingly sets out to do all it can to defend and encourage the institution of private property, especially in the form of small ownership, where normally there are no wage-earners. In Italy the number of such small owners or part owners still forms a very large proportion of the population: small agricultural proprietors or half-share farmers, small shopkeepers owning their own shops, small independent business men of all kinds, artisans owning their own tools. This is the class which fascism honours most. It is the class in which the sacred institution of the family merges with that of property. Here too we have genuine freemen, forming the backbone of a country—and, as far as the agriculturist is concerned, producers for consumption rather than producers for profit. In central Italy particularly, this class flourishes, so that each village almost is an agricultural co-operative society of small proprietors and a colony of small owners of shops and of artisans—while, in between the villages, the larger estates form virtually a series of another kind of co-operative society, composed of half-share farmers clustering round the central estate buildings. In these districts the general standard of living is high, the houses clean, the cooking excellent with generally an abundance of good food and drink, and there is an air of well-being and contentment about, of activity and joy in life. These peasants are no dull sods of the earth, but intelligent and progressive in their arts, refined in manner, naturally artistic and musical, wise in the secrets of nature, the representatives of an old race which has preserved its vitality and the inheritors of a wonderful patrimony of tradition, the accumulation of generations of experience of life. Compared to the class of wage-earners in Italy or any other country, they are an altogether superior people. In Italy now, all that can be done for them is being done for them by a government which beams on them benevolently, and every effort is being made to strengthen and increase them as a class, to spread the social and economic system they represent into those parts of Italy less characterized by it. The practical abolition of death duties in the first and second degree by the fascist government was aimed chiefly at benefiting this class, apart from the moral significance of the measure as a defence of the family; and under the fascist corporative system, this class has become organized for the first time and so placed in a position the better to defend itself against the inroads of industrialism and big business. It would be out of place here, however, to detail the manner in which fascism is promoting the defence and spread of this class in Italy. It is sufficient to say that it is a many-sided policy which is not neglecting the need felt in the country districts for better facilities for culture and amusements, as well as financial credit. The great fascist After Work Institution, which operates all over the country, in town and countryside, is endeavouring to bring to the latter some of the amenities of the former. In fact, to watch fascism operating in the countryside is rather like seeing the dreams of George Russell's (Æ's) rural civilization gradually materializing.

Together with the class of small, almost self-sufficing family proprietors, fascism aims at favouring the genuine co-operator, especially the co-operatives of production. These co-operators, members of a single trade, own their capital in common and share out the profits. They also represent a class of freemen; and they are encouraged by every means accordingly. Add to these classes the professional classes (doctors, lawyers, artists of all kinds and degrees, the ministers of religion, engineers, etc., etc.), the majority of which have taken up their profession in response to the inner call of special interests and inborn talents (here, even in conditions of dependence, we have that kind of service which approximates to one of perfect freedom), and we get a section of the nation which, together with the larger property owners, fascism wishes to see representing, as a condition of a really healthy State, the overwhelming majority of citizens. Between the two classes of property owners and professional men, the artisan is the connecting link; and, it is claimed, the interests of most of these people (the big proprietors and perhaps some of the big professionals are an exception) almost automatically coincide with the national interests. Taken as a whole, among these classes wealth is extremely well distributed. Most of their production is production for consumption or for expenditure on necessaries and small comforts. Profiteering among them is, generally speaking, insignificant—too insignificant to be regarded as a national danger. When they flourish, therefore, national needs almost look after themselves, if not quite. They represent the ideal of the "distributive" State. Indeed, in this respect fascism approaches the ideal of that group of writers in England, of whom Chesterton and Belloc are the better-known names.

When, however, we come to examine the case of the larger owners of capital, the need of a supplementary principle to that sanctifying the institution of private property comes to be felt; and fascism proclaims this supplementary principle as one of the cardinal principles underlying its economic policy, namely, that all forms of property be regarded also as a public trust. No man may do exactly what he likes with his own. That would be licence. No man has the right to do anything which is harmful to the collective interests. It is not a question merely of respecting a neighbour's equal rights before the law, but a moral obligation so to contrive one's life that one's interests become, as far as is humanly possible, coincident with the public interests. This represents the limit of a man's individual economic rights; and the principle itself is a definite corollary of the fascist definition of liberty already given, namely (to use the words of St. Paul) that liberty is freedom from the bondage of sin. The bonds of moral obligation limit licence but not freedom. So the obligation to use one's capital in a manner coincident with the collective interests, to regard one's private property as being simultaneously a public trust, is no infringement of liberty or of proprietary rights.

The manner in which fascism in Italy is attempting to enforce this principle will be briefly described below. But before doing so there is another principle to be laid down. It is this: that the pursuit of a maximum aggregate national wealth, as an economic end, should be subordinated to the pursuit of a healthy social system. In other words, general well-being is more dependent on a healthy social system than on great aggregate riches. Well-being does not necessarily vary in proportion to the collective income. The latter enters into the problem as an important element; but the factor of a healthy social system, of which in turn a well adjusted distribution of wealth is another factor, is a still more important element. To give examples of what is meant: a community in which there was one exceedingly rich family, one thousand moderately rich families and twenty thousand families living on the margin of subsistence might have a total collective income greater than another community composed of one hundred and one moderately rich families, ten thousand families less rich and ten thousand families just comfortably off. But the latter community would reflect the greater well-being—and its greater well-being would be all the greater, relatively speaking, if in the first community the great majority was dependent on the few and in the second the great majority was composed of independent producers. To give another example: the income of Great Britain is variously estimated at five to fifteen times as great as that of France. But it is exceedingly doubtful whether the general well-being in Great Britain is even equal to that of France. Those, indeed, who have a wide experience of living conditions in both countries generally agree that the well-being in France is the greater; and the difference to France's advantage lies in the better distribution of wealth and a better social system. France is a country of small proprietors and co-operators. It is still a country where the family is considered the essential unit, rather than the individual; and where the social relationships between different classes still preserve some of the old traditions, handed down from the Middle Ages, tending to make the conditions of those classes economically dependent upon others more humane, less stereotyped, less that of master and man, and consequently less exasperated. The latter case is still clearer in Italy and Spain. But the national aggregate wealth of Italy and Spain is so much smaller than that of France that greater weight has to be given to this factor than in the case of France. France probably represents the country in Europe to-day where, on a balance of factors, the well-being is greatest.

This leads us to the consideration of those classes whose economic lives directly depend on others—the proletariat class. This class cannot be done away with altogether. They are the poor, even when they are comparatively well off, who are always with us. No society can dispense with them altogether. How then to deal with them other than by the general policy of keeping their number down as far as possible in proportion to the total population? The fascist answer is: by insuring them as decent conditions of employment as possible (that goes without saying); by granting them certain definite rights in the form of a labour charter; by giving them the sense of their interests being identified with those of the industry in which they are workers and—more important still—of being soldiers in the service of their country; by widening the opportunities of advancement within their class and of escaping from it altogether; and lastly, most important of all, by bringing the employer and the employed together socially so that they get to know each other, so that the personal element enters into their mutual relationship, so that wage-earning work becomes proportionately humanized. By these means some kind of approach to that kind of service which is perfect freedom can be made for this class. Take, for instance, the lot of domestic servants. Granted decent conditions of work, every domestic servant knows that his or her situation depends entirely on the manner in which he or she is treated. Domestic servants need respect, not patronage. They need to feel themselves members, albeit subordinate members, of a family, whose interests are identified with theirs. The happy servants of a household are those who feel they occupy a position of trust, of gratitude and respect, well earned and acknowledged, like that occupied by an old family nurse: one of the few common survivals in industrialized countries of the servant whose dependence has remained perfectly humanized. There are, of course, exceptions; and in the less industrialized countries the exceptions are often the rule. But where the humanizing intervention of a baby is absent, domestic servants are tending to slip more and more into the position of exasperated, class-conscious drudges, willing workers only in proportion to the bribe offered or extorted.

Fundamentally it is all a moral question. Where there exists a genuine Christian spirit (not a reflected one, nor one applied according to a set of formulas or favourite Biblical texts) the question resolves itself in proportion to the closeness of the personal relationship between the master and the man. The spirit above all else is therefore what is needed. But in proportion to the degree of separation between the class of employee and the class of employer, so a system is required to bridge the gulf of mutual incomprehension; and the fascist corporative organization of society in Italy is designed first and foremost to fulfil this purpose. Secondly, it is designed to enable the State, as representing the collective interests (and no other body can do this), to control individual (class or trade) egoisms which of their own accord fail to canalize themselves into channels coincident with the collective interests; in other words, to enforce the principle of property regarded as a public trust. The corporations are designed to become both the major means and, what is even more important, the founts of knowledge and experience on the basis of which interference by the State on behalf of the collective interests may be under; taken with progressive wisdom and effect. For even though we acknowledge the need for State intervention with respect to private business, in order that society may be rid of the abuses, it is not sufficient to promulgate laws of "thou shalt not this" and "thou shalt not that." The complexity and expertness of modern business makes such negative injunctions (even if they assume a positive form) both easy to elude by persons minded to do so, and easily futile by reason of their ingenuousness. If the means of production, distribution and exchange are to be *socialized*, without having recourse to the means advocated by socialists (namely, nationalization and municipalization), the control by the State must be positive. And if it is to be positive and if it is to be wise (lest the fowl that lays the golden eggs be sacrificed) it must be a control from within and not one from without. Hence it must be a control which exhibits a definite form of co-operation between the representatives of the State and the representatives of all the factors of private initiative and production. Nobody must be left outside the system. Private economy and public economy must be thoroughly integrated, in such a way that both the various factors of production (i.e. the various factors of labour and capital) may be integrated with respect to each industry and branch of industry; and there must likewise be integrated the rights of the individual and the State.

This is the principle on which is based the corporative organization of society of the fascist State. The specific form of organization to be adopted may, of course, vary with the needs and character of different peoples. But some kind of organization based on the above principle is an essential of the fascist State. Within the limits of this principle and of the general principles, mentioned above, on which this principle is itself based, and by means, chiefly, of the organization itself which arises out of this principle, the problems to be solved must be solved progressively as accumulated and progressively accumulating experience dictates. This is the fascist alternative to socialism.

The following, by way of illustration, is a short description of the corporative organization as it is being developed under fascism in Italy. The reader should, however, carefully bear in mind that fascism does not expect the Italian model to be copied slavishly elsewhere.

The capitalists of every branch of industry form a union. So do, for the same industry, each category of employees engaged in it—one union and one union only for each category. The elected representatives of each union are brought together to create a corporation for their particular industry, in the form of a permanent organization of which they constitute, so to speak, the Board of Directors. The President of the Board, however, is a State official, nominated by the Ministry of Corporations. The corporation itself, though run by its own staff of officials, under the main direction of its members, is a definite organ of the State, a decentralized department, so to speak, of the Ministry of Corporations, and is responsible directly to the Minister of Corporations. As for the unions, members of each corporation, their articles of association, which must provide for a number of social, economic and technical activities, must receive official recognition from the Ministry of Corporations, while the corporation undertakes to supervise and co-ordinate their work. The main business of the unions, however, is to defend the economic interests of the class they represent. The main work of the corporations on the other hand is to harmonize these interests in so far as they conflict, and to carry out duties of a social and technical kind. Under its supervision labour exchanges for the industry are established, statistics of all kinds kept, technical schools created, commissions of enquiry appointed with a view to diminishing costs of production and "rationalizing" the industry, etc. It sees that the unions adhere to the law, carry out their obligations with respect to the insurance, etc., of workers, and to the strict application of collective contracts and the terms of the Labour Charter, which defines the principles of equity and justice in the domain of production. So too it co-ordinates the social work undertaken by the unions with the work of the national after-work and maternity and infant welfare institutions and affords the worker protection and advice, though a special national institution for which it acts as a decentralized office, with respect to the recovery of insurance benefits, medical assistance, emigration, etc., etc. Then it sees to it that employers carry out the terms of collective contracts entered

into between its members with respect to all workers indiscriminately engaged in the industry, even to those who are not members of the recognized unions forming the corporation. No
worker engaged in the industry is thus denied the benefits of a
collective contract. These contracts themselves are frequently
drawn up under the auspices of the corporation; and the latter
acts as a means of conciliation between capital and labour in
regard to any disputes which may arise in the event of either
party wishing to refer to it the dispute. Finally, plans are on foot
by which in conjunction with the Prefect of the Province, who
is the chief local representative of the State executive, prices
may be regulated with a view to eliminating profiteering and
usury.

The various local unions are federated into national unions
and again grouped into thirteen great confederations of production, six representing capital, six labour and one the professional
orders (civil servants receive a separate organization altogether).
Inversely the corporations, which are national bodies, have each
local decentralized organizations corresponding to the local
unions; while in Rome there is constituted under the Ministry
of Corporations a central corporative council, which acts as a
kind of social, technical and economic parliament, composed of
the representatives of capital and labour appointed by the various corporations, of the central co-operative institute (which
acts, so to speak, as the corporation of the various co-operative
societies) and of the federation of professional men. It is pre-
sided over by the high officials of the Ministry of Corporations,
the Minister and the under-secretary of State, and there are co-
opted to work on it, besides, a certain number of experts and
representatives of other ministries. This central council has
quasi-legislative powers within the limits set by the legislative
measures passed by Parliament. With it and by its help the Ministry of Corporations co-ordinates and controls the whole of the
corporative organization of the State as outlined above.

Strikes and lock-outs are forbidden; and in the event of a dispute between capital and labour arising, which the good offices
of the corporation has failed to settle, the question is passed to

be adjudicated upon to the ordinary civil Courts of Appeal constituted for the purpose into a Magistrature of Labour. Such courts have plenty of experience in assessing civil claims and are well adapted to perform this special function. The judges are aided by expert assessors appointed by the disputing parties and decide the question on a basis of equity, *all things considered—* that is, the ultimate interests of the respective parties to the dispute, of the industry and of the nation, after reviewing all the technicalities of the question as well as the state of trade and of employment, the cost of living, the prices and profits of the industry, etc. The general principles laid down by the Labour Charter constitute the principal landmarks by which the judges may be guided towards a just decision.

By means of this elaborate but flexible organization, which is entirely financed by the union rates and is susceptible to gradual improvement, supplemented by individual laws and by enterprises directly and indirectly run by the State and municipalities, it is calculated it will be possible to see to it eventually that all property shall conform to the standard of a public trust. If things, moreover, go on as steadily as they are doing at present in Italy, men who are already in their middle age will see before they die a society in which every producer is a member of a corporation (including the co-operative producers) and every consumer a member of one or more consumers' co-operatives. For the first class it will have become naturally easier to be, *qua* producers, good citizens, on account of the corporative life which they will find themselves leading, willy-nilly, and more difficult to be bad ones, on account of the controlling influence of the State. For the second class prices will tend to correspond to the minimum; and because unfair prices and undue profits will have become the exception, money incomes will have much less unequal, while the rich who remain will have corresponding social responsibilities. These results, besides, will have been brought about by co-operation between the State, private capitalists and labour. The State will have become a predominating factor of control, but it will not have taken the place of private initiative. All factors of production will have been consulted and all legitimate private interests (that is, private interests that do not clash with the general interests) will have been duly respected. That is the driving idea behind the whole scheme. For further details the English reader cannot do better than consult the volume entitled *A Survey of Fascism*, published under the auspices of the International Centre of Fascist Studies in Lausanne (Ernest Benn, Ltd., London, 1928), or, alternatively, Alberto Pennachio's *The Corporative State* (New York, 1927), published by the Italian Historical Society of America. Both these publications have an excellent chart illustrating the organization in diagrammatic form.

As far as direct State enterprise is concerned, the Italian Labour Charter lays down the guiding principles very clearly: "The corporative State considers that private initiative in the field of production is the most efficacious and most useful instrument in the interests of the nation . . . the whole body of production must be considered as a united effort from the national point of view . . . the private organization of production being a function of national interest, the organizer of any economic undertaking shall be responsible to the State for the direction given to production . . . intervention by the State in economic production should take place only when private initiative is lacking or is insufficient or when the political interests of the State are involved." Hence fascism is actually reluctant to engage on schemes of nationalization or municipalization. A *prima facie* case in favour of such activity requires first to be demonstrated—and of course there are a great many things which fulfil this proviso. As time goes on a great many other things may come to be added. And in addition to enterprises directly State-run, there is an intermediate type of enterprise which fascism favours rather than have recourse to the former. Such bodies the Italians call *enti parastatali*, which might be translated as "semi-State institutions," such as the Bank of Italy, which is an autonomous body controlled by the Treasury, or the Social Insurance Institute, which constitutes a State monopoly respecting all forms of social insurance run on a mutual basis by which it is meant that profits must be devoted either to diminishing insurance rates or increasing the benefits or extending assistance to the insured by way of clinics and hospitals and sanatoria and means of profitable recreation, etc., or extending the scope of insurance, or directly combating the causes of disease, or financing better housing conditions for the insured—that is, in one way or another, directly or indirectly, returning the money with interest into the pockets of those who have provided it in the first instance. Many other examples of this kind of State enterprise in fascist Italy could be quoted, each possessing a special character. The State railways, for instance, are run in Italy as an autonomous company, profits being devoted either to increasing the wages of its employees or lowering tariffs or improving the plant or extending railway communications or running road transport to supplement the railways or even to investments in other semi-State institutions such as the State petroleum company (instituted with the object of breaking the monopoly as far as Italy is concerned of the great world petrol trusts—later it may develop into a State petrol monopoly) and thereby securing cheaper supplies of a class of goods required in large quantities by the State railways. Much can be done by the State too by way of co-ordinating charitable work, eliminating overlapping and providing additional funds—witness the great after-work and maternity and infant welfare institutions which have been created by Mussolini's government—while it is a fascist principle that the State must take upon itself the initiative, with or without private co-operation, for all kinds of public works—road building, land reclamation, the construction of canals, aqueducts, railways, power stations, ports, workmen's dwellings, etc., etc., which may be calculated to pay the community hand over fist in the long run, which limits the extent to which capital may be exported or driven out of the poorer districts or diverted to luxury trades, but would not for one reason or another offer sufficient temptation to purely private initiative. The Banks of Sicily and Naples, which come under the direct supervision of the Treasury, have the special purpose of fostering enterprises of this kind in the poorer districts of the South.

The purely social aspects of the fascist corporative system should here be emphasized. Through the corporations the various classes engaged in each industry are brought together in a permanent and active form in social work. They learn thus to understand each other better; and the situation of the wage-earner tends to be humanized, as in this way he is brought into contact with his employers. The better class of the latter under the capitalist system aim, of course, often, on their private initiative, at doing this. But under the corporative system, the indifferent or bad employers cannot escape their moral obligations. Within the corporation too the limits of the differences of interest between capital and labour come to be understood and their common interests, which are the interests of the industry taken as a whole, come to be appreciated. An additional ladder is also thereby formed by which talent, economic, political, technical or social, may rise to prominence. Finally, the presiding influence of the State, intervening in favour of the national interests, promotes the growth in both masters and men of a national conscience in relation to their industry, so that their work tends to take on the character of a burden shouldered for the common good; and this in turn is a great help in the difficult task of humanizing the lot of the wage-earner. It gives him something of the ideals of a soldier and provides some compensation for any lack of interest he may have in the routine of his daily task.

The Italian Labour Charter, on which the working of the corporative organization largely hinges, is a remarkable document. It defines the basic rights and obligations of both capital and labour; and, as we have seen, forms the rules of equity according to which disputes between capital and labour are settled in the last resort. Fascism refuses to admit that the community should suffer while individuals settle their differences by a trial of strength. The State representing the community has the right to intervene, but it can only do so effectively if its decisions bear the hall-mark of justice. As we have seen, actions are moralized in proportion as they become universalized, so that a decision in the interests of the community represents a definite moral step forward over the victory of a sectional interest. But more is accomplished by the Labour Charter. The moral law, the universal law, enters into the question even more directly; and in order to safeguard a decision, based essentially on the moral law, from being arrived at in too great a sense arbitrarily, it is necessary for the guidance of judges that all the matters in dispute be made referable to a codified set of principles. This is what the Labour Charter purports to be. In itself it is no more than a declaration of rights; but the principles it enunciates have since been embodied in the laws of the land, which it is the business of the judges to administer. The decisions therefore are not subject to any equivocation.

This intervention of State justice in disputes between sectional interests within the State is a striking illustration of the fascist idea; and the principle might well be extended into the international field. Unless the moral law, documented in the form of a set of apposite principles, comes to be universally acknowledged, international life remains at the mercy of warring interests. What is good in the League of Nations is (apart from its utility as a piece of international machinery) precisely the good-will which lies behind it. What is lacking in the League of Nations, as an instrument for peace, is that, despite the good-will which lies behind it, the selfish interests of the big powers and of their *clientèle* of little powers—and especially of the "capitalist" nations, who control the available colonial territories and raw materials of the world—remain the driving forces of its action. Just as it is impossible to bring class warfare within a community to an end without defined principles of equity and justice, based on common moral and social needs without respect of persons, by which the merits of conflicting class claims may be assessed and adjudicated upon in the general interest, so international strife must continue until, as a first step at least, a charter can be framed (like the Labour Charter in Italy) by agreement among the powers, setting forth the principles of equity and justice as between nations in the form of a common code of morality. Such a code will not acquiesce any more in the notion of "having's keeping" than in the notion of "taking's having." The "proletariat" nations must have their rights defined and such rights must be what Shaw would no doubt call communistic, but what fascism would be content to call equitable. Life is dynamic and not static. Peace can only be secured temporarily by forcibly maintaining the *status quo*. If that is all that can be done, an explosion sooner or later—and all the greater and more disastrous the longer it is deferred—will be bound to ensue. Likewise, if nothing more can be done, the "proletariat" nations must perforce adapt their action to capitalist principles, just as the working proletariat, as Bernard Shaw has conclusively demonstrated, has been forced to play its own game of selfish action (ca'canny and all the rest—what Shaw calls "trade union capitalism") as their chief weapon of defence. A capitalist system makes capitalist morals compulsory for all; and when a trade union restricts production or enforces its claims by a strike, capitalists under the prevailing capitalist system should have nothing to say, if they had any grain of intellectual honesty, but that imitation is the sincerest form of flattery. Likewise, if a "proletariat" nation in the last resort enforces its interests by war, the "capitalist" nations should properly withhold from casting stones. They are really the cause of the whole pother. Fascist principles accordingly hold out a way of escape from international strife in proportion as they spread. It is a way which is not the same as socialism but is in certain respects similar. It claims, however, to be a better way because more practicable, more in conformity with human nature and with reality.

In some respects, indeed, fascism resembles guild-socialism. They both share the ideal of basing the organization of society on trade corporations and they agree on insisting that all private property should be regarded also as a public trust. Where they part company is chiefly on the question of democratic individualism. Guild-socialism like all forms of socialism clings to the idea that government should be, in effect, the resultant of con-flicting individual interests (in its case, trade interests). It would have the government responsible to the people organized indi-vidualistically and rejects the idea of the authoritative State, responsible to God only for the good government of the people in the general interests. On the other hand, it should by now be apparent that with regard to certain meanings of the term, fas-cism is not undemocratic. For one thing it is no respecter of per-sons in the sense of favouring individual sectional interests. It subscribes to the ideal of the French revolutionary army, namely, that the humblest private soldier should be allowed to carry in his knapsack the *baton* of a marshal of France. Thirdly, it advocates a government broadly based upon the people, one in which individual sectional interests are given a hearing and are invited to co-operate in the task of promoting the interests of the whole community. But it insists that the task of government is a specialist's task, and should be reserved for specialists in the form of an aristocracy of talent and moral responsibility. It insists that the State should not be divided against itself in its direction, and that it should form a united, integrated whole, a true unity in its necessarily human diversity, with its executive structure a hierarchy of authority, recruited from all classes of the population but deriving its authority from above and not from below.

CHAPTER VII

THE UNITARY AND INTEGRATED STATE
THE ITALIAN FASCIST CONSTITUTION

W E may now almost take leave of principles. The reader should be in a position, after noting what has gone before, to exercise his ingenuity in devising a constitution in accordance with the fascist idea, suitable to the conditions of his own country. The form which the fascist constitution is assuming in Italy does not pretend to universal application. It is but an example of what can be done. It is but one architectural construction in the fascist style. The question of monarchy versus republicanism is, for example, not affected by it. That is a question of national tradition or else one of expediency. On the other hand, should a republican constitution be preferred, it would have necessarily to conform more to the ideal represented by the aristocratic republic of Venice (except that it must not entail a closed, hereditary aristocracy) than to that realized in nineteenth-century republics which have grown out of the ruins of the old monarchies, and have been nurtured on liberal and democratic principles.

In Italy, the monarchical tradition—that is, in the royalist sense—is not very strong except in Piedmont. Most Italians feel, in their bones, that the principle of an hereditary royal house was disposed of, once and for all, with the expulsion of the Tarquins from Rome several centuries before Christ. They realize that the principle was only reintroduced by the barbarian invasions. They feel—and fascism reflects this feeling—that the legally sanctioned presence of an hereditary privileged caste, even if confined to a single family—is anomalous, theoretically unjust and even a trifle absurd. They look upon it as an institution not quite civilized, as the Roman and Greek conceived of civilization. Indeed, they look upon it as a relic of barbarism. They are prepared to accept it, on the other hand, as an exceedingly useful expediency, very much in the spirit in which the prophet Samuel reluctantly condescended to the anointing of Saul as the first King of Israel.

Monarchy has accordingly been accepted by fascism in Italy, mainly as a decision of expediency. A fascist republic would entail the selection of a President, probably for life, by some complicated machinery calculated to ensure that the President would be a gentleman acceptable to all patriotic trends of opinion in the country as a man embodying in his person the national tradition and one whose integrity of character was above suspicion. That, the selection of such a man on every occasion would not be beyond the capacity of some ingeniously devised system is proved by the extraordinarily successful record of the Doges of Venice over a period of more than a thousand years. Nevertheless, the death of each President would mean an interruption in the country's normal life; and this interruption an hereditary monarchy obviates. Under the monarchical system continuity is never broken; and this constitutes an extremely weighty practical argument in favour of monarchy. Moreover, in the actual historical conditions of Italy, the crown constitutes an important factor operating in favour of the country's unity. The House of Savoy has magnificent and universally acknowledged national traditions. It has served the country conspicuously well throughout its history. The unity of Italy was achieved largely through the wisdom and leadership of Victor Emmanuel II; and modern Italy is especially grateful for the part played by the House of Savoy during the past hundred years, since Italy initiated her struggle for independence and unity. It should be noted too, in particular, that it was owing to the courageous action of the present King that the fascist march on Rome in 1922 was carried through to a successful issue without open civil war, and without involving the army in politics. Finally, were any question entertained of the abolition of monarchy, the unity of the country, on which fascism lays so much stress, would be weakened, owing to the strong monarchical tradition in Piedmont and among large sections of the people elsewhere.

Consequently the Italian fascist constitution accepts the monarchy and would strengthen it. If the King himself is overshadowed in the popular imagination by the dominating personality of Mussolini, this is unavoidable. A man like Mussolini and the circumstances of a revolution are not everyday occurrences. But Mussolini is at pains to uphold the King's prestige and to bring his person and the institution he represents constantly before the public mind; and there is no doubt whatever that the monarchy in Italy to-day is stronger than it has ever been before.

Kingship in Italy, however, remains essentially constitutional. The King reigns but be does not rule, exactly, as in Britain. His one practical prerogative is the choice of his Prime Minister from among the more prominent members of the dominating party, exactly as in England. Where the difference comes in is not in the King's prerogative, but in the abolition of party government and in the position occupied by the Prime Minister himself under the fascist constitution.

And here we come to the consideration of a very important distinction. Unless this distinction is made, it is impossible to understand the true situation in Italy; and in order to understand it the reader must be possessed of an historical sense, the essence of which is to see things dynamically, that is, as moving in time. Fascism has abolished the party system; yet, at the same time— here and now—it is still only a party, the dominating party. A distinction must accordingly be made between what is meant by a fascist in the sense of one who accepts the principles of fascism and reflects its *Weltanschauung*, as set forth in the previous chapters, and what is meant by a fascist in the sense of a definitely accredited member of a revolutionary party, dominating the Italian State to-day. Until such time as the new constitution is quite complete and tried, until such time as the whole country has become for all intents and purposes completely "fascisticized" (and this may take a whole generation of time), the Fascist Party must necessarily fail to coincide for all practical purposes with the whole nation. But its definite intention is to bring about this coincidence. Like the Gods in Wagner's Ring, the Fascist Party is deliberately working for its eclipse as a party— for the downfall of Walhalla. When that day comes the King's prerogative of choosing the Prime Minister will be able to be exercised as a national choice from among the most prominent national figures, engaged in politics and belonging to a special constitutional body or council formed for the purpose of providing a panel out of which the King will be absolutely free to make his choice. This council is now known as the Grand Fascist Council. This name may even survive, in so far as fascism will have identified itself completely with the nation. But meanwhile the Grand Fascist Council, during the period of transition from the old pre-revolutionary order to the new fascist order, must necessarily remain a party as distinguished from a truly national organ. It is already, of course, a national organ from the strictly legal standpoint, and owing to the fact that its members are imbued with the fascist idea, which sets the nation above party or class. But at the same time, in the actual historical circumstances, while there are large numbers still of patriotically minded people who have not allowed themselves to be assimilated to the fascist idea, who still believe in party government either as a necessity or as a useful expediency, whose mentality is what the fascists dub as "demo-liberal," to be included in the panel, now composing the council, means membership of the exclusive Fascist Party organization. The time will come, on the other hand, if the fascist revolution accomplishes its purpose— the reader, I hope, will forgive me if I seem to be labouring the point—when the members of this panel, of this council, will cease to bear a party ticket, and will be nothing more nor less than the cream of political talent in the country; while the present Fascist Party will have become no more nor less than a national constitutional organization devised for the purpose of securing a progressive selection of statesmen up to the point in which a member may become entitled to enter the privileged lists of this council.

Thus—prescinding from the historical conditions of to-day—the fascist constitution in Italy has, first, a King: a constitutional monarch, reigning but not ruling, the principle of the nation's continuous life, the first and ultimate representative of the nation taken as a whole, and enjoying the prerogative of selecting his Prime Minister, who rules the country in his name, and is responsible to him and through him, as the temporal vicar of God, for the country's good government.

Next, there is a council, composed of about thirty members, the result of successive stages of selection, under the auspices of a national political organization, from among the various cultural and productive organizations in the country, and thus representing the pick of the political talent available, from among whom the King will choose his Prime Minister.

The Prime Minister is the head of a Cabinet of departmental ministers, and not merely a member, *primus inter pares*, of the Cabinet. The Cabinet ministers are selected by him, from wherever he thinks best, and are responsible to him for their departments, exactly as he himself is responsible to the King. Under the Minister of the Interior come the heads of the local provincial divisions of the country: the Prefects of the provinces; and under the Prefects of the provinces come the heads of the communes (large and small), known as the *"Podestà"* (corresponding to our mayors). Then, parallel with this organization, which represents the major line of executive officers, there is the corporative organization of the State, which we have already described: the Minister of Corporations, aided by his Council of Corporations, already described, responsible to the Prime Minister, and the chairmen of the various corporations, responsible to the Minister of Corporations. This may be styled the minor line of executive officers. Both lines, it will be observed, are organized on a hierarchical system of responsibility, their interaction co-ordinated by the responsible Ministers, the Prefects and the *Podestà*; and all these officers, each occupying his special place of authority and responsibility, form with the rest of the members of the Cabinet, the executive, which is the ruling power in the country.

The executive, however, is neither, nor pretends to be, omnipotent. Its power is checked by various constitutional means. First, there is the judiciary, an entirely independent body, as in Britain, which applies the law. The executive is as much subordinate to the laws of the land as the humblest citizen. The executive in other words possesses no arbitrary powers. Secondly, there is the legislature, which helps to make the laws and the approval of which is required for any new law. It is composed as in Britain of two chambers; the Senate and the Chamber of Deputies (for local government purposes, provincial and communal—there are likewise small assemblies corresponding in constitution to the Chamber of Deputies). These chambers are not the mandatories of a sovereign people, though they represent the people in different ways. They share, of course, some of the sovereignty (though in a minor degree than the executive) by virtue of their legislative powers—and through them, the people at large may be said to share in a still minor degree, in the sovereignty. But they do not pretend to constitute the main, real, sovereign power as they do under a democratic constitution.

The Senate is a body of life-members nominated by the King on the proposal of the Prime Minister. Princes of the blood royal sit in it by right. For the rest it is composed of persons over forty years of age who have conspicuously served the State in their various professions—members of the armed forces, the civil service, the judiciary, the executive, the professions: eminent politicians, business men, labour leaders, professors, artists, writers, etc., etc. It is accordingly a highly representative body of national achievement.

The Chamber of Deputies is composed, on the other hand, of the representatives of the various categories of givers and takers of labour, of the professional classes (i.e. of the thirteen great national confederations of labour; capital and professional men, outlined in the previous chapter) and of the more important cultural and welfare-work associations in the land. It represents, in other words, the various productive interests (possibly conflicting interests) within the nation. Each member is definitely known to represent a particular interest, and his business is to plead that interest; but naturally—in a clearly defined body such as this is—he will plead it in vain, unless he can show reason that the interests he wishes to promote are capable of being squared with the national interests.

The members of neither chamber originate as party men. The first are appointed as a reward of public service, and the lives of the majority have been lived altogether outside active politics. The members of the second, representing as they do organized interests, are not so much political choices as professional choices. The bodies they represent, being muted for the particular purposes for which they were constituted, naturally send up those men to represent them who, they calculate, are most capable of doing so. If a joint-stock company, for example, were asked to appoint a representative to a general trade conference, the Board of Directors may be relied upon to choose the man deemed most capable of representing the company's case. The shareholders are not concerned whether his politics are black, white or red. They are satisfied if he is a capable business man, loyal to the interests of his company and possesses the talents needed to voice those interests effectively. So the members of the Italian Chamber of Deputies occupy a very similar situation. And the manner in which they are elected is also very similar, with only one important difference. They are not, for instance, elected directly by the general body of those whom they represent, but by the central Board of the body they represent. The important difference lies in this: the Board selects three alternative candidates (very much as a diocesan council, on the death of a bishop, sends up three names to the arch-bishop, out of which the archbishop—if he has no reason to reject all three as unsuitable—selects the new bishop). Thus the three names go up for examination to the Grand Fascist Council, which thereupon makes the selection (i.e. the Grand Fascist Council has a function here corresponding to that of an arch-bishop). In this way the fascist principle of hierarchical govern-ment is maintained, and the man considered as most valuable, from the national as distinct from the local point of view, is pre-ferred.

The whole list of selected members is then submitted to a general plebiscite of the whole electorate—*yes* or *no*. The pur-pose of this plebiscite is to demonstrate that there exists a suffi-cient degree of consent in favour of the list to justify its repre-senting organized opinion in the face of any severe criticism. Under such a system, the government is practically bound to obtain the required majority in favour of the list of candidates submitted, unless its work was proving on all sides outrageously incompetent. Very similarly the annual general meeting of a joint-stock company almost invariably passes the accounts and report, and confirms the Board in office, unless there happens to be an evident and *prima facie* case for enquiring into the man-ner in which the company's business is being conducted.

Should, on the other hand, the electorate turn the list down, then a regular election with alternative lists is provided—on a system of proportional representation. This alternative result, however, should not be regarded as homage to the idea of pop-ular sovereignty. It should be regarded as merely a piece of use-ful constitutional machinery, thought out with a view to giving the constitution a certain elasticity and to providing a safety valve for any really dangerous popular feeling.

No new laws can be promulgated without the consent of both chambers. But the executive proposes the bills. The cham-bers discuss them, propose amendments, get their amendments passed if they can, criticize them. Their functions, beyond this, are to criticize, pass or reject the various ministerial and national budgets; to voice sectional grievances; and to provide a ladder for political talent. With that their functions end. They have not the right to overthrow a ministry, although, of course, should, through a process of continual obstruction, a deadlock arise, tending to paralyse the executive, the King would have no other alternative but to consider a change in his Prime Minister. But the King, as sole representative of the nation, taken as a whole, alone has to decide to the best of his ability any such questions arising.

Finally, all laws involving a constitutional change, have to obtain the consent not only of the legislative chambers, but of the Grand Fascist Council. The chief ministers belong *ex-officio* to this council and all ministers have the right to speak in both chambers.

Now, no human contrivance is perfect and no Italian fascist claims that this constitution is perfect. It would be quite easy to make out a theoretical case in which a deadlock might arise out of this constitution, which would be incapable of solution except by some kind of *coup d'état* or revolution. Likewise, it would be quite easy to argue that it might degenerate into a tyranny, were the King in collusion with an ambitious Prime Minister, an imbecile or utterly blind to the public interests. The same kind of thing might be said of every constitution. What Italian fascists claim in favour of this particular constitution is that it is a fair reflection of general fascist principles, provides a good balance of powers, is neither too rigid nor too flexible and is suited to the present needs and to the mentality of the Italian people. They claim, moreover, that it is democratic in the sense that it does not represent a closed caste system of government, that it enables grievances to be voiced, enables all kinds of influences to be brought to bear on the executive, provides means of constructive criticism, a safety valve for strong popular feeling, and a ladder for political talent wherever it may originate. It is anti-democratic in the sense that it endeavours progressively to ensure government by an aristocracy of talent and to protect the executive from gusts of popular sentiment. The passing unpopularity of a given measure, which nevertheless may be very much in the nation's interests, may be discounted. The power of organized sectional public opinion may likewise be to a considerable extent discounted. It provides a strong and vigorous executive; while the whole structure of the constitution may be said to be no less than the whole nation organized and integrated. Thus it prevents local constitutional bodies and sectional interests pulling effectively different ways, to the detriment of the interests of the whole nation. Nor is the government—the executive—a *deus ex machina*, called into being by the periodical convulsion of an election and then left as something superimposed above the life of the nation, but is part of an all-embracing mechanism, from which no citizen is ever wholly absent, which is in perpetual motion. It is indeed the nation completely organized, completely integrated—the concrete realization of that unity in variety which is the essence of a true organism, a more perfect realization than has hitherto been found of the ideal of a commonwealth. This, in any case, is what it purports to be. Under such a constitution, the nation may be compared to a pyramid, broadly based, but culminating in a point of authority—braced by a strong executive, but containing within the edifice so braced every variety of compartment suitable to individual tastes, provided those tastes do not run counter to the safety and stability of the whole edifice.

It is not claimed, however, that the edifice is not subject to further improvement. On the contrary it is claimed that as time goes on, its sufficient flexibility, combined with the system of a strong executive, will enable it to be improved in the light of experience and to be adapted to slowly changing circumstances. All systems of government fail if a nation is decadent, most succeed if the nation is growing in vigour. But if a nation is growing in vigour and possesses at the same time a well-devised constitution, its well-being will have the greatest chance of being rapidly promoted. There will then be no back-sliding, no waste, no partial paralysis of the forces working for good. All constitutions, according to fascism, are no more than devices to ensure the maximum well-being of a nation. In the midst of all constitutional machinery there is discernible within certain shifting limits, the centre of gravity of sovereignty—ultimate human authority. Provided that authority be exercised better in the interests of the nation, taken as a whole, than any alternative authority, it possesses a divine right to rule. That, it is claimed, is the only point worth taking into account in the question as to where sovereignty ought to reside. And that is really the beginning and the end of the whole fascist case, when it comes to the building of the constitution; and the word "ought" implies a moral problem. So we are thrown back again on the main fascist contention, the acceptance of which depends on the recognition of an objective moral law. Dispute this and the whole fascist case goes by the board. Accept it, and it becomes difficult to remain unconverted to the rest; for the rest is little more than the application of this fundamental principle to contingent circumstances, entailing questions involving, indeed, the practical judgment as to the exact measures which should be adopted— the how much of this and the how little of that (and hence the need of authoritative government—strong, disinterested and *competent*)—but referring back always to one absolute and immutable law, which every reasonable man is capable of apprehending.

With that we can leave fascism to the reader's critical consideration. The case is stated; and there only remains a little to be said by way of cautioning the reader against certain very ready pitfalls. For the unwary—for those who have not had the time or the opportunity of studying the actual historical conditions in which fascism has arisen in Italy—it is important that these pitfalls should be pointed out. Otherwise he will have good reason to blame me if he comes later to revise his opinions, formed in the first instance in ignorance of them.

CHAPTER VIII

PITFALLS AND PARADOXES

THOSE who boggle at the idea of an objectively discernible moral law, will find it easier to approach the issues involved dispassionately, if they remember to distinguish between the moral law in the absolute sense and the moral law as applied to contingent circumstances. It is the former (apart from revelation) which fascists, in agreement with the teaching Churches, affirm to be evident to all reasonable and healthy-minded persons. The latter, on the other hand, they admit may be subject to differences of opinion in proportion to the complexity of the circumstances; but here too, they would assert, the differences of opinion that may arise need not be considered so formidable as they are often alleged to be, provided people are educated to use their practical æsthetic sense, to grasp situations whole by intuition, to avoid undue analysis and introspection, to fall back on simple general principles of action when in doubt, and to recognize that since there are varying degrees of capacity to determine what is right and wrong in a given set of circumstances, reverence for authority, in the particular sphere in which any question arises—scientific, political or religious, etc.—is an admirable state of mind, which should be earnestly cultivated. The fascist, indeed, is in a state of hearty revolt against the self-appointed amateur pontiff, who is so much in evidence nowadays in this era of so-called "independence of thought"—a phrase which fascism regards as either meaningless or merely synonymous with a robust temperament. But when it comes to the natural moral law in the absolute sense, he insists that it is as dear to reasonable and healthy-minded persons as are the colours of the spectrum to those not born colour-blind. The virtues, for example, have only to be pointed out in order to be recognized as such—fortitude, courage, self-discipline, sincerity, honesty, purity of heart, love and hope and faith (which, by the way, is a virtue and not, as the modern man is apt to regard it, "the ability to believe in something which one knows to be untrue"). As for the general principles of conduct, such as those laid down in the Decalogue or as, for example, the fascist political maxim that nobody is entitled to do what he wills if such action is against the general interests, these two represent clear, self-evident landmarks of moral truth, which the science of casuistry is able to refine in relation to a particular set of circumstances and so supplement with a number of smaller landmarks. The distinction, however, between what is contingent and what is absolute is a key distinction, which must always be made in approaching a fundamental question of this kind in general and any moral problem in particular, or grave risk is run of confusing the issue. And since the understanding of fascism involves a fundamental question of this kind, it is essential that the non-specialized reader be reminded of the distinction.

The whole question of liberty is really a question in point; for fascism distinguishes immediately liberty, in the absolute sense, defined as the right to do anything which is not wrong, as distinguished from licence, which is the right to do anything, good or bad, and liberty regarded as what may expediently be permitted or forbidden in a given set of circumstances. Liberty in the absolute sense is accordingly always the reverse side of the medal on which is inscribed the moral law, while liberty in the contingent sense is the degree of liberty permitted by the law of the land (itself based on the moral law) in relation to particular circumstances, a degree which must vary according to the needs of the situation.

Many people attack fascism in Italy on account of the limits which have been imposed by Mussolini's government on the freedom of the individual. The only question involved here, however, as far as fascism as a theory of government is concerned, is the question whether liberty is or is not distinguishable from licence in accordance with the above definitions. If it is, then the fascist point is conceded. The question on the other hand whether, in the given circumstances of Italian life to-day, Mussolini's government has or has not overstepped the limits of what should prudently be left for individuals to decide in the public interest, is not a question involving the theory of fascism, but one of a purely practical nature involving the wisdom of Italian statesmen. To judge the merits of this case with any degree of justice, it is necessary to have a full inside knowledge both of the Italian character and of the actual situation in Italy in all its actions and interactions. And nobody is fitted to do this, with perhaps rare exceptions, save an Italian living in Italy, possessed at the same time of the education and opportunity required for weighing all the complex circumstances. All that the outside student need keep in mind is the above distinction itself, the fact that he is an outsider and therefore in an unfavourable position to judge the merits of the question, and the fact that Italy is still in the throes of a revolution, which, as in time of war, requires many more restrictions on personal liberty than would be required in normal times.

To take a concrete example. In Italy the laws governing the liberty of the press are embodied now, for the most part, in the penal code. Infringement of the law leaves the culprit open to prosecution and, if he is proved guilty, to the prescribed penalties. The laws in themselves may not, of course, receive, like all human-made laws, universal approval, in that they involve contingent circumstances of a general nature; but, if they are carefully examined, it will be found that they are not particularly controversial. They cover very much the customary ground. It is forbidden, for instance, to incite soldiers to insubordination, to incite one class against another, to give vent to blasphemous and obscene language, to indulge in pornography, libel and violent abuse of the principle of authority and of the symbols of authority, etc., etc. In any case, the subject-matter is very carefully defined; and I think it can be said without fear of contradiction that very few persons, whatever their persuasion, would find much in them to object to. But at the same time it is strongly felt that under modern conditions the press, which is immensely powerful, must be brought under a certain discretional control; and accordingly, side by side with the provisions regarding the press as embodied in the penal code, there is a special law of public safety which empowers the executive, through the Prefects of the provinces, to confiscate the whole issue of a newspaper should be considered in his discretion that the publication of a particular article is liable to lead to a breach of the public peace or to cause embarrassment to the government in its efforts to keep on friendly terms with foreign powers. These discretional powers afforded to the Prefects entail a certain number of arbitrary decisions; and in the revolutionary circumstances of the actual moment, no doubt these powers are exercised with a degree of rigour which in normal times—even under a fascist government—would be very greatly relaxed. Meantime, given the circumstances, the press—though by no means muzzled—is rendered in many cases irritatingly timid. This is recognized by fascists themselves as unfortunate, but unavoidable in the actual circumstances; for the circumstances of a revolution are such that there is a constant danger of enflamed opinion breaking forth into violent action. It is a question of Hobson's choice between ugly incidents of violence; and a degree of repression. The question of principle is hardly involved at all. It is a question of practical statesmanship.

Passing from the consideration of liberty to the consideration of toleration, the same fundamental question is involved. The fascist temperament is intransigent—and claims that everybody should be so—when it comes to matters involving right and wrong in the absolute sense. It is tolerant—or claims to be— of the individual falling below the absolute ideal in the struggle of life and buffeted by circumstances. Toleration, fascists declare, is often a word which merely camouflages, indifference. They insist that mankind must not be indifferent, that life is finest where conviction is strongest, where men and women are ready to die and suffer for their ideas. Applied toleration is a question of law and liberty—a matter for statesmanship. As a virtue it is a blend of magnanimity and of a capacity for experience and understanding. But that toleration which is born of indifference or of physical hypersensitiveness is no real toleration at all. True toleration is a virtue; and it is a virtue which can run quite well in harness with intransigeance. Like idealism and a sense of reality they complement each other.

The discussion of these points not only illustrates the fascist *Weltanschauung*, but should bring home to the reader the necessity of distinguishing fascism in its essentials from any particular form of fascism as applied to given circumstances by a particular people. The Italian temperament is very different from the Anglo-Saxon's. Mind and emotion in Italy are less interwoven. The Italian mind is the harder or colder one; but his emotions are more passionate, cruder perhaps, certainly less sentimental. The Italian loves colour and drama and rhetoric, and abhors formality as distinct from artistic form. He is more spontaneous and perhaps less refined. For this reason—that is, the reason arising out of differences of national character—Anglo-Saxons and other foreigners must be careful not to confuse fascism with all that there is of the Italian character mixed up with fascism in Italy. Much of the very exuberance of fascism in Italy is merely Italian exuberance, much of Mussolini's rhetoric untranslatable Italian word-picture making. Much is distorted by the reflection of the historical phase through which Italy is marching. Italians, for example, are an old race, deeply experienced in life, with an unrivalled history of achievement, a race intensely proud of their glorious past and intensely ashamed of having become, during their period of decadence and disunity, a prey to foreign invaders, subservient, finished, soft and poverty-stricken—a race chiefly renowned abroad as one of ice-cream vendors and strummers on the mandoline. And now that they exhibit a newly-found vigour, which they feel and know is second to nobody's, now that they have accomplished their political unity and found at last a common consciousness of nationality, and know that they have it in them to become great again, it is not surprising that they give expression to their feelings and convictions in a manner which is somewhat irritating to the nerves of people of older national organizations, nervous in the face of inevitable dangers to the *status quo*, suspicious of upstarts. Italy, to-day, is like Elizabethan England, a young, comparatively weak nation which has suddenly realized the importance of the qualities it stands for and the potential strength which it is capable of developing. It is in a mood to singe the King of Spain's beard. But unlike Elizabethan England, Italy, owing to her glorious past, suffers in her first steps towards her glorious future from the effects of an inverted inferiority complex. This often makes her exhibitions of self-assertion particularly irritating. Once explained, however, they may be understood and more easily forgiven. But all this has nothing whatsoever to do with fascism, except that the advent of fascism has coincided (inevitably perhaps, however distinct the two things may be) with the growth of Italian nationalism, which has given fascism its peculiar flavour in Italy to-day and has received from fascism an idea which, because of its universality, is fitted to become a matter of national pride. It has added fuel to the nationalist flames.

Fascism itself is more universal than nationalist. It is nationalist only in the sense that it believes in patriotism as a force for good, and insists on the merging of individual interests in the general interests and therefore in the integration of the individual in the State, which implies the national bond. It repudiates, too, the idea of a universal State which might come through the loosening of the bonds of authority, and the breaking down of national distinctions. On the contrary, it believes that the only right way of moving away from our present conditions of international chaos towards higher international unity, is by building upon the foundation of self-respecting, strong and highly organized national entities. Otherwise, it is claimed, the gain of unity would mean a much more serious loss, namely, loss of vitality and loss of local character. Thus the State itself must be based on the family, on trade and vocational corporations, on differentiated regional elements, brought together into a higher unity but not at the expense of the personality of each part and not therefore through the pulverizing process of universal individual suffrage. In other words, the process of growth from smaller to larger political entities must be one "akin to a honeycomb and not to a soup" (to quote from a contemporary Italian periodical)—an aggregation of larger and smaller cells within cells—a natural growth which the practical statesman will abet as each successive stage approaches, but for which it would be unwise to force the pace.

Fascism and nationalism, issuing in any form of dangerous or chauvinistic temper, must consequently be sharply distinguished. In Italy they are still inextricably mixed. But nationalism in Italy represents really a movement anterior in time to fascism. It is a phenomenon which may be regarded as one of fascism's precursors. It has provided fascism with some of its most able men; and these men though evolving with the times, have inevitably brought into fascism some of the temperament of their purely nationalist upbringing. The later and the earlier movements have acted on each other reciprocally, but the later—fascism—is richer in ancestry; and this very richness in ancestry is leading to its gradual shedding of those particular influences of each of its ancestors which are incompatible with one another. Thus fascism is slowly discarding nationalist chauvinism; it is emerging as something quite distinct. In its purity it is already visible to the acute observer. He can see what the process is bringing forth; but to anyone with a superficial knowledge of Italy or lacking in a sense of history, it is easy to be blind to its significance.

Italian nationalism, like its counterpart in the *Action Française* movement in France, had a bias in favour of grand old pagan traditions, loving the Roman Church not so much as the spouse of Christ, but as the heir to the Roman Empire. It respected the Church *qua* Church as embodying the principle of authority and order, but was afraid of its humanizing charity. It was, moreover, penetrated with modernism, just like the *Action*

Française. But the difference in this respect is interesting. Whereas in France to a great extent, and so in England and in America, modernism is rampant in the form of a movement among persons who have lost faith in the literal meaning of their Church's dogmas and are attempting to square their loss of faith with their sentimental attachments to the tradition in which they were brought up, in Italy the equally rampant modernism was and is a movement of men who have become sick of their positivism and agnosticism, and are attempting to embrace the Church's dogmas in a form acceptable to a weak digestion. In other words, modernism is a meeting-place of two movements working in diametrically opposite directions, the one away, the other towards orthodoxy. For this reason, fascism in Italy being an advance in movement upon its precursor nationalism, is also in process of shedding modernism and becoming orthodox.

The process, of course, is not complete. But it is extremely symptomatic, for it reveals fascism as the fruit of a type of mentality which finds rest within the orbit of a teaching Church. It is not necessary to say more than that; but that much is positively evident. As far as our present argument is concerned, it should be observed that a large number of Italians, brought up in the positivist atmosphere of the generation before the war, are moving through modernism into the Church of their fathers. What is impeding their progress is already not so much the difficulty of swallowing the literal meaning of the Catholic Church's dogmas, but a spirit of insubordination to the Church's discipline. They claim that under modern conditions much of what the Church exacts of its members in the form of discipline and observance, and many of its more elaborate rites, are too exacting or take up too much time. It is this they would see modernized, rather than the dogmas. And they wish to see the Church less afraid of modern culture and manners. The siege by the forces of disbelief of the Church's citadel they proclaim as raised and would like to see the clergy attacking rather than defending, and, for the purpose of attacking more effectively, discarding a lot of mediæval paraphernalia. They are like men who would gladly serve in the army, if there were less parades, if comfortable clothing were substituted for stiff, hot uniforms, and if the generality of officers were only more intellectually inspiring.

The above represents the practical side of this absorbingly interesting phenomenon. In the realm of strict philosophy, parallel with the nationalist movement, there arose the new idealism of Spaventa, Croce and Gentile. This likewise may be regarded as the road of escape for many thinking Italians from rationalism and scepticism. Progressively during the past twenty or thirty years the new idealism has purged itself of that part of its Hegelian content which is certainly incompatible with orthodox Christianity. But here too the process is incomplete; and although Gentile, who stands still for the doctrine of immanentism as contrasted with transcendentalism, is already, as a theorist, a back number in Italy, there is a large body of philosophic opinion which burks at the philosophic methods favoured by the Catholic Church, namely, scholasticism. They would like to see neo-scholasticism give way to a method less formally syllogistic and entirely make its own the modern mathematical school. They accuse the Church of clinging to a method too much akin to that advocated by many rationalists, who they doubt can be defeated—but only pinned to their positions—by present-day theologians trained in the Catholic Church's own seminaries and universities. They assert that on this field the battle can end only in a draw amid arid abstractions. They would like to see St. Augustine the patron saint of modern philosophy rather than St. Thomas, in the belief that the methods the former pursued are, in the phase through which the world is passing to-day, on the whole more capable of assimilating modern philosophical methods than the scholastic method. And this fact—prescinding from the logic of the situation—is a physical hindrance to their complete reconciliation with Catholic claims.

The nett result is that anybody who views Italy to-day is very prone to see no wood but the trees only. The situation is a maze of apparent paradoxes and pitfalls for the unwary. Numerous persons who call themselves fascist are only fascist in a negative sense. They agree with the rationalized formulas; but their mentality belongs to a past generation. Nationalists, neo-idealists, modernists, red revolutionary syndicalists in upbringing before the war, they carry the mentality produced during the primitive period of their lives into their fascist life of to-day, their middle age. They are theoretical fascists only. All this is apt to distract the impartial observer; and when to this type of fascist are added the numerous gang of persons who have joined the movement for interested motives only, and of others who have had no education to speak of, but find in the movement, without understanding it, the means of self-expression in action, confusion is apt to become still worse confounded.

This is indeed the fate of all movements. They must be appreciated dynamically. They grow out of a series of previous movements and these, before they are each assimilated into the new movement and before all are fused to form a new metal, so to speak, which stands out as something definitely differing from any other, they may be seen to be flowing on by themselves and overlapping one another. The new movement first operates instinctively and blindly. Thinkers strip their minds to explain the instinctive actions and, after a period of controversy, produce a more or less agreed theory to fit the facts. Then new men arise who fit their actions to the theories, but possessed of mentalities formed under a previous dispensation. Only the youth, who have known no other dispensation, who grow up in the movement after the theories have become fixed, belong to it naturally, their action and their thought complete at one.

So the course of a movement has often the appearance of a phenomenon of nature; and unless a great man arises, a man of action, born before his natural time, capable of dominating the situation and of interpreting the movement as it will eventually emerge in its purity, the movement will move forward at the cost of many setbacks. But in Mussolini fascism has found its man, with the result that it is moving towards maturity with an astonishing rapidity. Without him, things would have gone too fast at certain periods and this would in turn have resulted in long periods of reaction and apparent stagnation. And no doubt far greater excesses would have been indulged in. There is little doubt indeed, were it not for Mussolini, that the fascist revolution, like most other revolutions, would have progressed in a trail of blood. He has succeeded in containing it within limits which have kept it astonishingly moderate, considering the circumstances of heated controversy. He has succeeded in canalizing it, and, by preventing the worst excesses, in withstanding the forces of reaction. This point should not be lost sight of in view of the indignation aroused in the hearts of many people by such excesses as have certainly occurred and by the curtailment of certain liberties, which in normal times would readily be conceded.

Those, to conclude, who would really learn what fascism stands for, must abstain from merely collecting opinions in a world in flux. Thousands of people in Italy are "agin the government," for one personal reason or another—because their own selfish interests, which they may not even realize are selfish, are frustrated; because this and that is not permitted, the necessity of which is not appreciated, or on account of an actual error of judgment on the part of the government; because of envy or dislike (merited or otherwise) of fascist leaders; because of economic difficulties which ignorance attributes to be peculiar to Italy, etc., etc. Thousands too do not fully realize, for the reasons I have attempted to describe, exactly what it all means. All tend to interpret the movement from their particular angle and in accordance with the prejudices acquired during their youth. But, living in Italy, moving among the peasants, the artisans and professional classes, interpreting the spirit of the new laws in relation to the traditions of these classes, reading the mass of fascist literature, and especially the official literature and the text-books approved for the training of the new generation, fascism can be seen to emerge as something perfectly definite and, whether we like it or not, exceedingly pregnant with vitality. Its special interest lies in its attempt to find a new synthesis, which will resolve the apparent antinomies of modern life, whether of action or of thought; its blending of ancient and modern, of the values which enhance personality with those which act as a check on individualism by returning to the ortho-dox solution of the problem, practical and theoretical, in accord-ance with a dualistic conception of the universe, of unity and diversity. If the reader will help the writer by forgiving his blem-ishes of style (some due to the need of a concentrated account of things) and the many necessary omissions, which a book of this length must necessarily make; if he will realize that the prin-ciples enumerated are subordinate to the spirit of the movement which it has been attempted to portray; if, finally, he will lay aside his prejudices for the time being and look upon the move-ment as a phenomenon worthy of his unbiassed interest, I think the foregoing pages will bring him to realize the inner signifi-cance of fascism, whatever may be his finally considered judg-ment of its merits. And if he does that, the writer's purpose will be fulfilled.

INDEX